M000223128

STRATEGIC CHOICE UNDER UNCERTAINTY

Multinational Corporations and the Pressure to Disinvest from South Africa

---

Mzamo P. Mangaliso

University Press of America,® Inc.
Lanham · Boulder · New York · Toronto · Plymouth, UK

Copyright © 2010 by
University Press of America,® Inc.
4501 Forbes Boulevard
Suite 200
Lanham, Maryland 20706
UPA Acquisitions Department (301) 459-3366

Estover Road
Plymouth PL6 7PY
United Kingdom

Library of Congress Control Number: 2010921276
ISBN: 978-0-7618-5087-8 (clothbound : alk. paper)
ISBN: 978-0-7618-5088-5 (paperback : alk. paper)
eISBN: 978-0-7618-5089.2

CONTENTS

Contents

ACKNOWLEDGEMENTS

Like any book, this volume was a product of collective effort. It would have been impossible to write it without the assistance of colleagues, friends and family far and near. And since the book had such a long period of gestation—close to two decades in the making—there are numerous people to whom I owe a debt of gratitude.

Foremost are the respondents who participated in the empirical study conducted as part of this project: the executives both in South Africa and North America. Without their input, the ideas contained here would not have been grounded in the reality of everyday business decision making. In that regard I wish to acknowledge Reuel Khoza and the late Brian Bannerman, both of whom were instrumental in connecting me with executives in South Africa. At the University of Massachusetts-Amherst I would like to thank Bill Brommery, Elliott Carlisle, Stephen Coelen, Tom O'Brien, Tony Butterfield, and the late Stanley Young who played important roles in nurturing the ideas contained in the book. Several people contributed in the editing of the book, including Bob Ford, Lou Wigdor, and Tom Millerick. Each of them read every single chapter, making corrections and changes that added precision to the text. Without their clarity with language the book would have been less readable than it currently is. My gratitude also goes to my colleagues, Brad Knipes, Raza Mir, and the late Stan Young who collaborated with me in earlier versions of some of the chapter materials as indicated in the book. I also owe a debt of gratitude to the editors at Rowman & Littlefield Publishing Group, Samantha Kirk, Brian DeRocco, and Paula Smith-Vanderslice, for their counsel and not giving up on me when I missed the deadlines. The constructive criticisms offered by the manuscript reviewers made the book better.

The final credit for this book goes to my family. My wife, Zengie, has been my constant source of strength and encouragement for over thirty years. She has gracefully traversed the boundaries between the roles of wife, mother, friend, and fellow scholar so well. Evidence of the latter can be seen in the epilogue of this book in which she is the coauthor. I am forever grateful to have her as my soulmate in our journey through life. The arrival our two daughters, Bande and Unati, brought joy to our lives, which was further enhanced this year by the arrival of our grandson, Isaiah Asande Vuyo Virgil who represents the next generations. It is the family that gave me the inspiration I needed every morning when I woke up to add a little more to the book.

Of course, all of this would have been for naught without my parents, my mother, Ivy Nomfuduko (nee Msikinya), and my father, Thompson Situ-kutezi Mangaliso, who raised three of us during the dark days of apartheid. I especially credit my father for being such a good role model for us and providing our family with stability. He showed us, by example, that through education, dedication and hard work anything is possible.

I want to conclude by acknowledging that any errors contained in this volume—whether by commission or omission—are solely mine. I hope that any distractions they will cause will be more than offset by the positive contributions of the book.

Mzamo P. Mangaliso
Amherst, Massachusetts
October 20, 2009

PREFACE

Very few countries have experienced South Africa's level of environmental turbulence in the late 1980s. This was a period filled with what social critic and *Future Shock* author Alvin Toffler described as rapid, dramatic, and often erratic discontinuity. The drama manifested itself in political upheaval as the discredited apartheid regime faced increasing isolation from the international community, which regarded the system of government as a contravention of human rights.

Political developments elsewhere in the world may have catalyzed the changes that were about to take place in South Africa. Among these were the May/June 1989 events in Tiananmen Square in China, which demonstrated the shakiness of totalitarian systems, and the fall of the Berlin Wall, which heralded the collapse of the Soviet Union and the end of the Cold War (Segal 1990). The latter effectively removed the overrated threat of communism, which had been used by the apartheid regime as the reason not to negotiate with Blacks. Regionally, the balance of power had begun to shift decisively toward the liberationist forces, mainly the African National Congress (ANC), following the defeat of the South African Defense Forces at the 1988 Battle of Cuito Cuanavale in Angola (Matlosa 2001). In the country there was mounting political unrest from the mass democratic movement, trade unions, and the two main liberation movements: the ANC and the Pan Africanist Congress of Azania (PAC), which conspired to render the country ungovernable. The turbulence triggered by these combined forces resulted in the rapid decline of the value of the rand in global markets and curtailed any technological developments in the country. In short, as had become clear to many members of the ruling National Party, the writing was on the wall: the days of apartheid were numbered.

The turning point was reached when, in 1990, then President F. W. de Klerk made the bold announcement that Nelson Mandela and all other political prisoners would be released unconditionally, that all political movements would be unbanned, and that political exiles would be allowed to return home. As Matlosa (2001) notes, the De Klerk regime opened the doors of apartheid for dialogue toward a new political dispensation. This was realized with the formation of a Government of National Unity following the country's historic first democratic election in 1994. Subsequent elections in 1999, 2004, and 2009 resulted in an ANC-led government, with the ANC receiving about two-thirds of the popular vote.

With the end of apartheid, South Africa embarked on a voyage of recovery and reconstruction, which it navigates to this day. Over the past decade the new leadership has faced some of the toughest challenges of any transitional state in recent times—transformation from an apartheid state to a nonracial and democratic one, and attending to issues of restorative, reconciliatory, and compensatory justice. While these challenges have at times appeared daunting, the country has handled the transition relatively well. For one thing, the bloody war that was expected to pit Black against White never took place. Instead, the different racial groups appear to have put the past behind them and banded together for the common goal of making the country a model for transitional economies. The Truth and Reconciliation Commission's handling of past transgressions allowed both victims and perpetrators to come to a common understanding that once the truth was out, forgiveness would follow.

South Africa, whose gross domestic product (GDP) was roughly $468 billion in 2008, has long been acknowledged as the most prosperous country on the continent. It has a history of attracting immigrants from neighboring African countries and around the world seeking economic opportunities (*Newsweek* 2009). But the economic challenges facing the country are formidable. According to a recent government report, despite evidence that the number of people living in poverty has declined, as of 2005 close to half of the South African population was living below the poverty line (Appel 2008). Under the leadership of the first three presidents—Nelson Mandela (1994–1999), Thabo Mbeki (1999–2008), and Kgalema Motlante (2008–2009)—the economy continued to grow and prosper. But this is a far cry from the expectations of political pundits in the waning days of apartheid in the late 1980s. Will democratic South Africa slip into a parlous state so typical of the rest of Africa? Or is it possible that the rebirth of South Africa places the much-heralded dream of African Renaissance at the doorstep of reality? The fourth democratic elections, in April 2009, once again resulted in a majority victory of just under two-thirds for the ANC. Under the leadership of Jacob Zuma, the government has vowed to tackle the nation's persistent poverty and health problems, violence, and unemployment, particularly among youth. The Center for Development and Enterprise in Johannesburg has estimated that 65 percent of people between fifteen and twenty-four were unemployed in 2005 (CDE 2008). In many ways, therefore, the term of President Zuma will be a watershed for South Africa, shedding light on most of the above questions and a host of other issues.

In taking us back to the late 1980s, this book reports on a study conducted to find out just how the top managers of large corporations perceived the level of environmental turbulence in South Africa, and on their strategic choices in response to pressure from stakeholders to divest their holdings in the nation. In this book, the terms *strategic choice* and *uncertainty* are used differently than in the theory of subjective expected utility (SEU), which lies at the foundation of most contemporary economics, theoretical statistics, and operations research. Based on a sophisticated mathematical model of choice, the SEU theory presupposes conditions of perfect utility-maximizing rationality among decision makers who live in a world of certainty, or in a world in which the probability distributions of all relevant variables are knowable (Bomona & Johnston 1979). But in the real world of business, managers must make decisions under uncertainty, guided by the logic of bounded rationality (March & Simon 1958). When confronted with several options whose probability of occurrence is unknown, they still have to make strategic choices, albeit by invoking their heuristics, personal biases and instincts (Tversky & Kahneman 1974). Strategic choice is used to connote major administrative choices made, formally or informally, by senior corporate managers in respect to questions regarding domain definition and navigation (Buorgeois 1980, Child 1974, Hambrick and Mason 1984). The assumption is that corporate decision-makers bring their own cognitive biases to the administrative situation reflecting their idiosyncrasies with respect to their anticipation of future events, values and preferences (Child 1974, Hambrick and Mason 1984, March and Simon 1958).

Implicit in the notion of bounded rationality is that strategic choices made are not necessarily optimal since they would normally have evolved out of organizational political decision-making processes. Decision-making can be defined as a conscious choice of a course of action from available alternatives. Strategic decisions are those made at the top of organizations. They are usually big in level of resources committed, high in riskiness, and have a long-run time horizon. Such decisions can involve entering new product-markets, exiting from others; opening new facilities, or closing old ones; or making ground-breaking changes in policies governing human resource management. By their nature and the manner in which modern organizations are run, these decisions follow a partly rational, partly political process. And, by its nature, in the political process any number of courses of action would be plausible, albeit less optimal, that would lead to the same ultimate end-goal. This is the essence of the concept of equifinality as proposed by Katz and Kahn (1966) and it is quite contrary to the precepts of the SEU as noted above. In the case of the decision to stay or pull out of South Africa, we see just unsure executives were in the choices they were forced to make. Almost in an escalation of commitment sense (Staw 1981), some seemed to want to remain

In this book uncertainty is defined as the lack of sufficient information and knowledge to make a decision, or simply the difference between the amount of information required to make a decision and the amount of information already possessed by the organization (Galbraith 1973, Mangaliso 1995). Information and knowledge are therefore the obverse of uncertainty: as information and knowledge increase, uncertainty decreases (Thompson 1967; Daft and Macintosh 1981; Daft and Lengel 1986). Of course, as this book will explore, the literature on uncertainty reveals a great deal of diversity in how the concept has been employed in organizational analysis. Many authors remind us that serious attention must be paid to external environmental elements, especially in strategic decision making, because limiting the search for solutions primarily to internal organizational decision processes may be practically ineffective (Duncan 1972, Jabnoun, et al. 2003). This view is supported by other researchers who note the crucial link between the firm's ability to understand and respond to external conditions and its long-term survival (Atherton 2003, Zahra et al. 1997, Miller 1993). In spite of these cautionary clarion calls, for the most part the extant models in the lead-up to the end of the last millennium focused on building the internal capabilities and competencies of the organization (Prahalad and Hamel 1990; Jauch and Kraft 1986). It is for that reason that the focus of this study was on the macro- or external environmental dimension of uncertainty faced by the top management of large corporations in their South African operations. That dimension includes socio-cultural, political-legal, economic, ecological, and demographic factors.

CHAPTER 1

Introduction

The research in this book examines how perceptions of the external environment, strategy preference, and company performance are related to one another. It explores these relationships using perceptual measures of the variables obtained from a sample of senior corporate executives of U.S.-based, Canada-based, and South Africa–based multinational corporations (MNCs). The focal geographical area of the study is the environment of South Africa. A number of hypotheses are generated and tested in an attempt to map out a conceptual framework, which relates the three constructs to one another. In exploring the linkage between these constructs, this study lays the groundwork for the development of explanatory theories for future research.

Overview

Many studies in strategic management have focused on the relationship between the organization and its environment. Most have focused on two broad areas: namely, the relationships between organizational structure and the environment and between organizational structure and the strategy followed. Chandler's (1962) seminal research on structure and strategy received widespread acceptance for its contention that organizational structures are shaped by strategic choices. In that study, Chandler discovered that strategies of product-market diversification implied the prevalence of decentralized structures, and that a new strategy required a new or at least a reorganized structure so that the enlarged enterprise could function efficiently.

Other researchers have subsequently argued that it is equally plausible that a given structure is likely to constrain strategy by producing predictable classes of strategic behavior, i.e., that under certain circumstances strategy can follow structure (Galbraith and Nathanson 1978; Burgelman 1983; Peters 1984; Miller 1987). Organizations cannot, however, be fully explained by the strategy-structure analysis without reference to their milieu. Thompson (1967), in fact, was among the first researchers to point out that organizations must be considered as open systems in order to fully understand how they survive and prosper in the long run. Environment and strategy are inextricably bound together. Environmental conditions affect strategy; and strategy must relate the firm to its environment. Consistent with this line of thinking, other researchers have also studied the relationship between the organization and its environment (Lawrence and Lorsch 1967; Burns and Stalker 1961; Perrow 1970; Child 1972). Their basic conclusion was that the environment poses certain problems for the organization which must be dealt with structurally.

In the 1980s a number of researchers provided abundant evidence that the environment plays an important part in strategy formulation. For example, Jemison (1981b) conducted a field study of the relative importance of internal organizational activities versus environmental interaction as a source of influence on strategic choices. His findings supported the position that environmental interaction plays an important role in determining organizational actions and, in fact, that it is the primary factor in determining strategic choices. Other researchers studied the relationship between strategy making and environment (Miller and Friesen 1983, Frederickson and Mitchell 1984, Rhyne 1986, and Miller 1987). They proposed that an increase in environmental turbulence and hostility is related to strategy making in successful firms and, therefore, that there should be particular forms of alignment or congruence present among certain attributes of the environment and strategy-making behavior. That would make possible the effective selection and implementation of strategy.

In spite of this evidence, there is still a paucity of empirical research devoted to the relationship between strategy and environment. In his literature review, Bourgeois (1980: 32) concluded that "strategy and environment have been joined empirically . . . but there has not been much work that joins the strategy formulation process and the environment." Most of the studies in this area have a number of shortcomings. Some have restricted their analysis to the business (Mascarenhas 1985) or even the operational level (Swamidas and Newell 1987). Others have simply clustered all organizations together as if they perceived and experienced the environment in exactly the same way. If Woodward's (1982: 272) premise that turbulence lies "in the eye of the beholder " is accepted, then the lumping of organizations together may be misleading since turbulence, hostility, and other factors are not constant features of a firm's environment. Instead, they can be considered as dependent upon the individual's prior beliefs and value structure (Fishbein and Ajzen 1975, Downey, Hellriegel and Slocum1975, Downey and Slocum 1975). Furthermore, the perceptual viewpoint has been supported over the objective viewpoint by other scholars who consider environmental elements as stimuli, lacking inherent meaning or information value until structured by the individual perceiver (Kobrin 1982; Hambrick and Snow 1977; Anderson and Paine 1975; Miles, Snow and Pfeffer 1974; Child 1972). These scholars have argued that organizations respond not to the "objective" environment but to the environment perceived by management. The resultant perceptual differences, in turn, affect strategic choices, as was revealed in a study by Khandwalla (1976). This study found that managers who perceived their environment as complex and dynamic (therefore uncertain) tended to employ more comprehensive strategies. In this regard, Miles and Snow (1978, p. 20) note that, ". . . [t]he organization responds largely to what its management perceives; those environments that go unnoticed or are deliberately ignored have little effect on management decisions and actions."

Another shortcoming of these studies is that they often have small sample sizes and are regional—both being characteristics that make generalization difficult. Furthermore, some studies have used middle managers as respondents and, as Mascarenhas (1985) conjectured, lower-ranking officers usually do not have as panoramic a view of the organization as that of managers nearer the top.

Significance of the Book

There is considerable conceptual and empirical justification for this study. Very little research on turbulence has used an international framework to (a) empirically delve into the question of how perceptions of extra-organizational, environmental forces affect strategy preferences and performance, and (b) generate and test a set of hypotheses emanating from such a dual Organization Theory/Strategic Management framework.

Because most of the empirical research published in the environment-strategy–performance interface has been conducted in the northwestern hemisphere, it will always be susceptible to criticisms of parochialism. Such skepticism will continue to dog social science research until, and unless, more validation can be obtained through research that traverses both the east–west and the north–south hemispherical divides. As the century progresses, business will increasingly cross national borders. Practitioners will constantly look for answers as business brings together people with different languages, cultures, values, and traditions. Practitioners will seek explanations that will help them to understand newly emerging phenomena and predictions to help them cope in the global marketplace. Empirical research is needed to confirm, deductively, if theories that are held to be true in one country in the world also hold true in another.

The research reported here accomplishes this goal by investigating the perception of executives across both dividing lines: the Atlantic Ocean and the Equator. Senior corporate executives in both South Africa and the United States were surveyed to give their subjective assessment of their South African operations. This research demonstrates the vulnerability of business to ideologically unacceptable government practices. An important implication of this research is the apparent powerlessness of business decision makers to put their objectively rational plans into action under turbulent conditions.

The choice of South Africa as the country of reference offers a unique opportunity for a number of reasons. In recent years the international community has focused sharply on the role of business organizations in South Africa because of the *apartheid*[1] policies of the National Party government, which came to power in 1947 (Sincere 1986). Elsewhere in the world, MNCs have been implored not to interfere in the internal affairs of host countries. Not so in the case of South Africa, where many MNCs implicitly or explicitly indicated that their presence could influence the South African government to abolish apartheid policies (Crichton 1986). Many U.S.-based MNCs, for example, were encouraged to sign a code of conduct later called the Sullivan Principles. The code was a set of equal-opportunity principles developed by the Rev. Dr. Leon Sullivan, an African American Baptist Minister who sat on the board of directors of General Motors. The original six principles called for: (1) the desegregation of the workplace; (2) equal and fair employment practices for all; (3) equal pay for equal or comparable work; (4) initiation of training programs for Blacks; (5) more Blacks in management positions; and (6) the improvement of the quality of employees' lives outside the work environment. These principles were amplified a number of times to sharpen the goals of socio-economic transformation. Indeed, the fourth amplification of the Sullivan Code committed its signatories to lobbying for sweeping social change, including the ending of all apartheid laws (Little 1978; Crichton 1986)[2]. Rev. Sullivan toughened the Code in May 1985 when he called upon the signatories to practice corporate civil disobedience against all apartheid laws and issued an ultimatum that if apartheid were not eliminated by May of 1987 he would call upon all U.S. companies to pull out of South Africa (Crichton 1986; Orkin 1986; Leonard 1986; Sincere 1986). In June 1987, at a press conference, he called on all U.S. corporations to withdraw from South Africa because the regime had failed to bring down apartheid (*New York Times* 1987). A number of companies that left South Africa during this period gave a variety of explanations for their decision to leave. These included poor economic conditions; a worsening socio-political climate; continued political unrest; increasing pressure from pro-divestment groups, and many other reasons (Kneale 1987). Nonetheless, there still remains much to be researched in this area.

Next, the choice of executives from corporations based in the United States, Canada, and South Africa as respondents for the study provides interesting similarities and contrasts. The United States and Canada share one of the world's longest borders; they are the two largest trading partners in the world; both hold essentially similar human values and a belief in basic freedoms; both espouse democracy and the free-enterprise system (Pasquero 1988; Robins-Mowry 1988). Finally, both have been featured in lists of the top ten trading partners with South Africa (Koenderman 1982). However, they are also subject to different forces and pressures. Until the passage of the Comprehensive Anti Apartheid Act (CAAA) by the U.S. Congress in the fall of 1986, U.S. corporations faced minimal governmental restrictions on their South African operations (De St. Jorre 1987). The Sullivan Code is and always was a privately sponsored, voluntary code of conduct. The Canadian government, on the other hand, adopted a code of conduct in 1978 for Canadian companies operating in South Africa (Newman and Bowers 1984). Although this code was similar to the Sullivan Code in substance, its introduction by the government was significant. And later, the Canadian government, well known for its tough anti-apartheid stand, took court action to ensure that some of the restrictions imposed on Canadian corporations vis-à-vis their S.A. operations were enforced[3]. Unlike the Unites States, Canada is a member of the Commonwealth Nations and, as such, follows the British industrial tradition.

In the past, it was assumed that corporate executives from Canada and the United States were a monolithic group. However, comparative analyses of these two groups have disproved this belief, demonstrating certain philosophical differences in how U.S. and Canadian top executives perceive the priorities of business (Milman 1986; Carter 1987; Robins-Mowry 1988). A study by Orpen (1987) revealed that South African managers perceived those priorities significantly differently from their North American counterparts. Note that even within country groups there is a great diversity in the backgrounds of executives. In Canada, important differences exist between French Canadians and English Canadians; in South Africa there are cultural and philosophical differences among Afrikaans-and English-speaking members of the White population who constitute a majority of corporate executives (see Crapanzano 1987). These differences and similarities have made executives from these countries interesting subjects for a comparative analysis.

Finally, the tendency for many business organizations to become multi-market, multi-product firms as they grow in size has been well documented (Chandler 1962; Rumelt 1974; Montgomery 1979). This tendency makes it difficult to classify such organizations by industry. In comparing locally based corporations with local subsidiaries of overseas-based MNCs, Capon et al. (1987) have suggested that the nation-state can provide important controls on the business environment. During the period of this study, South Africa provided an opportunity for such comparative research.

Variables Used

Environment

Earlier scholars have suggested that both external and internal factors of the organization be included in the conceptualization of the environment (Thompson 1967; Lawrence and Lorsch 1967). More recent literature, however, has argued that only external factors should be included since including both might lead to confusion, especially when the respondents will have no help in the interpretation of the instrument (Mascarenhas 1985). To avoid this problem, this study focuses only on the external environment.

External environments or organizations have been conceptualized in various ways. One important dimension is the degree of environmental stability. The early researchers of this theme, Emery and Trist (1965), suggested the concept of *turbulence*. Broadly defined, turbulence is a measure of change in the factors in an organization's environment. One end of a continuum represents high turbulence, a dynamic state where all factors are in constant flux; the other end represents placidity, a static environmental state where no turbulence exists. For this research, environmental turbulence was operationalized in three dimensions upon which organizational theory and the strategy literatures have focused most, i.e., *dynamism, hostility*, and *heterogeneity* (Miller and Friesen 1983; Mintzberg 1979; Khandwalla 1976; Child 1972).

Strategy

An important research issue in the study of strategy is the level at which it is operationalized and measured. Ansoff (1965), Andrews (1971), Vancil and Lorange (1975), Hofer and Schendel (1978), and Grant and King (1982) are among the most prominent researchers to draw a distinction among corporate, business, and functional-level strategy. This study focuses on corporate-level strategy, which defines the domain of the enterprise (Bourgeois 1980).

The five generic corporate strategy types developed by Harrigan (1985b) provide the conceptual underpinnings for strategy statements in the questionnaire developed for this study (see Appendix A). These strategy types are divestiture, retrenchment, selective growth or shrinkage, hold, and opportunistic investment. The Harrigan scheme was selected because her classifications are broad enough to encompass a wide range of situations. The operational definitions of the five strategies are as follows:

1. *Divestiture strategy*—a selling off or liquidation of a strategic business unit (SBU) or subsidiary of the parent company when the environment does not show signs of hospitality in the future.
2. *Retrenchment strategy*—slowing down any expansion and even pruning some of the less profitable operations in an attempt to reverse a consistent trend or poor performance.
3. *Selective growth/shrinkage strategy*—pursuing a mixed approach of beefing up operations within some market niche where operations seem more profitable and/or shrinking investment in less attractive businesses.
4. *Hold strategy*—deferring consequential actions until some key uncertainty is removed.
5. *Opportunistic investment strategy*—aggressively increasing the firm's asset base during deteriorating economic conditions (e.g., by offering to purchase the competitors' assets). A firm adopts this strategy when it believes that there are long-term advantages in beefing up its investment base in a given environment.

Performance

Five perceptual measures were used to measure performance: after-tax return on total assets (ATROTA); growth in sales (GROSA); overall performance (OVERPER); after-tax return on sales (ATROSA); public image and goodwill (PUBIG). It is expected that, in making these perceptual judgments, the respondent would, consciously or unconsciously, have been influenced by market-share objectives, investment size, expected return on investment (ROI), etc.; exogenous factors such as the inflation rate; and other short-term windfalls arising from discrepancies in accounting conventions. In earlier research, measuring variables in the way described above has yielded reasonable validity (Dess and Robinson 1984; Pearce, Robbins, and Robinson 1987).

Research Questions

This research attempts to answer the following questions:

1. Are there significant differences in strategy preferences between executives who perceive high turbulence and those who perceive low turbulence?
2. Are there significant differences in the perception of the environment between executives based at the overseas subsidiary as opposed to those based at corporate headquarters?
3. Is strategy preference a function of level of commitment and/or performance?

We believe that answers to these questions will shed light on underlying factors linking strategy to the environment. That might help in the formulation and implementation of effective strategies that are compatible with the relevant environmental conditions. The overall benefit would be the enhancement of social and economic performance.

Organization of the Book

The book encompasses nine chapters. Chapter 2 traces the evolution of the concept of uncertainty from the natural sciences to the social sciences. This is followed by a discussion in Chapter 3 of subjective certainty and the effects of entrenched subjective cognitive maps in executives' minds. This chapter is followed by an extensive discussion of responsiveness to environmental turbulence in Chapter 4. Chapter 5 begins to review the literature pertinent to the study and develops five hypotheses that will guide the empirical inquiry. Chapter 6 explores the topic of corporate social responsibility by analyzing the Sullivan Principles and the history of the involvement of multinational corporations in South Africa. Chapter 7 lays out the methodology used in the study and research design. Chapter 8 is the analysis of the research findings, which presents the data obtained from the questionnaires and information obtained from the interviews. Chapter 9 discusses these results, their implications for the field of management, and offers conclusions. The book concludes with Chapter 10, the epilogue that gives an assessment of the developments in post-apartheid South Africa. The appendices and bibliography contain reference materials intended to facilitate future research.

CHAPTER 2

Uncertainty in Management[4]

Since ancient times, the human species has been concerned with explaining the mysteries of the universe. Over time, as better information and new evidence became available, answers to these mysteries began to emerge, substituting previously held beliefs with new ones which, in turn, drew out a new set of curiosities. These curiosities have included whether the earth is flat or round; whether the sun revolves around the earth or vice versa (heliocentric vs. geocentric beliefs); questions about the origins of the human species (evolution vs. intelligent design); the existence of intelligent life on other planets and galaxies. These and many other questions have been asked, each eliciting differing, and very often opposing, answers. The common theme running through these questions is the innate human desire to reduce uncertainty on matters of cause and effect. In this chapter we define uncertainty, expound on the dimensions and sources of uncertainty, compare the different categorizations of uncertainty, and offer some insights on the strategies used by organizations in dealing with uncertainty.

Toward a Definition of Uncertainty

In common language usage, the term uncertainty is used to denote a state of unpredictability or a situation where there is not enough information to formulate an opinion or make a decision. In the management literature, uncertainty is usually related to a lack of knowledge about the organization's environment. As Carpenter and Frederickson (2001) observe, uncertainty is a consequence of environmental factors that generally result in a lack of information needed to assess means-ends relationships, make decisions, and confidently assign probabilities to their outcomes. It follows, therefore, that better information about the environment reduces uncertainty and leads to better strategic choices. Helmer (2003) draws a distinction between conditions of certainty, uncertainty, and risk, noting that these three are usually presented as three mutually exclusive dispositions concerning any given outcome. Certainty occurs when the relevant dimensions of the outcome are completely known. Uncertainty exists when the relevant dimensions are not known and where it is impossible to attribute a meaningful probability function to the outcomes. Risk exists where the relevant dimensions of the outcome are not known, but it is possible to meaningfully attribute a known probability function to the outcomes. It is worth noting here that the question of known versus unknown probability functions pits the expected utility (EU) theory of Von Neumann and Morgenstern (1947) against the subjective expected utility (SEU) theory of Savage (1954). EU assumes that the probabilities of outcomes are objectively known, while in SEU probabilities are not necessarily objectively known. In SEU the distinction between known and unknown probability functions is pointless, because subjective probabilities are assumed to be always known to the decision-maker. Some researchers prefer to fold the terms uncertainty and risk into the term *ambiguity* defined as, "uncertainty about probability, created by missing information that is relevant and could be known" (Camerer and Weber 1992: 330).

The Challenge of Uncertainty

Coping with uncertainty has been identified as one of the major administrative challenges faced by organizations (Thompson 1967; Starbuck 1976; Miles, Snow and Pfeffer 1974; Gifford, Slocum and Bobbitt 1979). It is perhaps in this regard that strategic management evolved as a field with one of the goals being to help the firm overcome the challenge of uncertainty by shaping its competitive landscape, hence the coming into being of the various generic strategies and strategic types in the 1960s, 1970s and 1980s (Ansoff 1965; Hofer and Schendel 1978; Miles and Snow 1978; Porter 1980, 1985; Jauch and Kraft 1986). This is discussed in the next chapter. Although there has been an explosion in the amount of writing on the subject of uncertainty, little is known about the processes whereby managers respond to uncertainty in formulating their corporate strategies (Parnell, Lester and Menefee 2000). A number of analysts have suggested various ways of overcoming uncertainty, which include buffering the organization's technical core; having the appropriate mix of organic and mechanistic structures; or providing the appropriate kind of information in terms of its scope, timeliness, and level of aggregation (Burns and Stalker 1961; Chenhall and Morris 1985; Mangaliso 1995; Thompson 1967). But uncertainty is a multidimensional phenomenon especially if viewed both from the perspective of those who effect it and those who experience it. Managers respond to what they perceive and perception of uncertainty is an individual psychological trait rather than an environmental attribute (Hambrick and Mason 1984; Miles, Snow and Pfeffer 1974; Downey 1974; Downey, Slocum and Hellriegel 1974).

Uncertainty has been subject to study in other fields of scholarly endeavor. In the economics literature, the foundational theory for explaining how decision-makers make choices under uncertainty is the subjective expected utility (SEU) theory (Bonoma and Johnston 1979; Currim and Sarin 1983, 1984). Even though the SEU is a robust theory, some inadequacies have been identified in its ability to serve as a descriptive model for decision making under risk and ambiguity since the exact probabilities cannot always be assigned to events, in effect rendering the uncertainty itself to be uncertain (Kahn and Sarin 1988). An alternative explanation comes from the prospect theory, the fundamental tenet of which is that people overweight outcomes that are considered certain relative to outcomes that are merely probable (Kahneman and Tversky 1979). The tendency to deal with ambiguous situations this way, called the certainty effect, contributes to risk aversion in choices involving sure gains and to risk seeking in choices involving sure losses.

The original discussions of uncertainty may be traced back to the discovery of undeterminable position of an arrow in flight by the Hellenistic philosopher Zeno in the 5th century B.C. As physics evolved into the study of particles, Heisenberg (Heisenberg 1958, Wheeler and Zurek 1983) pointed out that the conventional physics methods were not sufficient enough to simultaneously explain both the position and the momentum of a particle. As physics evolved into the quantum theory of particles, Heisenberg pointed out that conventional physics methods were not capable of simultaneously explaining both the position and the momentum of a particle (Heisenberg 1958, Wheeler and Zurek 1983). This observation led to the famous Heisenberg uncertainty principle (HUP) which, simply stated, claims that at a given point in time either the *position* or *momentum* of an electron can be measured with accuracy. But the accuracy with which both can be simultaneously measured is limited since any attempt to determine the location or momentum will influence the particle such that experimenter's tool will modify the original conditions (Bordley 1998, Heisenberg 1958; Horgan 1992). The HUP thus has two important assumptions, namely, *duality*, which contends that light exists both in wave-form and particle-form; and *indeterminism*, which is the acceptance of the impossibility of specifying simultaneously a particle's location and its momentum. Might it thus be possible for the same kind of effects that make quantum mechanical probabilities to violate this principle to also make behavioral probabilities to violate the same principle in social contexts? In other words, might there be a behavioral analogy to the HUP in organizations? As long ago as the

1930s the uncertainty principle was extended to biology and psychology by Nobel Laureate Niels Bohr (*SNL* 1936). He noted that analysis involving human behavior is infinitely more complex than physics because things you may wish to examine are changed by the very act of examination. That is why some scholars have cautioned against the rush into extrapolating the rationalistic paradigm of the natural sciences into the social sciences (McKerrow and McKerrow 1991).

Dimensions of Uncertainty

Uncertainty is not a uni-dimensional construct but one that is decomposable into several underlying dimensions (De Meyer, Loch and Tich 2002; Milliken 1987; Sutcliffe and Zaheer 1998). For instance, Dixit and Pindyck (1994) differentiate between input uncertainty, the origins of which are largely exogenous to the firm, and internal or technical uncertainty, which is endogenous. As McGrath, Ferrier and Mendelow (2004) note, these two kinds of uncertainty often create opposing pressures. Exogenous uncertainty seems to create the "wait and see" condition which affirms the desirability of waiting until a key source of uncertainty is resolved before a decision is made. Endogenous uncertainty creates pressure for the "act and see" condition in which the desire is to speed up the discovery process to resolve the uncertainty. Milliken (1987) proposes three underlying dimensions, which she calls *state uncertainty*, defined as the inability to assign probabilities to states of nature; *effect uncertainty*, defined as a lack of knowledge about cause-effect relationships; and *response uncertainty*, defined as the inability to predict outcomes of a decision. De Meyer, Loch and Tich's (2002) proposes four types of uncertainty that managers usually confront, namely, *variation* – defined as minor variations from scheduled values; *foreseen uncertainty* – where alternative contingency plans are necessary for other possible outcomes; *unforeseen uncertainty* – where decision-makers are unaware of an event's possibility and has no Plan B; and *chaos* – in which the project goals are completely invalidated by unforeseen events. Research conducted by Cheng (1987) in an electronics firm seems to corroborate the notion of variation uncertainty, showing that the accuracy of a capacity plan was a quadratic function of the degree of variation in work contents and was significantly affected by product demand. Research reported by Courtney, Kirkland, and Viguerie (1997) and Courtney (2003) distinguishes between four levels of uncertainty, viz., *Type 1* uncertainty which derives from a single forecasted vision of future events; *Type 2* uncertainty which occurs when future events can be described in a few discrete scenarios or outcomes; *Type 3* uncertainty – when a range of potential futures exist and in which actual future events lie in a continuum; and *Type*

4 uncertainty which occurs when there are multiple dimensions of uncertainty.

Building their typology from Williams (1985), Sutcliffe and Zaheer (1998) propose three types of uncertainty, viz., *primary uncertainty* – defined as the lack of knowledge about the state of nature; *secondary or competitive uncertainty* – which refers to a lack of knowledge about the actions of other economic actors; and *supplier uncertainty* – which arises from the possibility of opportunism on the part of the exchange partner firm. Writers in sociology define uncertainty as the character of situations in which agents can neither anticipate the outcome of a decision nor assign probabilities to the outcome (Beckert 1996:804). For them, the reason for uncertainty can be seen in the complexity of causal relations in the social world, which leads to unintended consequences and prevents the anticipations of outcomes. Table 2.1 summarizes these dimensions and categorizations of uncertainty.

Sources of Uncertainty

Several sources of uncertainty can be identified in the management literature. One source stems from an imbalance in the information required at a given time in order to make a decision, or what some have termed "information load" (Gifford, Slocum and Bobbitt 1979). It is exemplified in the work of writers who define low uncertainty as the availability of enough information and high uncertainty as having too little information (Lawrence and Lorsch 1967; Duncan 1972). The lack of information necessary to make decisions with certain outcomes leads to incompleteness of knowledge of cause and effect, and the inability to forecast future events with any amount of confidence (Dosi and Egidi 1991; Thompson 1967). Even when information is available, another source of uncertainty is the limited cognitive abilities of decision-makers to fully process that information, so that the larger the gap between the complexity of a situation and the agents' competence in processing information, the higher the level of uncertainty (March and Simon 1958). Following Simon's (1981) distinction between substantive and procedural rationality, some writers have called the first source *substantive uncertainty*, and the second source *procedural uncertainty* (Dosi and Egidi 1991). Another source of uncertainty is the lack of a discernible pattern or randomness of events or cues around the decision to be made. From this perspective uncertainty is considered to be the inability to assign probabilities to event outcomes: the more difficult it is to assign

Table 2.1: Categories of Uncertainty

Authors	Basis for categorization	Categories of Uncertainty
Early Researchers (c. 1960s)	Locus of uncertainty	Internal, external
Duncan (1972)	Similarity in environment sectors and state of change	Simple-static, complex-static, simple-dynamic, complex-dynamic
Aldrich, et al. (1984)	Amount of information on environment	Attribute, population, domain
McCann & Selsky (1984)	Complexity in environment and adaptation to change	Type 1,2,3,4 and 5 (Hyper-turbulence)
Jauch & Kraft (1986)	Effect on goals	Performance, objective
Milliken (1987)	Uncertainty as a flow: understanding, effect, response	State, effect and response
Dixit & Pindyck (1994)	Origins of uncertainty exogenous or endogenous	Input, internal/ technical
Sutcliffe & Zaheer (1998)	Lack of knowledge of nature and stakeholders	primary, secondary, supplier
Courtney, et al. (1999)	Amount of information on environment	Level 1, 2, 3 and 4
Mercer (2001)	Internal capabilities to understand uncertainty	Hidden, expected outcomes, random
De Meyer, et al. (2002)	Amount of information on environment	Variation, foreseen, unforeseen, and chaos

probabilities to event outcomes, the greater the uncertainty. The extent to which the elements of an environment are patterned is used as an indicator of the degree of environmental uncertainty (Emery and Trist 1965; Terryberry 1968). For instance, because of the difficulty to predict the performance of stocks with high variance in returns, stock volatility indices have been used as an indicator of uncertainty (Snyder and Glueck 1982).

Strategic Responses to Uncertainty

The strategic management literature offers many recommendations for coping with uncertain environments. For the present purpose we arrange these into two categories, namely, *normative* responses and *preemptive* responses. Normative responses are those that follow strategies prescribed by conceptual theorists and that have been proved to work through empirical research and observation. In preemptive responses, organizations focus on specific segments of the environment, where they will be able to direct unique strengths with which to mediate, dictate, and take advantage of environmental turbulence.

Normative Strategic Responses

The normative or prescriptive responses are primarily derived from the works of Porter (1980, 1985), Miles & Snow (1978) and other scholars who have subjected the prescribed typologies to empirical analysis (Anderson & Zeithaml 1984; Hill 1988; Jones & Butler 1988; Miller 1988; Nayyar 1994). While these theorists do not agree as to what strategic actions are appropriate under the different environmental conditions, what they propose can be grouped into generic strategies and organization-environment fit strategies. With generic strategies, given the likelihood of intense competitive rivalry among firms, the basic focus of the firm should be to develop a position of competitive advantage in the industry, either through a variation of economies of scale as is seen in the case of defenders and cost-leaders; or through some variation of economies of scope that is evident in prospectors and differentiators (Miles & Snow 1978; Porter 1985). Under the organization-environment fit perspective, the successful firm is one which is able to develop a two-way fit between itself and the environment. This it does through "forward-fit" strategies, e.g., product-market strategies, R&D investment, and environmental scanning; and "retro-fit" strategies such as streamlined organizational structure, adaptive control processes, and optimal production systems.

While the normative perspective provides a valuable framework for analysis and strategizing, it is perceived to be weak on several counts. The notion of a formal strategy has come under severe attack by the proponents of logical incrementalism (Quinn 1978), who suggest that total posture planning for firms is a waste of corporate energy, and should be eschewed in favor of a more inductive and incremental approach to precipitating events. Proponents of emergent strategies advocate a "crafting strategy" where the previous action of managers alters their future action as surely as a potter's tacit knowledge shapes every pot in a uniquely different manner (Mintzberg 1985).

Preemptive Responses

This is a contingency-based perspective which incorporates both the resource based view (Barney 1986; Hansen and Wernerfelt 1989) and the core competency view (Prahalad and Hamel 1990) of the firm. These views see the firm more as a bundle of valuable, rare, inimitable and imperfectly substitutable resources and knowledge-based strengths, which need to be harnessed and sustained in order for the firm to grow and prosper. Theorists who hold this perspective believe that organizational cultures (Barney 1986), routines (Nelson & Winter 1992), core competencies (Prahalad & Hamel 1990), competition-based advantages (D'Aveni 1994), human resource systems (Lado & Wilson 1994), and entrepreneurial strengths (Rumelt 1987) reside uniquely within the individual firm. Firms which develop them as a strategic weapon may be in a stronger position to reap advantages from turbulence than those that adopt a reactive posture. The preemptive strategies are intuitively appealing, but they have not been supported by as much empirical research as the normative theories. Preemptive prescriptions may be more difficult to operationalize for research, for the same reason they are more effective in operation.

Operational Level Strategies

How managers actually go about the business of dealing with uncertainty at the operational level presents several challenges. Courtney *et al.* (1997) discuss methods of strategy development that take into account the level of uncertainty the organization faces. According to them, conventional strategies are easily applicable to Level-1 uncertainty, where the future is clear and predictable. Level-2 uncertainty, where there is a limited set of mutually exclusive possible outcomes, requires decision analysis, option valuation models and game theory approaches to decision making. Under Level-3 uncertainty, where the range of future outcomes cannot be accurately identified, more sophisticated methods of forecasting and scenario planning are required. These authors suggest analogies and pattern recognition methods as the best strategy for decision making under Level-4 uncertainty since there is no basis to forecast the future in chaos.

Other researchers offer interesting ways of strategy formulation under uncertainty. For instance, Mercer (2001) suggests that the strategy to handle uncertainty needs to have complementary short-term and long-term objectives. At any level of uncertainty, the short-term plans should be incorporated with long-term strategy such that objectives for both of these strategies are not conflicting. Atherton (2003) provides an analysis of the nature of knowledge in small businesses, arguing that knowledge on internal and external uncertainties can be represented as a two-by-two matrix anchored by transactional vs. strategic as end points on one dimension, and objectivity vs. subjectivity as anchor points on the other dimension. The outcome of this research is that small businesses should find a balance based on the effect applied by environment. Lewis (2004) looks into different industries within Europe in order to come up with strategies for businesses that reduce uncertainty and equivocality. He collects data using research instruments, such as questionnaires and provides strategies to the management to address the issue.

Discussion and Future Research

Some amount of uncertainty must be accepted as a given in every aspect of strategic planning (Bernhard 2003). But greater amounts of uncertainty require correspondingly greater information with sufficient scope, delivered in a timely way and with the appropriate level of aggregation for managers to be able to make the appropriate strategic choices (Mangaliso 1995, Chenhall and Morris 1985). Until recently, the biggest roadblock has been the availability of real-time reliable information that would provide the platform for strong enough scenarios to make confident organizational planning projections. But, as more and more information becomes available to managers, the crux of the strategy process will shift to how well the firm can use this information to reduce the amount of uncertainty it faces in its environment. This, in turn, will depend largely on how well the organization can derive utility from the knowledge generated from the information at its disposal and integrate it in its decision-making processes (Spender 1996).

Our interest in writing this chapter began with the observation that, unlike in the natural sciences, the concept of uncertainty has not received systematic research attention in organization theory. An initial literature search confirmed that management research on uncertainty can best be described as patchwork, varied, scattered and non-cumulative. Consequently, one finds several clusters of researchers who write seemingly unaware of a large amount of writings already in existence on this topic. Several of the studies we read, in their rush to link uncertainty to other causal or consequential variables, ended up only giving superficial attention to uncertainty. The net result is unconnected but overlapping writings which are at once duplicating one another while at the same time contradicting one another. The present chapter was an attempt at ameliorating the situation by obviating this discrepancy. We did this by scanning the relevant literature in organizational behavior, organizational theory, operations and strategic management, and other related literatures. The initial outcome of this research showed an astounding variation in the conceptualization and treatment of uncertainty. We next classified the research into definitions, sources, and classifications of uncertainty. The result of our effort, though far from exhaustive, is a much more unified presentation of the essential nature of uncertainty. Future research endeavors must extend this analysis in order to further add to our understanding of the concept of uncertainty in other ways. For instance, can uncertainty be reduced across the confines of space and time? What are the implications of subjective versus objective certainty? Are decision-makers justified in using subjective certainty under conditions of uncertainty? Does the existence of uncertainty create loopholes in which executives can introduce their subjective political agendas? What about the role of ethics and fiduciary responsibility in all of this? Research that can answer these questions will go a long way toward advancing our understanding of the concept of uncertainty.

CHAPTER 3

Subjective Certainty in Organizations*,5

Over the years, many organizations have demonstrated inertia towards radical changes in the environment. Unfortunately, the result of this inertia or inability to adapt to changing environments is evidenced in many corporations going out of business or being bought by stronger rivals. In this chapter, we argue that this inability to react is due to the organization's entrenched subjective cognitive map. Ironically, the entrenched cognitive map provides the organization with structure and coherence to cope with the environmental uncertainly, both external and internal (Thompson 1967). However, in order to introduce flexibility and help the organization to be able to quickly adapt to the rapidly changing environment, we suggest that the shared subjective map has to be changed as well.

Environmental Change – Cause for Failure

One of the remarkable phenomena of the period leading to the end of the 20th century was the increased number of corporate failures. For example, of the original Forbes 100 companies in 1917, sixty-one had ceased to exist by 1987; and of the thirty-nine surviving firms, only eighteen remained in the Forbes 100. Another indicator of corporate failure is that of the original five hundred companies that made up the Standard and Poor's 500 when it was introduced in 1957, only seventy-four remained on the list by 1997 (Wadhwa 2009). Of these seventy-four, only twelve out-performed the Standard and Poors Index itself over the 1957-1998 period. Furthermore,

---

* This chapter is based on a paper co-authored with the late Dr. Stanley Young of the University of Massachusetts-Amherst.

only two of these twelve—General Electric and Johnson and Johnson—are
not part of industries which themselves out-performed the Index (Foster
2001; Standard & Poor's Index 1957-1998). One of the main contributing
factors to corporate failure during this time was the inability of firms to
adapt to changes in the environment (Duncan 1972, Downey, Hellriegel, &
Slocum 1975, Mintzberg 1994a, Bernasek, Shiller, Zook, Varian & Porter
2001). A number of reasons have been suggested for this inability, including
political and economic opposition, questions as to the desirability of such a
change, or the natural inertia or conservatism of individuals in organizations, etc. (Corboy & O'Corrbui 1999, Van Zwieten 1999). As a consequence,
the history of organizational life illustrates firms are just as likely to go out
of business because they failed to adapt to changed environmental conditions or because they failed to develop new and appropriate strategies
(Parnell, Lester, & Menefee 2000). This chapter focuses on one of the root
causes of corporate failure: the inability to adapt to environmental uncertainty. The chapter is predicated on the following three propositions:

1. A shared subjective cognitive map exists within the organization to
    cope with environmental uncertainty, both external and internal, which
    has to be changed if a new strategy is to be adopted.
2. Strategy is typically seen to represent a permanent guide for the func-
    tioning of an organization.
3. The proposal to change an existing strategy usually arises under uncer-
    tain environmental conditions, and often does not provide a clear-cut
    solution to the organization's problem situation.

The implication of the first proposition is that in order to change strategy
one has to change the shared subjective map. In this case, the significance of
the concept of shared subjective uncertainty will be reversed.

Limitations of Rationality

One of the traditional problems of strategy analysis has been how to deal
with the issue of environmental uncertainty and how to improve the ability
to predict and respond to future events (Abels 2002). In his book, *Risk, Uncertainty and Profit,* noted economist Frank Knight (1921) distinguished
between risk and uncertainty. He defined risk as measurable, and uncertainty as the sort of situation that a casino gambler faces. Knight defined
true uncertainty as doubt about the future, which cannot be reduced to
known probabilities and cannot be insured against. The chance of some-
body inventing the cure for cancer in the next twenty years is one example
of uncertainty. In business, uncertainty is endemic. Firms have to build factories and install machinery years before they find out how many items

they can sell. If events take an unexpected turn they can end up with too much capacity or too little.

Writing in his book, *General Theory of Employment, Interest and Money,* John Maynard Keynes (1965) expanded on the Knight thesis and noted that, according to conventional text book theory, firms should treat uncertainty as risk, assign probabilities to each possible outcome and choose the investment plan that maximizes expected returns. Keynes (1921) had earlier argued that this sort of ultra-rational decision-making was impractical, and that the outstanding fact about business is the extreme precariousness of the knowledge on which investment decisions were made:

> If we speak frankly, we have to admit that our basis of knowledge which rests on estimated yield ten years hence of a railroad, copper mine, textile factory, the good will of patent medicine, an Atlantic liner, of the building of the city of London amounts to little and sometimes to nothing (Keynes 1921: 134).

He further noted that, given these constraints, decisions to invest can only be taken as a result of animal spirits of spontaneous urge to action rather than inaction, and not as the outcome of the weighted average of quantitative benefits multiplied by quantitative probabilities. Nevertheless in the strategic management literature one still finds the normative ideal of the linear model of perfect adaptability, the desirability of scanning and interpreting future events and responding in real time so as to maximize the opportunities to minimize the risks in the environment (Aguilar 1967; Mintzberg 1994a; 1994b; 1994c). This uncertainty suggests that one might deal with the issue of uncertainty through more sophisticated statistical information processing systems or quantitative devices. One might expand environmental data collection processes or utilize more sophisticated analytical devices such as the Delphi technique, statistical futurism, game theory, scenario analysis, focus groups, etc. (Rowe and Wright 1999; *LRP* 1992; Ansoff & Sullivan 1993; Seaton 2002). There is a continual effort to improve the possibility of predicting, with a certain degree of objective certainty, what future events may occur (Kreinovich 2000; Anderson 2000, Lewis & Harvey 2001). One critique to this approach is provided by Herb Simon (1982) in terms of his concept of bounded rationality. He maintains that the ability to process information in an organization is limited by the decision makers' cognitive abilities. According to him, therefore, one cannot assume that the decision outcomes are based on perfect information, rather they are based on limited information availability. Consequently, managers can only analyze events and make decisions on the basis of that limited information or bounded rationality.

While one can hardly argue about the desirability of achieving a certain degree of objective certainty as to future events, the real question is its feasibility. This simply goes back to the Knight and Keynes observation that this is not likely to happen in the near future. The argument of this chapter is that rather than relying on the possibility of a strategic management team being able to develop in any complete fashion an ability to predict with certainty future events, what the firm relies on is the development of what we shall call the *subjective certainty* in the firm. Here one must distinguish between objective and subjective certainty. *Objective* is the ability on the basis of certain epistemological and methodological rules to establish what is true or certain about certain external phenomena. *Subjective* on the other hand is a feeling of absolute conviction that what one believes is true and valuable.

Subjective versus Objective Certainty

The importance of subjective and objective dimensions of decision-making in organizations was broached in a discussion by Thompson (1967) in his book, *Organizations in Action*. Adapted from Thompson's book, Figure 1 is a two-dimensional matrix that shows the possible decision situations with two variables defining the dimensions. These are beliefs about cause-effect relationships (subjective knowledge) and existence of accepted standards (objective knowledge). The two dimensions are dichotomized so that beliefs about cause/effect relationships may either be complete or incomplete, and existing standards may be clear or unclear. Combined, these two dimensions define four possible decision situations. Objective certainty occurs when cause-effect knowledge is complete and the standards are clear. This is a simpler and more straight-forward situation in which rational decision making is appropriate and computational strategy can be used. The situation becomes more complex in situations where cause-effect knowledge is complete but the standards are unclear. This is a situation of subjective certainty which should be subjected to social tests and where the final strategy is arrived at through a process of give-and-take. On the other hand is a situation where the standards are clear but cause-effect knowledge is incomplete. This is a situation of subjective uncertainty, which requires revisiting the goals and objectives of the organization or the application of what Thompson calls the instrumental tests. The final quadrant is a situation where cause-effect knowledge is incomplete and the standards are unclear. This is the quadrant objective uncertainty or façade where decision-making follows inspirational strategy—hoping for the best but preparing for the worst.

Shared Cognitive Subjective Map

The psychological necessity of having a cognitive map in order to respond to the external environment requires no detailed analysis (Schwenk 1984, Tversky & Kahneman 1974; 1980; 1982; 1983; 1996). People do not approach their environments with blank minds and merely record physical sensory data and respond to it in a distinctive manner (involuntary nervous response). As Scheibe (1970) has observed, what human beings do, how they behave, depends on what they want, their values, and what they consider to be true or likely; their beliefs about themselves and the world, and their psychological ecology.

Figure 3.1: Subjective vs. Objective Certainty

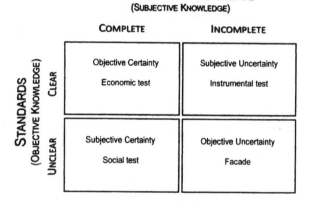

Adapted from Thompson (1967)

In the organization, when making decisions managers estimate the probability of the likelihood of a scenario or event to occur based on the scenarios 'availability' in the manager's memory (Tversky & Kahneman 1982). That is, the ease with which a scenario or event can be called to mind increases the subjective probability estimates of its likelihood (Ross & Sicoly 1982). This learning process, based on the memory's availability (recollections), creates a "strategic bias" in the managers' decision processes (Bukszar 1999). When based on collective memories, this bias becomes part of the organization's cognitive map.

For their firm's strategy, therefore, managers rely on this assured and yet subjective cognitive map. The map is normative. At any given time there

exists an established orthodox manner in which the managers are to conduct their mutual and collective efforts in terms of executing the firm's
strategy (Cohen 2001). Over a long period of time on the basis of trial and
error, a body of knowledge and a set of core competencies have been built
up within the firm, which provides the firm a unique competitive advantage
at its continual profitability, its unique capability and continued success
(Porter 1980; Barney 1991; McGee & Sawyer 2003). It is assumed that the
basis of the organization's past and continued success rests on the continued use of this conventional orthodoxy. These sets of beliefs are assumed to
be rational, realistic, successful, pragmatic, efficient and effective. They constitute, in part, the intellectual and social capital of the firm and, if followed,
will presumably always lead to organizational success. The content of such
an organizational strategy is typically incorporated as part of the organization learning process in a set of written memos, mission statements, policies and procedures, and unwritten shared understandings of tradition,
norms and conventions (Patterson 2002).

Seen from this perspective, the organization's strategy becomes important for several reasons. It reflects the context in which the firm finds itself,
and the unique past history of the firm. It provides a road map that informs
the managers about the organization's priorities, what it considers to be of
value, how to decide among competing alternatives, how to behave and relate to others, etc. (Raymond, Julien & Ramangalaby 2001). Overall, this
map is a guide that provides the manager with a sense of correctness, and
management practices with a coherent rationale and justification for action
(Clarke & Mackaness 2001). It provides, through the collective learning and
shared experiences, a mutual understanding and order in the face of internal and external uncertainty. An organization by its very nature requires
the corporate activities to be exercised in an orderly and predictable fashion. Managers cannot renegotiate daily the essential activities of organizational life of which strategy is probably the most significant (Greve 2002).
It would be too disruptive to be continually questioning organizational activities. Have we defined our goals correctly? Is this environmental event
significant or not? Do we have sufficient information? Managers would be
too concerned about the negative consequences of making the "wrong" decisions, and the anxiety would make them retreat into obsessive report
analysis and number crunching, which would cause long delays before any
action is taken—a condition described in the literature as "analysis paralysis" (Peters and Waterman 1980; Eisenhardt 1989; Langley 1995; Forbes
2005).

The shared subjective cognitive map is a body of knowledge, which the
individual accepts because is convinced about its correctness and rightness.
In general, managers believe in it and invest themselves in it. This makes it
possible for managers to continue to operate in the face of uncertainty, in
the absence of complete data, facing the possibilities of failure and with the

conviction that no matter what the problem is, the traditional strategy will somehow pull the organization through (Clarke & Mackaness 2001, Greve 2002). It is during periods of organizational crisis that managers are most likely to hold on to traditional strategies in as rigorous a fashion as they can—as the darkness closes in, one raises the spears higher. This map provides certainty in a world in which managers will never have perfect information or be able to respond to a changing world in a completely timely fashion. They will never be able to predict what the nature of the world will be in five or ten years from now and prepare themselves accordingly (Anderson 2000). Thus, given challenges to management by the government, unions, employees, competitors; and the uncertainty in which we live, if one holds one's confidence in the conventional strategy, the organization will see it through.

Legitimate and Illegitimate Change

We now turn to the second proposition—that strategy represents a permanent part of corporate operations. Part of the organizational culture is to delineate what dimensions of organizational practices can be changed and/or improved, and which should be maintained or preserved.

Legitimate Change

In organizations, such issues as corporate strategy, managerial authority lines, managerial development, and organizational functional perspectives are thought to be permanent aspects of the corporate mantle and are therefore not to be changed. There is usually an established organizational change process that defines how, when, where, what and on what basis certain practices should be changed. This is a legitimate change process. Legitimate changes are those changes that are to be encouraged, and that are expected to lead to progress, profitability and long run organizational well-being. Perceived illegitimate change, on the other hand, relates to those dimensions of organization that are to be constant and stable, "where all to be learned about has been learned," and attempts to change these will lead to chaos, inefficiency and a loss of progress or profits (Woiceshyn 2000).

Usually, change is routinized (Perrow 1974, 1977, 1985; Tuominen, Rajala, Möller, & Anttila 2003). Great companies such as Unilever, Procter and Gamble, General Electric, and many others have rather elaborate systems in terms of developing and introducing new products into the marketplace. This is an ongoing and continuing process. Cost reduction may be a continuing change process in many firms and may result in changes in job requirements, loss of status or pay, changes in staffing arrangements, all of which may be opposed by individual workers or groups of workers. However, such opposition is viewed by the organization as illegitimate opposition. Department stores continually change their fashions, others are continually improving their software and industrial engineers continually improve productive processes and/or equipment. Supermarkets may continue to revise an array of products they display on their shelves. All these types of changes are legitimate, routine and frequently institutionalized; they are part of the core strategy.

Illegitimate Strategic Change

In reference to the third proposition, we suggest that the organization's strategy is part of the beliefs of the organization's members (Dutton & Jackson 1987; Dutton, Walton & Abrahamson 1989). As a result, a typical proposal to change strategies based on conditions of environmental uncertainty will be rejected when it challenges the shared subjective beliefs of the employees about the fact that the current strategy is a permanent feature of the organization. The organization's members therefore view such "imposition" as betrayal or an illegitimate element in the organization (Fiske & Taylor 1991).

There have been circumstances in which some fundamental aspects of the corporate strategy, which as "beliefs" were assumed not to be changed, have been changed. This change creates a paradox, which underlies the tenets of strategic management. On one hand management traditionally strives to deliberately uphold the current intended strategy and its implementation through various forms of employee orientations, training, and discipline (Mintzberg and Waters 1985). But when radical change is necessary, management has to deny these practices, which they previously sought to uphold. This is the change problem with which this chapter is concerned. It is the situation in which someone is attempting to change a strategy which was understood in the past not to be changed. Thus, as many analysts have observed, such situations can arise when the intellectual and social capital—the core competencies which in the past gave the firm a competitive advantage—no longer add value because of changes in the environment (Byrne 1996; Prahalad and Hamel 1990). In the 1980s, for example, there was a noticeable contrast between the American and Japanese firms. Chrysler and GTE were plodding along while their Japanese counterparts, Honda and NEC, were surging ahead of them with vigor and determination. Most of the failing U.S. companies were unwittingly yielding their competitive advantage by surrendering their core competencies through outsourcing as Chrysler did when it outsourced its engine manufacturing to Mitsubishi (Prahalad and Hamel 1990). And then there is the example of the

Morgan Stanley Bank, which restricted its marketing to doing business with *Fortune 500* companies, because it could not adjust to serving the most dynamic sector of the economy, small technology companies. A yet more recent example was the merger of Chrysler and Daimler-Benz which experienced difficulties because Chrysler was a marketing company whereas Daimler-Benz was an engineering one, and neither wanted to subjugate its functional dominance to the other (Hansell 2000). On a more macro and international scale, was the disinvestment campaign against businesses with ties to South Africa. What changed the highly profitable business environment in South Africa is when it was revealed that the profitability was predicated on the exploitation of Black workers and the violation of their human rights and dignity. As seen in Chapter 6 of this volume, many corporations were reluctant to adjust to this new reality or were content with incremental changes when radical change approaches were needed.

The Challenge of Change

Why is change so difficult? When the top management team attempts to introduce a drastic change in strategy, in the absence of a widespread sense of a sinking ship, such changes are viewed on the part of organizational participants as illegitimate and fiercely resisted (Waldman, Ramirez, House & Puranam 2001). Strategies cannot be arbitrarily modified. Simply pointing out that alternative strategies exist is insufficient to bring about change. When it is not entirely clear that significant strategic change is necessary, the conservative elements of the organization will argue that the solution to the problem is simply a more efficient execution of the existing strategy. One will not give up a successful, historical, established strategy, when the alternative strategy's success is uncertain and illegitimate. Even when the strategy being pursued shows signs of failure, researchers have found that instead of cutting their losses and dropping a failed course of action, people will continue to pursue it due to escalation of commitment (Staw 1981). This phenomenon has been found to occur in several instances, such as investment decisions, decisions to enter or to exit a given product-market (as the SA examples indicate), decisions on career choices, and other public policy decisions. In strategy, managerial effort has paid more attention to the implementation of the existing strategy rather than to the formulation of alternative strategies. Also, there is the conflict between those who believe that a more successful execution of the existing strategy will save the firm as against those who want to develop an alternative strategy. As the history of firms indicated at the outset of this article, it is just as likely that firms will deliberately pursue the originally intended strategy rather than change it.

A good example is Montgomery Ward which, at the turn of the twentieth century, was the largest mail-order business in the United States, supplying rural and small-town households around the country with goods produced in America's factories (De Long 1997). But Montgomery Ward found it difficult to adjust to the new format of specialty stores, superstores, and discount department stores that were introduced in the 1960s. Value began to migrate throughout the 1980s from the outmoded business designs represented by Montgomery Ward and others to new, more competitive ones such represented by Wal-Mart, Target, Home Depot, and others that were better able to satisfy customers. In conclusion, this argument proposes that typically, firms are not completely adaptive but rather incorporate mechanism wherein they are only adaptive within the boundaries of their existing strategy.

Change Strategy

Organizations from time to time either change or adjust their strategies as a direct response to environmental changes (Barr 1998). But, is it possible to induce a successful change process in terms "altering or modifying" the firm's strategy from one to another (second-order change)? Some literature suggests that second-order change is atypical even in times of environmental upheaval (Greenwood & Hinings 1988; Tushman & Romanelli 1985). Empirically Meyer and his colleagues found that second-order change occurred only about 30 percent of the time (Meyer, Brooks & Goes 1990; Meyer Goes & Brooks 1994).

We propose that to achieve a successful change in strategy, one might think in terms of doing socio-analysis (Young & Litterer 1991). Socio-analysis involves (1) diagnosis, (2) isolation of error, (3) consciousness raising, and (4) insight for problems of abnormal organizational behavior. Diagnosis involves data collection, pattern identification, interpretation and error isolation. With sufficient data, one should be able to isolate the organization's pathology, that is, where the cognitive map driving the existing operation of the organization is wholly inconsistent with the environment in which the organization finds itself. It is really an isolation of organizational dysfunction, of unreality or mythology. Managers may postulate motives, goals, or values which are not achievable or desired. Psychological inconsistencies have to be experienced. While one may note the conflict, the individual may not see it or be willing to change until he/she experiences the dysfunction. This requires the insight to connect one's own cognitions and failed actions, which is the final stage of the process. Given the specific delusion that is or has been isolated, the analysis is to supply valid knowledge or a new set of assumptions which the managers can now adopt.

Conclusion

What this chapter attempted to demonstrate was that over time, a shared subjective cognitive map emerges as to how the strategy of the firm should be executed. It is this *subjective certainty* what makes possible for the firm to continually operate in terms of whatever external events occur. Because of the conviction that historically this strategy is correct, attempts to change it will, psychologically, institutionally and sociologically, cause collective problems to arise. When top management attempts to change the strategy, it should beware of the fact that it is going to conflict with the shared collective map and the staff may view the need for change as simply another environmental event which is probably false and is to be ignored or avoided in some fashion. There is a tendency to view organizations, at least from a normative perspective, as being rational, adaptive and responsive mechanisms. One premise of this review is that the organizational change literature maybe somewhat deficient as to the nature of organizational pathologies. Of particular concern are those maladies, i.e., maladaptive and rigid behavior, which are hidden in the collective long-term memory of the enterprise and are not easily accessible to the conscious review of organizational participants. This subjective aspect of organization may present some of the more difficult dimensions of change in favor of new and different organizational strategies. Finally, one has to confront the problem of conflict between issues of objective and subjective certainty insofar as certain objectives create challenges over long-held beliefs about the firm, the marketplace, economy, competition, etc., such a challenge erects problems on psychological loss, a loss of self confidence, defensiveness, inertia and inability to act. One was to realize the firm's strategy combines objective and subjective elements and the strategy staff host able to work with both.

CHAPTER 4

Responsiveness to Turbulent Environments[*,6]

While posing a real problem for management practitioners, environmental turbulence finds only fleeting and fragmented mention in the mainstream academic literature of management. This chapter discusses turbulence, traces its origins, and subjects it to critique. Based on observations of responses to it and several theoretical streams, including new theories such as hypercompetition and chaos theory, a framework of responsiveness to turbulence is presented and discussed, and a set of propositions presented. The rationale behind the framework is that successful responses to turbulence are contingent on socio-cultural as well as technical-economic conditions in the environment.

Background

The relationship between planning and firm performance has long been the subject of intense debate (Andrews 1971; Miller and Cardinal 1994; Mintzberg 1994a). The debate reflects one of the major concerns of strategic management: aligning the skills and resources possessed by the organization with opportunities and constraints in the environment (Jemison 1981a; Miles and Snow 1994; Schendel and Hofer 1979). This alignment with an uncertain and fast-changing environment engages the organization's core competencies in the pursuit of corporate goals (Andrews 1971;

---

* This chapter is based on a paper co-authored with Dr. Raza A. Mir of William Paterson University, Wayne, New Jersey; and Dr. Bradford J. Knipes of Westfield State University, Westfield, Massachusetts.

Mahoney and Pandian 1992; Prahalad and Hamel 1990; Thompson 1967). A variety of contingencies determine the fit sought by organizations, and one of these contingencies is environmental turbulence.

Environmental turbulence is a phenomenon that is increasingly being recognized as having an important moderating influence in the relationship between planning and performance (Ansoff 1991; Goodstein and Boeker 1991; Miller and Friesen 1983; Mintzberg 1994b; Theobald 1994). It has been mentioned with increasing frequency as researchers have grappled with how organizations should cope with rapid changes in the environment. For instance, according to some observations, environmental turbulence was involved in the changing managerial roles within Japanese corporations (Johnston 1995); the reconstruction of management in post-Communist Eastern Europe (Johnson and Loveman 1995); the "greening" of organizational studies (Shrivastava 1994); the systemic organizational upheavals in the United States and their effect on big corporations (Quinn and Mason 1994); organizational reengineering (Hammer and Champy 1993); and the TQM movement (Klimosky 1994). This may be the reason why some of the most prominent scholars in the field have warned that environmental turbulence will continue to challenge organizations (Ansoff 1984, 1991; Drucker 1980; Huber 1984).

Despite these admonitions, there appears to be little research on managing in turbulent environments. The academic literature aimed at helping managers learn to cope in turbulent environments is sparse (Camillus and Datta 1991; Ellis 1982; Theobald 1994). Consequently, most managers either suffer from the effects of paralysis by analysis, or simply resort to tried and tested approaches to strategy such as centralization, standardization, and efficiency maximization, which are largely inappropriate in turbulent conditions (Bourgeois, McAllister, Mitchell 1978; Cameron, Kim, and Whetten 1987; D'Aveni 1989; Khandwalla 1978). Largely following the threat-rigidity response pattern, these strategies often act as blinkers which provide focus on direction, but block out the peripheral vision so crucial in turbulent environments (D'Aveni 1989; Mintzberg 1990; Staw, Sandelas and Dutton 1981).

Turbulence thus poses a fundamental challenge to strategic management by mediating the planning-performance relationship (Miller and Cardinal 1994). If turbulence can be accepted as real, then the entire premise of strategic planning may be challenged as merely an exercise in organizational self-delusion (Mintzberg 1991). This chapter explores the theoretical streams of research that have informed the debate, and offers a map for the researcher studying the impact of strategic planning on firm performance. The intention is to engage the academy in discourse concerning the origins of environmental turbulence, its manifestations, and implications for organizations.

Understanding Environmental Turbulence

Characterizations of environmental turbulence are as numerous as they are disparate. Some sources define turbulence as a wild, unruly, and disorderly commotion, a great perturbation (Webster's English Dictionary); others as changeability, speed, and novelty in the environment (Ansoff 1984). Still others define it as environments in which the speed of change and inter-connectedness of elements are high (Emery and Trist 1965). In empirical studies, some researchers have operationalized turbulence through the perceived relationship between centralization and effectiveness (Huber, Miller and Glick 1990), while others see it as a key moderator in the planning-performance relationship (Miller and Cardinal 1994; Pearce, Robbins and Robinson 1987). According to Pfeffer and Salancik (1978), turbulence is change coming from anywhere, without notice, producing unanticipated consequences both to those initiating it and those experiencing it. Some characterize turbulence as difficult-to-predict discontinuities in the environment (Aldrich 1979; Keats and Hitt 1988), especially in situations where there is room for strategic choice within a highly deterministic environment (Hrebiniak and Joyce 1985). Environmental turbulence causes factors in the environment to become more uncertain and the value of important variables to become more erratic (Smart and Vertinsky 1984). As Metcalfe (1974) noted, the sequential escalation of the interrelatedness of the *complexity* and *dynamism* in the causal texture of the environment results in greater uncertainty, which, in turn, creates problems for complex organizations. Bourgeois and Eisenhardt (1988) refer to the analogous high-velocity environment characterized by rapid discontinuous change in demand, competitors, technology, or regulation, so that information is often inaccurate, unavailable, or obsolete. In this chapter, we define environmental turbulence as *the complex interconnectedness of environmental elements which exhibit rapid, unpredictable, and discontinuous change that makes the future hard to predict.*

Related Literatures

Environmental turbulence can be explained from several literatures and research streams. These include resource dependency, decline, crisis management, volatility, uncertainty, chaos theory, and postmodernism.

The underlying premise of the resource dependency literature is that decisions are made within organizations under the assumption that the environment is a system-like context of resources, social structures, and the natural environment (Aldrcich 1979; Aldrich and Pfeffer 1976; Lawrence and Lorsch 1967; Pfeffer and Salancik 1978). In order to survive and prosper, the organization must acquire the resources that are critical to its functioning from an environment which is uncertain. This makes the availability of resources uncertain, which, in turn, calls upon the organization to find a way of reducing this uncertainty. But there are also other organizations which are competing for the same resources. The organization must reduce its dependence on these organizations and maximize dependence on itself (Pfeffer and Salancik 1978). Change is assumed to occur via autonomous variations in any element of the environment and is continuous and potentially predictable (Lenz and Engledow 1986). But when environments become turbulent in the manner defined earlier, then the assumption of continuity and predictability of change breaks down. Resource dependency does, however, encourage organizational learning through opportunistic surveillance, and protection of the technical core of the organization through buffering (Pfeffer and Salancik 1978; Thompson 1967).

The decline literature is one that many authors tend to associate with diminishing resources in the organization's task environment, which tends to result in decreasing internal resource munificence over time (Cameron, Kim and Whetten 1987; Cameron, Sutton and Whetten 1988; D'Aveni 1989; Harrigan 1985b; Starbuck and Hedberg 1977). The typical response to declining resources is workforce reduction, which invariably leads to a variety of adverse effects (Greenhalgh, Lawrence and Sutton 1988). If the environment continues to be turbulent, then downsizing and efficiency maximization strategies are only "fuel for temporarily perpetuating the lingering paralysis" (D'Aveni 1989: 599). While Harrigan (1985a) recommends the timely use of exit strategies as appropriate in declining industries, Zammuto and Cameron (1985) recommend domain consolidation and reduction of scale of operation in order to protect the firm's core product-market domain. In general, it can be said that both decline and turbulence have negative effects on the organization. The difference is that decline tends to be felt by employees who are mostly at lower levels of the organization, while turbulence is felt mostly by the top management team (Cameron, Kim and Whettem 1987).

The crisis management literature is grounded on the understanding that crises are events inside and outside the organization that represent threats to organizational survival (Smart and Vertinsky 1977; Starbuck, Greve, and Hedberg 1978; Zammuto and Cameron 1985; Shrivastava and Mitroff 1987). They occur as a result of simultaneous and interacting failures in internal and external environmental elements (Perrow 1984). Turbulence is described more as a consequence of the crisis than its causal antecedent. The challenge for management is to devise ways of anticipating, preventing, and managing these corporate crises. Several models for doing this are suggested in the literature (Mitroff and Pauchant 1990; Meyers and Holusha 1986; Shrivastava 1987), most of which deal with the need for organizations to undergo a "paradigm shift," or a fundamental rethinking of organizational goals and practices.

Volatility is typically defined as the change in the rate of change: as long as the rate of change is constant, it is predictable and therefore not problematic (Bourgeois 1978, 1985; Snyder and Glueck 1982; Tosi, Aldag, and Storey 1973). Although research on environmental volatility can be traced back to the contingency theorists of the 1960s, the state of the art is still unclear (Snyder 1987). Debate seems to center around the question of whether environmental volatility can be measured objectively. As with the crisis literature, the concept of volatility seems to involve change that is unpredictable, coming when it is least expected, and with varying degrees of frequency and amplitude (Bourgeois 1985; Snyder and Glueck 1982; Tosi, Aldag, and Storey 1973). The distinction between turbulence and volatility or crisis in terms of duration is that a crisis or a volatile situation is usually of shorter duration; with turbulence, no end seems to be in sight (Smart and Vertinsky 1977).

The next important consideration of environmental turbulence comes from the uncertainty literature (Daft 1986; Downey and Slocum 1975; Duncan 1972; Galbraith 1977; Thompson 1967). As indicated in the preceding chapter, uncertainty is the absence of information; the difference between the amount of information required and the amount of information available; or a state that exists when an activity is embarked upon with less than complete knowledge about the probability of its outcome (Daft 1986; Downey and Slocum 1975; Galbraith 1977). Further reading of the literature on uncertainty (Bourgeois and Eisenhardt 1988; Downey and Slocum 1975; Duncan 1972; Thompson 1967) leads one to conclude that an implicit causal relationship exists between turbulence and uncertainty: environmental turbulence is regarded as a precursor to environmental uncertainty, varying in direct proportion to it. Yet a distinction is made that turbulence is the state of the world, whereas uncertainty is a state of mind. As Downey and Slocum (1975) note, uncertainty is a set of stimuli which lack meaning for informational value until perceived by an individual. A turbulent environment requires a high degree of abstraction by decision-makers in order to produce manageable strategic maps. As the level of uncertainty increases, so does the individual's lack of knowledge and thus the need for higher-quality strategic maps in line with the law of requisite variety (Ashby 1956). Responses to uncertainty may vary, from defensively buffering the organizational core (Thompson 1987), to proactively seeking potential synergistic benefits from the source of the turbulence itself, to capitalizing on competitors' weaknesses (D'Aveni 1994).

Another stream of research that feeds into environmental turbulence is based on chaos theory (Baumol and Benhabib 1989; Levy 1994; Stacey 1991; Thietart and Forgues 1995). While not a new theory itself, the application of chaos theory to management research has been helpful in illuminating the concept of environmental turbulence (Levy 1994). Conceptualized mainly as a study of complex, non-linear dynamic systems, chaos theory may be seen as an opportunity for extension of systems theory into the non-linear realm of organizations (Katz and Kahn 1966). Organizations are enmeshed in chaos with tension between forces which push the organization toward order and stability, e.g., planning, structure, coordination, control; and forces which push the organization toward instability and disorder, e.g., innovation, entrepreneurship, experimentation. A balance of these forces is necessary. Organizations need a sufficient level of order and structure, but too much would destroy the organization's creativity. Organizations also need a certain amount of chaos since it is the only way to find new forms, but too much would undermine their very existences (Thietart, et al. 1995). Chaotic systems exhibit a sensitive dependence on initial conditions: small errors in the estimation of the present state result in exponentially large errors in the estimation of future states. As a result, long-term forecasting becomes impossible under chaos. Turbulence tends to drive the system toward chaos. In such situations successful firms are those that adapt and react faster than the competition, and the best way of coping is through learning. But, according to some observers, systems do not remain chaotic for long (Phelan 1995). Business environments appear to go through long periods of incremental change, punctuated by the occasional discontinuous disruption, the essence of the "punctuated equilibrium" (Gersick 1991; Tushman and Anderson 1986). Under normal, stable conditions, however, it is recommended that firms shift the allocation of resources more toward strategic planning.

The last stream of research, postmodern theory, drawing from Baudrillard's (1986) assertion that "[t]he secret of theory is, indeed, that truth does not exist" (1986: 141), suggests that all attempts by managers to "know" are rendered futile by the existence of an ultimate unknowability (Harland 1987). In effect, postmodernism equates strategic planning with a "truth claim" made by the organization, and suggests that in an enacted environment, such claims are at best a product of organizational navel gazing, and at worst, an enforcement of discipline and order in the organization, that ends up stifling all organizational creativity (Rosenau 1992).

The above discussion was an attempt to demonstrate that the discourse on turbulence is informed by numerous streams of research. Table 4.1 is a summary of the discussion. While this list of research streams is not complete, it represents the diversity of sources. Despite arguments to the contrary, it is our belief that environmental turbulence is on the increase (Drucker 1980; Mangaliso and Lane 1992; Miles and Snow 1986). Since its impact on contemporary organizations will be telling, we believe it is imperative that management researchers become more deliberate in studying the concept. The radical socio-political and technological changes sweeping the globe will continue to put a strain on the organizations' capacity to cope.

Table 4.1: Turbulence-Related Literatures

Stream	Authors	Premises
Resource dependence	Aldrich and Pfeffer 1979; Pfeffer and Salancik 1978; Thompson 1967	Environment is system-like context of resources, social structures, natural environment. Organizations use their resources to actively shape their environments or protect their core by buffering.
Decline	Cameron, et al. 1987; 1988; D'Aveni 1989 ; Greenhalgh et al. 1988; Harrigan 1985b ; Zammuto and Cameron 1985	Diminishing resources in organizations' task environments lead to adverse effects such as layoffs and mutual blame. Typically felt at lower levels of the organization. Turbulence is felt at higher levels.
Crisis Management	Meyer and Mitroff 1987; Mitroff and Pauchant 1990; Perrow 1984; Shrivasta and Mitroff 1987	Events inside and outside organizations represent threats to organizations' survival. Organizations must anticipate, manage, and prevent corporate crises.
Volatility	Bourgeois 1978, 1985; Smart and Vertinsky 1977; Snyder 1987; Tosi, et al. 1973	Problem with volatility is that change in the rate of change in the environment leads to unpredictability. Unlike turbulence, volatility is of finite duration.
Uncertainty	Bourgeois and Eisenhardt 1988; Daft 1986; Downey and Slocum 1975; Duncan 1972; Galbraith 1977; Thompson 1967	Exists when knowledge about activity is incomplete, probability of outcome not known. A set of stimuli that lack meaning until perceived by individuals. Uncertainty is a state of mind; turbulence is the state of the world.
Chaos Theory	Baumol and Benhabib 1984; Levy 1994; Stacey 1991; Thietart and Forgues 1995	Organizations viewed as complex, non-linear, dynamic systems that exhibit characteristics of both chaos and stability. High levels of turbulence lead to chaos which makes long-term forecasting practically impossible. Short-term planning enhanced by simulation.
Postmodernism	Baudrillard 1986; Harland 1987; Rosenau 1992	Truth is unknowable. Attempts at long-range planning like "navel gazing." Only stifle organization creativity.

Evidence and Criticism of Turbulence

Evidence

From the foregoing discussion it can be understood why an analysis of the firm's environment should be a *sine-qua-non* in the overall schema of strategy-making. The history of organizations in the U.S. and elsewhere bears testimony to the fact that ignoring this can be fatal to the firm. Many organizations have been driven out of business due to ignorance of environmental developments and inability to adapt to them. Large firms such as Paramount Studios, Warner Bros., and MGM in the movie industry were shaken when the television networks CBS, NBC and ABC entered the same scene. Facit was unprepared for the onslaught of the word processors. GTE failed to capitalize on the miniaturization revolution of the 1980s, losing its leadership role in the microprocessor market (Prahalad and Hamel 1990).

Some firms have been able to *harness* turbulence to their advantage by strategic product entries, divestments, mergers and acquisitions. For instance, the recent takeover of Lotus by IBM, or AT&T's use of value-based management systems to turn the divestiture of the "Baby Bells" to advantage may be seen as *turbulence-mediated turnarounds* rather than mere reactions to turbulence. But turbulence has not been limited to the economic, political and technological dimensions. In the legal or regulatory sphere, many airlines did not quite fathom the impact of the 1978 Airline Deregulation Act. The opening up of Eastern European markets may be seen as turbulence-mediated opportunities in the international arena. These opportunities have led multinational corporations to swiftly redeploy their resources strategically in these incipient markets (Johnson and Loveman 1995).

In the turbulent socio-political environment, who could have predicted the myriad stakeholder coalitions that pressured Nestlé, S.A. to stop marketing infant formula to third world countries as a substitute for breast feeding? Who could have anticipated that the international anti-apartheid sanctions and divestment movement would coalesce with a broad range of stakeholders and successfully pressure many multinational corporations to reluctantly withdraw from South Africa (Mangaliso 1992, 1997; Crawford and Klotz 1997)? Evidently, social responsibility, or the imperatives derived from it, has the potential to generate turbulence, as Exxon and Union Carbide found out. The overwhelming evidence of turbulence in real-life situations, as well as the fundamental impact it has on planning systems has led many scholars to concur that the environment is shaped by specific conditions within it, and that better understanding of organizational dynamics requires a fuller understanding of the determinants of environmental contexts, i.e., the economic, technological, socio-political and ecological environmental contexts (Glueck 1976; Whittaker 1978).

Criticism

While turbulence has been studied intensely, its premises have not gone unquestioned. As has been pointed out, the metaphor of turbulence was borrowed from the natural sciences by Emery and Trist (1965). While it offers explanatory value, it may not be invested with the analytical rigor that goes into the making of a theory. Scholars have criticized the usage of turbulence in the management literature on two premises: relativity and metaphorical generalizability.

Relativity

Some scholars (McCann and Selsky 1984; Mintzberg 1991; Woodward 1982) point out that the Emery and Trist typology does not give a complete account of real-world manifestation of the environment. They do not see turbulence as a universal phenomenon. Indicating that turbulence is not a discrete state passed through by all members of the environment, these authors assert that turbulence is a relative phenomenon. Other organizations may see dynamic, complex conditions simply as opportunities for innovation and growth. The major shake-out in the computer industry and its move away from mainframes may be a serious threat to IBM, but a golden opportunity for corporations like Dell and HP/Compaq. In short, turbulence is in the mind of the strategist. Mintzberg (1991 1994b) has gone so far as to state that turbulence is a figment of imagination since no one has made an attempt to measure it. Still others (Ansoff 1991; Mangaliso and Lane 1992) have argued that the evidence provided by upheavals in several industries in the late 1980s and 1990s warrants further studies of environmental turbulence.

Metaphorical Generalizability

In the physical sciences, turbulence is the movement of fluid masses in all directions, with much mixing and many collisions. When this happens, eddies, vortices, waves and `white water' are some of the patterns which form. Turbulent flows occur when the combination of density, depth and velocity overcomes the viscosity (Hurlbut 1976). A closer reading of the physics literature reveals that two kinds of turbulence are distinguishable: streaming flows and shooting flows. The Emery and Trist (1965) metaphor of turbulent environments seems based on streaming flows. Shooting flows, as generated in rapids and falls at very high velocities, may have opposite implications for management, whereby collaborative and planning-based systems are indicated. Although Emery and Trist do talk about the system developing collaboration and other adaptive mechanisms for coping with increased turbulence, they do not explain what happens when the coping capacity of the members is completely overwhelmed. This issue was taken up by McCann and Selsky (1984) who proposed the existence of another type of environment which they called the *Type 5* or hyper-turbulent environment. In this environment, the degree of turbulence is seen to have exceeded the coping capacity of the system as a whole. New and radically different phenomena such as social triage begin to manifest themselves. Coping mechanisms in hyper-turbulent environments include the formation of social *enclaves* by survivors and social *vortices* which suck the failed organizations down under. On the whole, corporate strategies for dealing with hyper-turbulent environments can be seen in such real-world phenomena as mergers (social enclaves) and divestitures (social vortices). The notions of environmental turbulence and hyper-turbulence have important implications for the strategy-making process.

Toward a Framework of Responsiveness

As the preceding sections suggest, responses to turbulence traverse a contingent and negotiated realm. Organizations need to make customized choices depending on internal resources and external contingencies. Given the contested nature of the debate, it is important to resolve the normative and preemptive perspectives so that responses to turbulence are intelligible both to practitioners and to researchers.

In suggesting a framework of responsiveness to turbulence, it is important to anchor the concept in specific environmental contexts. In today's globalizing world, organizations operate in environments which are characterized by a great amount of diversity, and this diversity cannot be fully captured in a single continuum. In this chapter, we have chosen to use two environmental dimensions that we believe are most fundamental in their impact on the functioning of the business firm. Following Mitroff and Kilmann (1984), we have named these dimensions the technical-economic dimension, and the socio-cultural dimension. While these dimensions are not exhaustive and may thus be said to be an oversimplification of the reality of the business environment, we believe that they achieve a useful parsimony. Unlike Mitroff and Kilmann (1984), we believe that cognitively, technical-economic and socio-cultural issues do not exist as opposite ends on the same continuum, but are independent dimensions.

The technical-economic dimension refers to the non-living domain of the business environment, including technology, machinery, manufacturing, production, distribution, information, finance, accounting, and marketing. Indeed, TQM and reengineering may be seen both as responses to technical-economic turbulence by those who practice them, and as sources of turbulence to those who are victims to them. While it can be said that technical-economic turbulence is an all-pervading artifact of the business environment, its differential impact on different industries is apparent. For instance, the steel industry does not have to contend with the rapidity of technological innovation that is the norm in the computer industry. Similarly, marketing-based innovation would impact the beverage industry far more than it would the oil industry. Clearly, proactive strategic responses to the environment will be mediated by the nature of technical-economic turbulence present in the industry.

The socio-cultural dimension deals primarily with the human domain of the business environment, which is driven mostly by non-economic considerations. Humans act opportunistically—within bounded rationality—in the pursuit of their selfish goals and objectives (Williamson 1985). The socio-cultural dimension encompasses political (in)stability, culture, morality and ethics. Even with globalization, organizations must alter their production, distribution and marketing strategies in response to local socio-cultural quirks. Strategic decision-making must respect the socio-political turbulence that pervades the global marketplace. Multinational corporations have far fewer issues of political uncertainty and policy upheaval in mature secondary markets like the EC than they do in the incipient market economies of Eastern Europe. Conversely, embryonic markets offer far greater potential for growth than mature markets.

Based on the above two dimensions, our framework of strategic choices in a turbulent environment is presented in Figure 4.1.

Quadrant 1: Placid-Placid Environment

The simplest environments are those characterized by both technical-economic and socio-political placidity. Such environments are usually seen in protected economies or in industries where entry barriers are very high, such as the diamond industry (Bain 1956). Here, the strategic choice would be to focus on maximizing the Ricardian rents that can accrue from the business. The Top Management Team would be able to assume a long-range planning horizon, focusing on such goals as resource generation, allocation, and growth. Firms operating in such environments may be best served by *bureaucratic* strategies, emphasizing consolidation, control, and cost reduc

Figure 4.1: Framework for Dealing with Turbulence

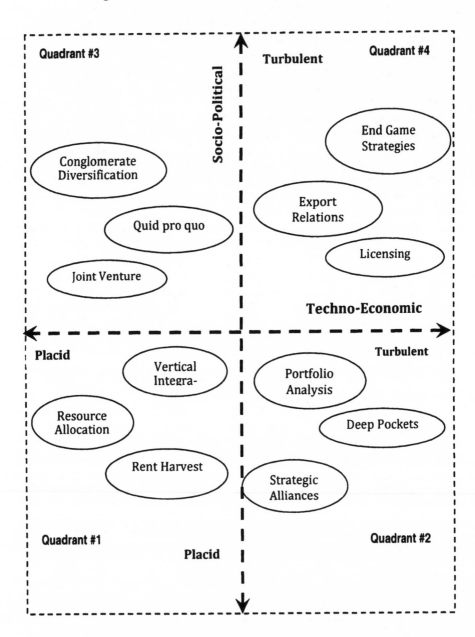

tion to maximize efficiency and sustain competitive advantage. We consider the term "bureaucratic" to be appropriate even though, in contemporary popular literature, it has been misconstrued to focus only on its negative aspects such as extreme pigeon-holing of responsibility, insensitivity, maliciousness, rigidity, and hostility (Goodsell 1985). There are also positive aspects of bureaucracy which ensure that millions of routine jobs are performed reliably, including mail delivery, approval of applications, quality control checks, and answering consumer complaints. We have used bureaucracy in the Weberian sense to connote division of labor, emphasis on efficiency, dedication to profession, and respect for authority and position in the chain of command (Weber 1958), all of which are positive attributes in environments that are placid.

Three key sub-strategies can be identified for firms operating in placid-placid environments. Given the certainty of resources in this situation, the issue of *resource allocation* becomes important. In this environment, the success of a firm is predicated upon internal and reflexive activities aimed at improving efficiency, such as managing cash-flows, inventory control, and labor relations. Similarly, according to transaction cost economics, the market or hierarchy question would favor the hierarchy because control would be internalized (Coase 1937; Williamson 1985). In the make-or-buy decision, where a firm has to weigh the benefits of integration against subcontracting or using other market agencies, the firm would choose to make something. Generally, the *vertical integration* strategy would be preferred, with the firm taking charge of upstream or downstream activities in the value chain (Porter 1985).

Finally, the placid-placid environment must be recognized as ephemeral. In a world characterized by creative destruction, such a benign environment may conceal the storm which follows the calm (Schumpeter 1934). Organizations operating in placid-placid environments, therefore, are advised to exploit their *rent harvesting* strategies before the available rents are eroded by competitive entry. This may be very clearly seen in the pharmaceutical industry where firms try to maximize the rents from various star drugs while they are patent-protected, and then invest these rents in product development, in anticipation of severe falls in market share and revenues following the expiration of patent protection. The foregoing discussion may be summed up into the following three propositions:

P1: In placid-placid environments, successful firms focus on resource allocation, which includes managing cash-flows, inventory, and labor deployment.

P2: In placid-placid environments, firms will seek to minimize costs and maximize efficiency through vertical integration.

P3: Because of the ephemeral nature of placid-placid environments, successful firms will adopt rent harvesting strategies in
order to prepare for future uncertainties.

Quadrant 2: Placid-turbulent Environments

While the placid-placid environments may have been artificially prevalent
in the 1970s with best examples in the command economies of Eastern Europe, such environments are few and even more ephemeral these days.
Many organizations that operated in Eastern Europe's command economies
have had to deal with fundamental paradigm shifts that they were scarcely
equipped for. In market economies, technology has often been observed to
step in and upset the homeostatic conditions that would normally be found
in a mature marketplace. A situation where socio-political placidity coexists
with technical-economic turbulence—as is presently the case in a significant segment of the U.S. economy—lends itself to the execution of *option-
based strategies*. The strategic choices of organizations operating in such
environments can be viewed through what has come to be known as the
"option lens," which considers strategy as a process of resource deployment
options (Bowman and Hurry 1993). A super-set of strategic options is
created, which can be held in abeyance until the right opportunity arises.
When this occurs, full-scale deployment of resources is unleashed. The option lens offers a better view of organizational resources in placid-turbulent
environments.

Three key sub-strategies can be identified in the option-based realm.
First, *portfolio analysis* can be seen as one way of keeping various strategic
choices alive and viable. A portfolio may be seen at once as the firm's investment in a basket of securities (Majd and Pindyck 1957; Myers 1984); or
as the actual, minimal presence in various industries in anticipation of future increased involvement (Bowman and Hurry 1993; Hurry, Miller and
Bowman 1992). For example, various pharmaceutical companies keep minimal investments in a variety of bio-technology firms in anticipation of
major breakthroughs. Such a strategy is especially useful when the organization is operating in a broad industry environment characterized by technological upheaval, like the computer industry. This strategic choice is also
influenced by the amount of capital at a firm's disposal. The amount of
available resource is not entirely a function of a firm's size, but of the existence of *deep pockets* (D'Aveni 1994). The issue is not how much a firm has,
but how the reserves are deployed within a universe of opportunities. Deep
pockets provide the ability for swift global entries, defensive price strategies and political leverage in a hypercompetitive world.

Third and last, firms that exist in environments characterized by t-
echnical-economic turbulence would benefit from synergistically exploiting

the advantages of *strategic alliances* (Gulati 1994; Parkhe 1993). Strategic alliances have been proliferating at an exponential pace in the 1990s, and one reason for this has been the need to pool organizational resources, especially in high financial or intellectual capital arenas, where individual entry is daunting. For instance, in the pharmaceutical industry, where the cost of new product innovation has been estimated to be in excess of $500 million (Malknight 1995), it is not uncommon to see two large multinational corporations announce collaborative research proposals to work for new drug development. Such an arrangement is usually followed either by co-marketing arrangements or division of the global marketplace for marketing rights. In the semiconductor industry, which can be characterized as turbulent because of rapid, unpredictable technological changes, firms have increasingly turned to collaborative and co-operative inter-organizational ties for research and development (Aldrich and Sasaki 1995; Tushman and Anderson 1986). Sometimes the costs become so large that the government must step in to facilitate the process, as seen in the case of the U.S. semiconductor industry. A government-supported consortium—SEMATECH—was established in 1987 when it became obvious that none of the individual firms had sufficient resources to commit at the scale required to remain competitive with Japan (Spencer and Grindley 1993). SEMATECH may have been influential in sparking a resurgence of the U.S. semiconductor industry by 1992. In sum, strategic alliances form a powerful tool for operating in technical-economically volatile markets, but usually need an environment of socio-political stability to be fully effective. The following three propositions follow from the above discussion:

P4: The most effective strategies in environments characterized by socio-political placidity and technical-economic turbulence are those based on portfolio analysis techniques.

P5: In environments with socio-political and economic-technical placidity, firms enhance the long-run sustainability of their competitive advantage by diversifying their investments.

P6: Firms which compete in environments with socio-political and technical-economic placidity enhance their competitive positions by engaging in collaborative strategies such as strategic alliances.

Quadrant 3: Turbulent-Placid Environments

The issue of socio-cultural turbulence in an atmosphere of relative technical-economic stability is often seen in the case of multinationals which are planning to expand into terrains that are relatively unexplored for their product range, with a severe shortage of local and specific information. The foray of the Western multinationals into Eastern Europe in the mid-1980s was characterized by this tentativeness. It is argued that such situations offer *collaborative strategies* as the most logical strategic choice for organizational survival and success.

The unequal distribution of knowledge among organizations can best be tackled by entering into partnerships, which may offer both stability and a pool of knowledge. However, given the delicate and transient nature of some strategic alliances, they may not be the most suitable form of partnership. Organizations operating in socio-political turbulence, but technical-economic stability may need to concede the "political imperative," (Doz and Prahalad 1991) to the local subsidiary in the joint venture.

Three sub-strategies may be identified in this realm. The first, *quid-pro-quo,* holds the local subsidiary accountable for organizational performance, either through equity sharing or another form of compensation. For instance, Pepsi was able to enter Russian markets with a franchising arrangement despite the extreme shortage of hard currency in Russia, because it actively helped the Russian government top find international markets for naval defense equipment.

Such a strategy may not always be feasible, especially in regions that lack a dominant business with which to enter into a quid-pro-quo relationship. Another strategy is to enter into a *joint venture* with the organization, whereby a third organization is created. When liability for the joint venture is limited to the newly created entity, turbulence may be minimized. Most organizations operating in the Middle East surrender majority equity rights to their local subsidiaries in exchange for marketing rights and bureaucratic liaison.

In environments subjected to selective, industry-based sanctions, companies may reduce their risks by a conglomerate diversification strategy, spreading their investment into a variety of areas. For instance, Japanese organizations facing a threatening US tariff escalation on luxury cars would benefit from active presence in other segments of the automobile market, or from diversifications like those of Honda (generators, lawn mowers). General Electric Company, faced with protests to get out of nuclear warhead manufacturing, benefited from their acquisition of the National Broadcasting Company (NBC). The following three propositions sum up the thoughts presented above:

> P7: In environments characterized by socio-cultural turbulence and technical-economic placidity (Q-3), the most appropriate strategies are the *quid-pro-quo* strategies in which a firm gives in order to receive.

P8: In order to stave off the effects of socio-cultural turbulence in Q-3 environments, the most appropriate strategy to adopt is the joint-venture.

P9: To reduce risk in Q-3 environments, firms seek unrelated or conglomerate diversification.

Quadrant 4: Turbulent-Turbulent Environments

When socio-political turbulence is accompanied by a great deal of technical-economic turbulence, the chaotic system that develops makes long-range planning impossible. This is the quadrant where learning becomes important, a situation which gives credence to Mintzberg's (1991) scorecard of "Learning: 1, Planning: 0." Here, the firm must develop *distancing strategies*, whereby the gains of entry and presence are significantly given up in an attempt to reduce the risk associated with operating in highly uncertain markets. For instance, firms in industries such as computer software, music, and motion picture distribution, etc., find it difficult to operate marketing alliances in relatively unknown markets because of lax copyright laws and the consequent fear of infringement of intellectual property rights. Distancing strategies may be seen as traversing a spectrum, from an organization seeking to limit its knowledge-based and capital-based commitment to a region, to outright divestiture of resources in an attempt to protect existing markets.

One strategy that may be adopted by new entrants into markets in the turbulence-turbulence quadrant of Figure 3 is to develop *export relations* with local trading houses. Such arrangements are often characterized by low margins and tenuous market presence, but offer at least a limited opportunity in an area where a more organic presence is unfeasible. On the other hand, for firms already present in the market, technology may be *licensed* out to other areas, where potential is limited but misuse is nonthreatening. Many Hollywood movies, which outlive their product life cycle as entertainment vehicles in the U. S. and Europe, generate revenue in global markets. Their simultaneous release in the U.S. would have risked piracy[7].

Last, when neither export options nor licensing arrangements are feasible, a firm may consider the option of *endgame strategies*, whereby total divestiture from a particular market may be necessary either to prevent further escalation of losses or to protect proprietary information. The decision by the EC not to do business with non-ISO9000 certified firms may be a response to environments that are turbulent on both dimensions of figure 3. Another example is offered by Polaroid Corporation and later Eastman Kodak, which decided to exit the South African market when it became clear that their products were being used to further the political objectives of the apartheid regime. The following propositions capture the essence of the preceding ideas:

P10:   Firms entering turbulent-turbulent or Q-4 environments will seek export relations with local trading partners.

P11:   For firms already operating in quadrant 4-type environments, the best way to protect their product and preserve their presence in the market is through licensing.

P12:   When conditions of turbulence escalate beyond the organization's coping capacity, the most appropriate strategies are endgame strategies such as divestiture that help to minimize losses.

Discussion

Before discussing the implications of the framework offered in this chapter, it is important to acknowledge its weaknesses. Our framework suffers from the same weakness as others (e.g., the BCG matrix) in that it is simplistic: A two-by-two representation of reality is bound to leave out many of the in-between conditions, the gray areas. For instance, between the extremes of placidity and turbulence, Emery and Trist (1965) suggested two other states: placid randomized and disturbed reactive environments. If these two were to be added, we would then end up with a much more complex 4x4 matrix. We chose to stay with a 2x2 matrix in the interest of parsimony. As Mitroff and Kilmann (1985) note, it is the essence of the discussion rather than the subtleties that is important. Others have advocated for simplification as a necessary starting point in the process of theory development (Lant and Mezias 1990). Obviously, the strategic responses are not strictly confined to their categories in the model. Rather, these are likely associations, and the suggested propositions need to be evaluated and empirically tested.

Since environmental turbulence is now a fact that organizations have to live with, several implications may be drawn. As a cover story in a *Fortune* magazine once warned, organizations will have to "hold on, it's going to be a bumpy ride" (Richman 1995). First, managers and researchers must recognize that turbulence will place demands on organizations that are not necessarily consistent with their organizational strategies. This implies that organization leaders must infuse a culture of adaptations, flexibility, and speed of response. Second, managers will have to continuously explore new ways of doing things through innovation, entrepreneurship, and experimentation. It will be necessary from time to time to establish temporary equilibria as a precondition for adapting to the vagaries of a constantly changing environment. Third, the increased unpredictability of the environment implies that managers must have in their arsenal a battery of responses which they can utilize when needed. Furthermore, a new organizational paradigm would permit the development of catalogues of configurations from which organizations will have to choose when environmental forces are more powerful than organizational viscosity (Thietart and Forgues 1995). Fourth, the complexity, diversity and turbulence in the environment mandates a duplication of those conditions within organizations— a sort of "law of requisite turbulence" to paraphrase W. R. Ashby (1956). As stated earlier, organizations must have the right mix of stability and chaos to be able to survive under conditions of turbulence.

Implications of a paradigmatic shift as a prerequisite for managing under turbulent conditions are profound. For one thing, the process of organizational sense-making—in the same sense as the economic principle of comparative advantage—seems to suggest that when two firms are adept at making sense of different environments, they can offer critical support to each other in conditions of turbulence. This does not mean that firms must coalesce, alter market structure, or arrange monopoly power as a prescription for survival. It means that in a world of "interculturalizing" business interests, a firm entering a new market often gains greater advantage in a collaborative relationship with another firm which may already be in possession of the necessary adaptive information. Examples of such strategic alliances include AT&T with Olivetti (Italy) and MCI with British Telcom in telecommunication; US AIR with British Airways and Continental Airways with Alitalia in the Airline industry; and Alfa-Romeo (Italy) with Nissan (Japan) in automobiles.

The impact of a combination of socio-political and technical-economic forces originating in the organization's environment is best illustrated by South Africa in the 1980s when a number of multinational corporations reluctantly succumbed to the divestment movement and withdrew their business from that country. This issue is reported more fully in this volume. In Eastern Europe, the creation of new 'market economies' has led to a variety of options for diversifying MNCs. Within organizations, it has been demonstrated that cultural heterogeneity can play a part in economic performance (Franke 1991). Thus, a firm's strategic responses must pay due respect not only to the technical-economic imperatives of survival, but also to the socio-political imperative of legitimacy. A firm that is prepared for the impact of public policy is most suited for survival.

Conclusion

It has often been observed that organizations operating in turbulent environments neglect experimentation, risk-taking, and the examination of non-core activities. The planning process becomes short-term crisis management, making long-term strategic planning a casualty. The most difficult job for a management team facing turbulence may be the traditional one: re-evaluating and redefining what business they are in, what other businesses they should be in, or even whether they should be in a particular business at all. They should maintain the methods and techniques that help them to succeed in relatively placid environments, while being vigilant of signals that indicate a paradigm shift for emerging environmental contingencies. The graveyards of organization history are filled with "successful" organizations which failed to undertake paradigm shifts in conditions of turbulence. It is perhaps this activity above all which determines whether a firm succeeds or even survives. We concur with those who believe that the only sustainable competitive advantage organizations have in turbulent environments is the ability to enhance learning (Mintzberg 1991; Stata 1989). Learning will be enhanced through discourse about how organizations will function in the ever increasing turbulence of tomorrow's environments. We hope this chapter will advance that process.

CHAPTER 5

Strategy and the Environment

Strategic management has been flooded by an infusion of research from diverse areas. Contributing researchers have drawn their concepts from as near afield as marketing (Biggadike 1981); industrial organization (Porter 1981); and administrative behavior (Jemison 1981a). Others have drawn their concepts from other, broader social disciplines—for example, psychology, sociology, social and cultural anthropology, economics, and political science (Neghandi 1975). Unfortunately, this literature has been uneven and, to a large extent, noncumulative.

The different contributing researchers have employed different paradigms, units of analysis, causal presumptions, and research biases. The metaphoric usage of many of the concepts, along with nuances and conjectures from the various disciplinary roots, has hindered attempts to develop the unified, systematic body of knowledge so vital to the pursuit of any area of academic research. Consequently, although the practitioner has benefited from promising theoretical developments and valuable insights, there remains much heterogeneity and divergence in the field. A clear pattern of research findings from one study is frequently muddied by contradicting evidence from the next (Starbuck 1976). This predicament may be one of the factors which have led some scholars to proclaim that strategic management is "bankrupt" (Hurst 1986), that "we need a revolution in strategic planning" (Stubbart 1985), or that the field is in a state of "conceptual confusion" (Van Gils 1984: p. 1073).

Most of this confusion stems from the usual definitional and measurement problems that are characteristic of much research in organizational behavior (Miles, Snow, and Pfeffer 1974). For example, in his discussion of problems with semantics in management, Urwick (1960) noted that no less than 23 different meanings were associated with the term "management" (Jemison 1981a). The goal of this chapter, therefore, is to review the litera-

ture relevant to this area of research to provide a conceptually secure platform from which further discourse can be launched.

To achieve this goal, the chapter will sketch the evolution of Strategic
Management from its Business Policy roots. Next, we will discuss some salient features of the environment. After that, we will consider strategic responses to such environments, followed by an exploration of the literature
on the interaction among environment, strategic planning, and performance. After highlighting the critical role of the subjective side of strategy
making, we will briefly survey the literature in the international, intercul-
tural context. We will conclude with recommendations for a course of future theory building.

A Brief History of Strategic Management

As noted in the previous chapter, the term strategy owes its origins to the
Greek words *stratos* (army) and *agogos* (one who leads). *Strategos,* or the
army general, is the highest ranking military officer. In the management
literature, strategy represents the art of the general (Collis 2005). As a concept, strategy was first introduced to management during the 1950s (Hurst
1986). But as the field of Strategic Management rapidly emerged in the
1960s and 1970s, a growing number of researchers and practitioners
sought to improve their understanding of the forces that shape the strategies of complex organizations (Miles, Snow, and Pfeffer 1974). That is when
Business Policy—the precursor to Strategic Management—was introduced
in many MBA curricula as a capstone course in the training of future corporate leaders (Schoenberger 1992). Strategic Management grew in importance in response to the growing need organizations had to address the
environmental issues that affected them so that they could survive and
prosper in the long run (Miles and Snow 1978, Hofer and Schendel 1978).

During the 1960s, when strategic management was evolving from business policy, the environment was relatively stable and benign (1986). Most
large-scale enterprises were relatively undiversified, operating as single or
dominant businesses (Channon 1973; and Rumelt 1974). The Western
world's pervasive optimism derived from the notion that managers could
control the growth and destiny of their organizations. Up to that time, management theory had relied heavily on universalistic principles propounded
by such theorists as Taylor (1911), Fayol ([1916] 1949), and Weber (1947).
In addition, organization studies concentrated on examining the impact of
internal variables, such as size, technology, workflow, and leadership style,
on the organizational structures, behavior patterns, and effectiveness. This
so-called "closed-system" approach pervades the works of Woodward
(1965) and Perrow (1967), and studies on leadership at the Ohio State Uni-

versity and the University of Michigan (Stogdill 1965; Likert 1967). At this time, the environment was assumed to be static and was, therefore, ignored (Miles, Snow, and Pfeffer 1974).

As the 1960s unfolded, however, the dysfunctional consequences of pedantic adherence to guidelines based on environmental determinism soon became evident in the face of two major developments: (a) rapid growth in the size and diversity in the marketplace, and (b) rapid environmental change. The growth in size of many of the large scale enterprises and their diversification into widespread geographic markets and products, well documented in classical management studies, led to the development of the venerated four-stages model (2) (Chandler 1962; Stopford and Wells 1972; Channon 1973; Rumelt 1974; Montgomery 1979). Ansoff (1984) attributed this rapid growth to the marked acceleration of change within firms and the accelerated application of science and technology to management. Simultaneously, researchers and scholars began to observe a shift from labor- to capital-intensive industries (Drucker 1986) and a tendency toward the growth of the tertiary segment. The upshot of these developments was that the guidelines and norms that had previously been taken for granted were increasingly questioned.

The second development, perhaps more central to this study, was the dynamic changes in the environment. These were reported with increasing frequency in management journals (Emery and Trist 1965; Metcalfe 1974; Metcalfe and McQuillan 1977; Tushman and Anderson 1986). The relatively smooth growth of the world economy after World War II became a thing of the past. There was growing acceptance among many contemporary theorists that not only was the environment changing, but that the rate of change was also rapidly increasing. As Emery and Trist (1965) noted, "The environment contexts in which organizations exist are themselves changing, at an increasing rate and towards increasing complexity."

It is in the context of these changes, therefore, that the evolution of strategic management must be understood. As a field of study, strategic management has been defined in several ways. Some scholars have defined it as the process by which general managers of complex organizations develop and utilize a strategy to co-align their organization's competencies with opportunities and constraints in their environment (Jemison 1981a; 633). Other scholars have defined the term normatively, as a three-step, systematic approach of managing strategic change (Ansoff 1984). These steps consist of positioning the firm through strategy and planning; responding strategically in real-time through issue management; and systematically managing resistance during the implementation phase.

In the last thirty years so much has been written about organizational environments that, beyond the terminological confusion, there is now considerable acceptance that organizational environments are tending towards a higher rate of change (Metcalfe and McQuillan 1977; Lenz and Engledow

1986). Furthermore, many scholars and futurists have predicted that these changes will not be smooth but full of discontinuities (Drucker 1969; Whittaker 1978; Tushman and Anderson 1986; Tichy 1983). Drucker has described the period from the 1970s onward as an "age of discontinuity" (1969) and a period of "turbulence" (1980; p. 3), where what may be individually rational is collectively irrational.

According to scholars of macro-organizational theory, as organizations move into this kind of environment, the collective effect of panic reactions will nullify any immediate gains and further undermine the stability of the whole system (Metcalfe and McQuillan 1977). To manage organizations at this level of complexity, these scholars have developed Macro-Organizational Management (MOM) techniques, while other scholars have suggested other forms of co-operation (McCann and Selsky 1984) and coalition (Harrigan 1985a).

Environment

According to Duncan (1972), the environment consists of relevant physical and social factors outside the boundary of an organization that are taken into consideration during organizational decision making. Duncan distinguished between the external and internal environment, but his definition of the former seemed to treat the environment as a single entity "out there." Contemporary scholars, however, have moved away from this single-entity conceptualization. Several researchers have suggested that the external environment consists of different sectors, which exist in two strata (Bourgeois 1980; Starbuck 1976; Dill 1958; Miles, Snow, and Pfeffer 1974).

Types of Environments

In his landmark review of organizational environments, Starbuck (1976) delineated two types of environments. The first consisted of elements with which the organization was in direct exchange. The second included elements that compete with the organization for resources being directly exchanged. Environmental strata surrounding organizations are given different names by different scholars: Bourgeois (1980) speaks of task and general environment; Pearce and Robinson (1985) refer to operating and remote environments; Hall (1972) calls them specific and societal environments; Neghandi's (1983) external environment consists of the task and societal strata.

The task/operating/specific environment—the stratum closest to the organization—consists of the actual organizations, groups, and people with whom the organization must interact to survive and prosper. Duncan (1972) seems to be referring to the task environment when he writes about competitors, resource suppliers, and technological developments. The general, remote, or societal environment—which makes up the outer stratum—consists of sectors that provide an important background influence on the entire management process and yet affect the organization only indirectly. This stratum usually includes social, political, economic, technological, and ecological factors (Whittaker 1978). In short, the general, remote, or societal environment indirectly affects all organizations in a given society, and the task, operating, or specific environment affects the individual organization more directly. As pointed out earlier, this study focuses on Bourgeois's (1980) general environment.

However, although there seems to be general agreement on environmental stratification, there remains scant agreement over what comprises each stratum. For instance, some scholars (Dill 1958) include regulatory groups in their classification of task environments, while others (Dess and Beard 1984) exclude regulatory groups. Some emphasize technology in the task environment to the degree that a company must meet the technology requirements of its own industry (Duncan 1972). Others consider technology to be a component of the general environment to the extent of the level of scientific and technological advancement in a given society (Kast and Rosenzweig 1973).

In the present study, the external environment will be the focus and will be defined to include all factors outside the firm that can lead to opportunities or threats. Many of these factors are typically beyond the firm's control (Jauch and Glueck 1984; Child 1972; Pearce and Robinson 1985). We will therefore refer to them as the external environment.

Environmental turbulence

The issue of turbulence has been discussed in the preceding chapter. We reiterate here that it is Emery and Trist (1965) who have generally been credited as the first scholars to recognize the salience of turbulence in the firm's external environment. Several other scholars subsequently added their own building blocks, which have augmented understanding of this phenomenon (Metcalfe 1974; Metcalfe and McQuillan 1977; Drucker 1980; Woodward 1982; McCann and Selsky 1984; Dess and Beard 1984; Smart and Vertinsky 1984; Cameron, Kim, and Whetten 1987). Recently, the rise to prominence of environmental turbulence has generated a great deal of conversation in the field as portrayed in the Mintzberg – Ansoff exchange in the early 1990s (Ansoff 1991; Mintzberg 1990). The following collage of typical comments made over the last decade by a variety of scholars bears witness:

> For the one certain thing about the times ahead, times in which
> managers will have to work and to perform, is that they will be
> turbulent times. . . . Sometime during the 1970s the longest pe-
> riod of continuity in economic history came to an end. At some
> time during the last ten years, we moved into turbulence.
>
> (Drucker 1980, pp.1–3)

> Environmental turbulence is a condition that will intensify, not
> abate. Excessively turbulent conditions that threaten to over-
> whelm adaptive capacity pose serious, but largely unexplored re-
> search and social policy questions.
>
> (McCann and Selsky 1984, p. 460)

> Managers build their private success models through experience,
> trial and error, successes and failures. When the environment is
> undergoing discontinuous change [or turbulence], the historical
> success model becomes invalid, and acts to block the newly rele-
> vant data.
>
> (Ansoff 1984, p. 334)

> The trends [facing multinational enterprises] imply increasing
> turbulence. A more certain and unstable environment may
> emerge for the MNE . . . and shifts in the external environment are
> going to come from anywhere, and without notice, to produce
> consequences unanticipated by those initiating the changes and
> those experiencing the results.
>
> (Gladwin and Walter 1980: p. 574)

Although phrased in different ways, the theme common to these excerpts is
that turbulence will continue to play a significant role as a major challenge
to modern organizations. It therefore is timely to study this phenomenon
and to study both how corporate executives perceive it and how they factor
those perceptions into their strategic choices. Despite the recognition given
to the significance of environmental turbulence, however, researchers have
devoted few studies to the concept.

Emery and Trist (1965), Terryberry (1968), Aldrich (1979), and
McCann and Selsky (1984) studied the interconnectedness among environmental factors as a major source of environmental turbulence. Other
scholars have studied the concept only as a facet of other, broader phenomena, e.g., crisis management (Smart and Vertinsky 1984), decline (Cameron, Kim and Whetten 1987), or environmental volatility (Tosi, Aldag, and
Storey 1973; Bourgeois 1978, 1985; Snyder 1979; Snyder and Glueck
1982). Note that environmental volatility and turbulence are similar in one
respect: they represent discontinuous (or revolutionary) breaks after tradi-
tion-bound periods of time. The difference lies in the duration of the discontinuity; in turbulent environments, no end seems in sight. As Smart and Ver-

tinsky (1984, p. 200) put it, "[F]actors become more uncertain; the values of important variables and the variables themselves more erratic in fashion." Emery and Trist (1965) stated that even the ground is in motion. However, given the relative nature of turbulence alluded to by McCann and Selsky (1984), it is not surprising that environmental turbulence has been defined in various ways by different scholars. Developing his conception from the Emery and Trist (1965) typology, Metcalfe (1974) defined environmental turbulence in terms of problems created by complex pluralistic systems, so that greater uncertainty is generated by the sequential escalation of the interrelatedness of the complexity and dynamism in the causal texture of the environment.

While acknowledging that many writers have drawn comparisons and differences between environmental uncertainty and turbulence (Cameron, Kim, and Whetten 1987), this study will adopt Smart and Vertinsky's (1984) view. They contend that the amount of turbulence in the environment is closely related to the degree of uncertainty faced by the firm. As indicated in Chapter 1, this study defines the concept broadly as a measure of change in the factors in an organization's environment. In operationalizing environments, authors have employed some combination of the three factors used in this study—dynamism, complexity, and hostility—in their codification (see Figure 4.1). Dess and Beard (1984) codified the three as munificence, complexity, and dynamism; Khandwalla (1972) referred to them as malevolence, uncertainty, and dynamism; Child (1972) spoke of illiberality, complexity, and variability; Miles, Snow, and Pfeffer (1974) codified the environment in terms of uncertainty, heterogeneity, and change.

Organizations as Open Systems

Burns and Stalker (1961), Chandler (1962), Katz and Kahn (1966), Lawrence and Lorsch (1967), and Thompson (1967) paved the way for a growing acceptance of the "open-systems" view of organizations. This view portrayed organizations as socio-technical mechanisms drawing resources from the environment at one end, and exporting goods and services into the environment at the other (Jelinek, Litterer, and Miles 1981; Miles, Snow, and Pfeffer 1974).

Figure 5.1: Attributes of the Environment

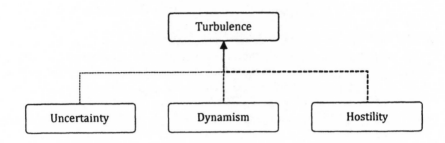

Adapted from: Pfeffer and Salancik (1978: 68)

Implicit here is that organizations differ from their environment; in other words, that there is a boundary between the two. Note that, due to the continuing flow of incoming resources from the environment, this boundary has become so blurred that many of the foremost scholars in this area of research have come to acknowledge that the two are inseparable (Biggadike 1981; Lenz 1981; Chaffee 1985). Some believe that the boundary between the organization and the environment is an arbitrary invention of the perceiver (Thompson 1967; Child 1972; Starbuck 1976).

Borrowing the analogy of a cloud, which Starbuck (1976) used to characterize the dilemma likely to be encountered in defining organizational boundaries, Miles, Snow, and Pfeffer (1974) portrayed the dilemma succinctly: Starbuck has compared the problem of defining the organization's boundary to delineating the boundary of a cloud. In delineating a cloud, we can measure the density of its moisture and, by selecting some specific level of density, determine what properly "belongs" to the cloud or to its environment. But with organizations, the boundary problem is more difficult. If we wished to measure the density of interaction and involvement, the measurements would change over time and across decision areas, thereby changing what is "in" the organization and what is "in" the environment.

In many respects, Lenz (1981) has asserted that the environment is both the "creator" and "creation" of management, and can thus be seen as objective or subjective/enacted. Assuming, however, that organizations can be distinguished from their environments, it will be helpful to describe the environment for the sake of analysis. This leads to the question of how the organization interacts with its environment. The literature on this issue can be classified into two schools of thought. The first focuses on the adaptation of the organization to its environment (Lawrence and Lorsch 1967; Child 1972; Ansoff 1984). The assumption here is to treat the environment as a constraint or problematic element to which the organization must adapt to increase its chances of survival (Staw and Szwajkowski 1975).

The philosophy of the second school assumes that organizations are rarely passive agents absorbing environmental pressures, but are active agents capable of shaping their environments to reduce uncertainty (Cyert and March 1963; Thompson 1967; Aldrich 1979; Pfeffer and Salancik 1978; Weick 1969). Whether it is by adapting to the environment or by intervening in it, the goal of the organization is to mitigate the level of turbulence (Emery and Trist 1965; Das 1986). Indeed, one of the central themes in the strategic management paradigm has been the imperative of posturing the organization to effect a match between its capabilities and its resources (strengths and weaknesses) on the one hand, and environmental conditions (opportunities and threats), on the other. Environmental assessment by the organization leads to adjustments in its environment that will create satisfactory alignments of environmental opportunities and risks with organizational capabilities and resources. This imperative has become enshrined in most Business Policy/Strategy textbooks under various models and acronyms, e.g., "SWOT," "WOTS-UP," and TOWS (Weihrich 1982, Barney 1986, Gray and Schmeltzer 1987).

How organizations choose to address their environments depends in large measure on the philosophy of their leaders on their conception of the environment. Lenz and Engledow (1986) have suggested five models of environmental conceptualization that can be used by managers in evaluating their environment. Although it is beyond the purview of this study to discuss the full merits of such a typology, we present it here since the choice of corporate strategy will be influenced by the philosophical and ideological orientations of corporate executives, as well as by the epistemological and ontological assumptions of the adopted model. A comparative overview of the essential characteristics of the Lenz and Engledow (1986) typology is presented in Table 5.1.

The next section presents a conceptual development of strategy and discusses the repertoire of strategy alternatives available for addressing turbulent environments.

Strategy

Conceptual development in any academic area is dependent upon a clearer definition of terms. Unfortunately, as an earlier example by Urwick (1960) demonstrated, much confusion persists in defining relevant concepts. The concept "strategy" is no exception. As stated earlier, the term can be traced to the Greek word *strategos*, which denotes the art of the general.

Strategy and Environment

Table 5.1: Types of Models for Environmental Analysis

Criteria	Assumptions about environmental structure	Ways to gain knowledge about the environment	Origins environmental change
Industry Structure Model (e.g., Porter 1980)	The dominant environment is a pattern of industry competitive forces stemming from the actions of "competitors"	Develop a formalized competitor analysis connected to strategic planning	Change is caused by industry and extra-industry evolutionary processes.; occurs at uneven rates.
Cognitive Model (e.g., Weick 1977)	Environmental factors and causal linkages among these are embodied in a cognitive structure, which is enacted in retrospect.	Encourage organizational learning via flexible, open inquiry and decision processes.	Change is reflected in revisions to/replacement of the cognitive structure as new meanings are imposed on organizational experiences.
Organization Field Model (e.g., Thompson 1967; Bourgeois 1980)	The environment is primarily composed of mutually interdependent formal organizations characterized by a hierarchy of internally homogeneous layers.	Design administrative structures to be consistent with environmental contingencies.	Change originates in the general environment and affects task environment phenomena.
Ecological, Resource Dependence Model (e.g. Glover 1966)	The environment is a system-like context of resources, social structures, and the natural environment characterized as a multilevel hierarchy.	Opportunistic surveillance. Encourage organization. Learning among organizational subunits.	Change occurs via autonomous variation in any element of the environment. Change is continuous and potentially predictable.
Era Model (e.g. Lodge 1975; Yankelovich 1982)	The environment is a distinct pattern of social structures, institutional relationships, roles, and values undergirded by psycho-culture, and/or ideology	Broad-scale environmental scanning. Monitoring of 'megatrends.'	Experimentation by individuals/formal organizations disturb an underlying ideology and social structures.

The term itself seems to have entered management literature from the military (Steiner 1979; Everend 1983) to denote that which one does to counteract what one's competitor does or is likely to do. Perhaps the best known definition of strategy is the one given by Chandler (1962, p. 13):

> Strategy is the determination of the basic long-term goals and objectives of an enterprise, the adoption of courses of action and the allocation of resources necessary for carrying out these goals. Decisions to expand the volume of activities, to set up distant plants and offices, to move into new economic functions, or become diversified along many lines of business involve the defining of new goals. New courses of action must be devised and resources allocated and reallocated in order to achieve these goals and to maintain and expand the firm's activities in the new areas in response to shifting demands, changing sources of supply, fluctuating economic conditions, new technological developments, and the actions of competitors.

This elaborate definition observes that an organization's members play an active role in strategy making and that their intention is to act on the environment. Furthermore, Steiner (1979) recognized that strategy is confined to higher echelons of the organization when he defined strategy as that which top management does that is of great consequence to the enterprise. Furthermore, a correspondence exists between the hierarchical level and the type of strategy in question: corporate strategy (What business should we be in?) gets formulated by higher echelons of management than does business strategy (Given the business we are in, how should we compete?). Tactics are formulated at the organization's lowest levels. Note, however, that research has increasingly shown that other levels of management can and do participate in the formulation of strategy depending on the circumstances and requirements of the firm's environment (Burgelman 1983, Mangaliso 1995, Wooldridge and Floyd 2008). This qualification aside, Chandler (1962) took the point about the firm's strategy even further when he asserted that the firm can succeed in spite of any number of tactical mistakes, as long as it follows the right strategy. Of course, one must always bear in mind the caveat alluded to by Thompson (1967, p. 148) in his discussion of whether or not such a thing as the "right" strategy even exists.

The contemporary conceptualization of strategy has brought about a dichotomy in the concept's definition. Raised by Hofer and Schendel (1978), this dichotomy addresses what the concept should include. Should it include both the ends (goals and objectives) that an organization wishes to achieve and the means (an integrated set of policies and plans) that will be used to achieve them? Or should it only include the means? Hofer and Schendel (1978) supported the view that strategy is a statement of means only. Other scholars who have followed suit include Glueck and Jauch (1984: 8) and Thompson and Strickland (1986: 7).

The multidimensionality of the strategy construct was demonstrated by Chaffee (1985). He grouped strategy definitions in the literature into three categories: the linear strategy, the adaptive strategy, and the interpretive strategy. The linear strategy model tends toward determinism and focuses on planning, while the interpretive model parallels recent interest in corporate culture and symbolic management. The interpretive approach further assumes that reality is socially construed (Morgan and Smircich 1980). The adaptive model recognizes the interplay between the organization and its environment, with the need for the organization to continually assess that environment (Miles and Snow 1978). The adaptive model is most appropriate for the present study.

Next is the issue of strategy content versus strategy process. Theorists who segment the strategy construct implicitly agree that the study of strategy should include both the actions taken (content) and the processes by which those actions are decided. Observe, for example, that the process by which a given strategy is arrived at may vary from company to company. It may take on different modes—e.g., entrepreneurial, adaptive, or planning (Mintzberg 1973); it may be synoptic or incremental (Frederickson and Mitchell 1984; Quinn 1980); and it may be influenced by a number of factors, including, attitudes of management towards risk, internal political considerations, external dependence, power, and socio-cultural variables (Pearce and Robinson 1985; Neghandi 1983). Furthermore, process may involve environmental scanning (Aguilar 1967; Fahey and King 1977) and comparison with organizational resources (Fry and Killing 1986).

Without trivializing the issues raised above, this chapter will neither give a detailed account of the intrinsic exposition of strategy (content) nor an in-depth discourse on how strategic choices are arrived at. Other studies have dealt with these issues. For example, comprehensive discussions of process and content studies are presented by Huff and Reger (1987) and Fahey and Christensen (1986), respectively. For excellent analyses of how strategic choices are arrived at the reader can turn to Child (1972); Montanari (1979); March and Simon (1958); Cyert and March (1963); Mintzberg and Waters (1985); and Quinn (1980).

Explanans of Economic Behavior

In their pioneering article, Hempel and Oppenheim (1948) declare that one of the foremost objectives of all rational enquiry is to explain the phenomena in the world of our experience by answering the question "why?" rather than only the question "what?" In philosophy of science, a scientific explanation of an empirical phenomenon consists of two parts. The first part comprises sentences that describe the phenomenon to be explained—

known as the *explanandum*. The second part—the *explanans*—comprises a set of sentences that give an account about why the observed phenomenon occurs, explain the antecedent conditions are that lead to it, and offer law-like general statements about the phenomenon. Strategic management has benefitted from the introduction of concepts and theories from other disciplines that can serve as explanans for the phenomena observed in the field and thus provide the rationale behind behaviors such as the choice of corporate strategies, structures and systems.

Two of the most important underlying theoretical anchors that will be highlighted here are the transaction cost economics (TCE) theory and the resource-based view or RBV (Williamson 1975, Barney 1984, Masten 1993). These two theories supplement each other in that while the TCE theory only offers a partial explanation of the nature of the firm, the RBV complements the nature side and goes far beyond on the question of the firm's essence, thereby providing a fruitful starting point for an integrative framework (Pitelis and Pseiridis 1999). We will not evaluate the efficacy, relevance, and limitations of these theories. Instead, we will explicate the extent to which these two theories are helpful in providing the logic underlying the strategic choices made. We draw on the classic literature in strategic management and the literature in other related fields to show that the two theories posit different types of coping mechanisms. We conclude with a discussion of the implications of these finding for future research.

Transactional Cost Economic (TCE) Theory

TCE theory has been used by organizational theorists to explain the way organizations function and the differences in their performance outcomes (Williamson 1975, Jones 1983, Jones & Hill 1988, Ouchi 1980, Robins 1987). In its most general formulation, TCE theory posits that activities will be optimally organized when they minimize the production costs and economize the transaction costs involved in producing the desired outcome. In this context, the firm is viewed as a "managerial hierarchy," or a particular form of organization for administering exchanges between two parties or firms (Coase, 1937). An exchange with other firms entails a variety of market-related co-ordination costs associated with the transactions that take place independently of managerial oversight (Williamson 1975, 1985). The managerial hierarchy therefore functions to economize in transaction costs. TCE is about discerning the tradeoffs between transactions that are coordinated through a managerial hierarchy or *fiat* on the one hand, and autonomous transactions coordinated through the market on the other. Firms exist precisely because of their access to *fiat*, which is an advantage in coordinating transactions in the face of market opportunism and uncertainty.

Firms are considered better at price negotiations and in oversight of the various post-transaction activities associated with the exchange (Gebauer & Scharl, 1999; Kraut *et al.*, 1998).

Note that the determination of transaction costs essentially depends on at least three factors: high asset specificity, high uncertainty, and bounded rationality. *Asset specificity* refers to investments in assets which are specific to the requirements of a particular exchange, or the appropriateness of some assets to be used in applications other than those initially acquired. Williamson (1985) distinguished four different types of asset specificity: site specificity, physical asset specificity, human asset specificity, and dedicated assets. Asset specificity results in sunk costs – the higher the sunk costs, the more costly the market transaction. *Uncertainty* occurs when one party possesses more information about price determination in a transaction than the other, which may lead to opportunistic behavior (Williamson 1985). Opportunism includes calculated attempts to obfuscate, disguise, distort, or hide information, all of which contribute to raising the cost of the transaction. *Bounded rationality* stems from the cognitive limits of the human mind's ability to process information and from incomplete information, skill and time—all of which lead to the impossibility of devising *a priori* fully specified contracts (March & Simon 1958). Because of these factors, market transactions become subject to opportunistic behavior, which makes them more costly than if the transactions took place within the firm's hierarchy.

Essentially, TCE theory is predicated on agency theory assumptions that reduce all transactions in economic interaction to a set of contracts between principals and agents (Jensen & Meckling 1976, Fama 1980, Eisenhardt 1989). Conceptually close to TCE theory, agency theory uses the metaphor of a contract to describe relationships in which one party delegates work to another through a contractual relationship (Bergen, Dutta and Walker 1992, Jensen & Meckling 1976). An agency relationship is said to exist whenever one party – the principal – depends on another – the agent – to undertake some action on the principal's behalf. Agency theory suggests that in an organization, the reason that problems arise is because principals entrust agents with tasks that they neither have the time nor the ability to do themselves. This gives agents an opportunity to misrepresent information and divert resources to their own personal use. Principals thus have a need to monitor agents or, alternatively, induce them to cooperate by designing incentive schemes. Agents also may be motivated to bond themselves to the principals if they want to avert monitoring. The challenge of organization design is to structure efficiently the agency relationship to minimize monitoring, bonding and related costs (Jensen and Meckling 1976).

Resource-Based View (RBV)

At the root of most of the writings on the resource-based view (RBV) of the firm is the landmark work of Edith Penrose (1959), who considers the firm a collection of tangible and intangible productive resources bound together in an administrative framework. The firm's boundaries are defined by its ability to maintain sufficient administrative coordination and authoritative internal communication (Pitelis and Pseiridis 1999). The RBV is closely aligned with the core competence concept of the firm advocated by Prahalad and Hamel (1990). Core competence emphasizes that a firm becomes superior to others not simply because it possesses better resources, but because it can also apply them more effectively (Mahoney and Pandian 1992). Collins and Porras (1995) define core competence as a strategic concept that captures the firm's capabilities – those things that the firm is particularly good at doing – that allow the firm to leverage or strategically apply them to a wide array of products and markets. The examples they cite include Honda in engines, NEC in semi-conductors and Sonoco in winding spiral tubes. In the same vein as core competence, the RBV perspective asserts that certain firm-specific resources or assets differentiate the firm from its competition, leading to above-normal returns and, hence, sustainable competitive advantage (Barney 1991, Wenerfelt 1984, 1995). These resources are usually classified into land and equipment, labor—including workers' capabilities and knowledge, and capital—both tangible and intangible (Mahoney and Pandian 1992). The RBV perspective presumes that firms are rent-seeking entities. Rent-seeking is defined as the search for resources and capabilities that enable the firm to develop, choose, and implement value-enhancing strategies to gain above-normal rents (Bowman 1974; Lado, Boyd and Hanlon 1997; Rumelt 1984). Mahoney and Pandian (1992:364) distinguish between three types of rents. The first is achieved by owning scarce resources such as valuable land, location advantages, patents, and copyrights that lead to *Ricardian rents*. The second, *monopoly rent*, is achieved through government protection or through collusive arrangements that present high barriers to entry. The third, *entrepreneurial or Schumpentarian rent*, is achieved through risk-taking and entrepreneurial insights in uncertain environments. To accomplish that goal, the firm must acquire or develop resources that are simultaneously valuable, rare, inimitable or difficult to imitate, and non-substitutable (Barney 1991; Rumelt 1984 Wernerfelt 1984). Again, as the advocates of core competence have noted, acquiring and developing resources is necessary but not sufficient for a sustainable competitive advantage. They must be leveraged and utilized to enhance the firm's core competence (Prahalad and Hamel).

In conclusion, while market failure explains the firm's existence under the TCE, the RBV posits that the reason that a firm conducts economic activity is not market failure but the firm's success in organizing its activities beyond the capability of markets to conduct (Madhok 2002). The TCE with its industrial organization economics perspective focuses externally on the industry and product markets while, according to Collis & Montgomery (1994), the RBV perspective combines the internal analysis of phenomena within the firm with the external analysis of the industry and the competitive environment. Both these perspectives must be considered in tandem to capture the firm's dual challenges of aligning its internal competencies and weaknesses with the threats and opportunities in the environment (the fundamental tenet of the SWOT analysis) (Ansoff 1965, Hofer and Schendel 1978). In that sense, the TCE and RBV can be seen as two sides of the same coin (Madhok 2002).

Strategic Responses

Little research has investigated the repertoire of strategic response options that organizations are likely to pursue under turbulent environments. For instance, Glueck (1976, p. 121) proposed a typology consisting of four grand strategies: stability, growth, retrenchment, and combination. This typology was considered useful in analyzing strategic responses under general rather than turbulent environmental conditions. Rothschild (1979, p. 3) proposed a five-level typology of corporate strategies: growth, hold, rebuild, harvest, and exit. This is similar to the five-strategy typology developed by Harrigan (1985b) consisting of the growth, selective shrinkage, hold, retrenchment, and divestment strategies. Although the Harrigan typology was meant for declining industries, it is applicable to turbulent environments. A summary devoted to each strategy, including its characteristics and circumstances for its application, is presented in Table 5.2.

The five-strategy typology just discussed is not a panacea for all turbulent environments, but does offer sufficient options for such environments. Depending on the degree of environmental turbulence, however, it is possible that a strategy that was successful in one corporation or situation may not be successful in another. It is also conceivable that analysts and managers in a given organization may choose to use combinations of these strategies and be successful (Glueck 1980). Note that these strategies can be arranged along a continuum ranging from risk avoiding (divestiture) to entrepreneurial (opportunistic). The term "entrepreneurial" is not used in the Schumpeterian sense here, but to denote those strategies that allow organizations to renew themselves and their markets by pioneering, innovation or

Table 5.2: Strategy Options

Strategy	When Implemented	How	Caution
Increase investment	When firm believes there are long-term advantages in increasing investments	Lower competitor's exit barriers. Purchase their assets.	Prudence required. Must make financial and business sense
Selective growth or shrinkage	If demand within some market niches seems to endure. If there is a possibility to reposition by shrinking less profitable businesses and expanding more desirable ones	Application of portfolio techniques, e.g., BCG, PLC, GE Spotlight, to identify candidates	Timing is the key. Capitalize on contacts or promising market before competition does
Hold	When in the best strategic posture but want to wait until some uncertainty is clarified to avert hasty decision	Firm won't expand its product line, but won't shut down plants	May lose market. Unclear when to take action, especially if only incremental changes take place in environment
Retrench	When firm's level of performance is consistently below expected. When there is a need for cash flow	Organization invests less money than it receives. Performance held up through increases in efficiency	May sometimes be falsely equated with surrender or failure
Divest	Firm wishes to recover its asset value. Environment is not improving. Poor economic performance	Sell off or liquidate subsidiary or SBU; implement portfolio analysis	Timing also key—pull out too soon: low rewards. Pull out too late: may wind up with excessive losses.

Adapted from Harrigan (1985b), Rothschild (1979)

risk taking (Schumpeter 1950, Miller 1983, Mintzberg 1973). Such strategies characterize management's acceptance of a particular product-market
domain and involve the commitment of resources to achieve organizational
objectives (Miles and Snow 1978).

Emery and Trist's (1965) premise of turbulent fields calls for a close
and continuous reflection on the consistency of the chosen strategy in the
various parts of the organization and, more broadly, of the world, and the
chosen strategy's compatibility or alignment with the environment. For this
reason, the present study focuses on improving the understanding of how
strategy preferences relate to the perception of environment and effectiveness. Bourgeois (1980) suggested a synthesis or "marriage" between the
two levels of strategy (he called them the primary and secondary strategies,
respectively) and the two levels of environment—the general environment
and the task environment. He proposed that the two constructs were related to each other as shown in Figure 5.2.

Relating corporate strategy to the general environment is the process
of domain definition. Domain definition is concerned with the organization's choice of domain or change of domain—such as that which occurs
when, for example, a firm diversifies into or exits from particular products
or markets. Examples include Miles and Snow's (1978) "entrepreneurial
problem" and Chandler's (1962) "strategic decision." Domain navigation
denotes competitive decisions made within a particular product-market or
task environment. Examples include Chandler's (1962) entrepreneurial
decisions and Porter's (1980) competitive or generic strategies. The distinction between the two processes is important since in domain definition one
is concerned with the "portfolio" issue (Hofer and Schendel 1978). Here at
the corporate level, the firm's strategy centers on pooling a group of "assets" (i.e., firms or subsidiaries) either to minimize total risk for a given level of corporate return or to maximize return for a level of risk (Hofer and
Schendel 1978; Kobrin 1982). The variables and issues studied at this level
should, therefore, be different from those studied in the domain navigation
process. Since further discussion of the domain navigation process would
be of limited value to this study, our research will focus on the connection
between corporate strategy and the general environment, i.e., the domain
navigation process.

Performance

Since its emergence as a field in the early 1970s, business policy has gradually shifted from having an essentially descriptive, clinical orientation to
greater concern with objectivity and methods of scientific measurement
(Cool and Schendel 1987). Nowhere has this been more pronounced than in

the measurement of performance. Performance measures are considered to be an indication of how effective the organization has been over a period of time. That criterion is usually measured in long-run terms, so that an organization that survives is considered to be effective (Gibson, Ivancevich, and Donnelly 1979). Effectiveness can also be applied to short-term situations when considering the accomplishment of short-term goals. Standard management texts portray organizations as being in control, and therefore effective, when the actual performance matches or exceeds the planned or expected performance (Schermerhorn 1986; Holt 1987).

Figure 5.2: Hierarchical Relationship of Strategy and Environment

Environment Level   Strategy Level

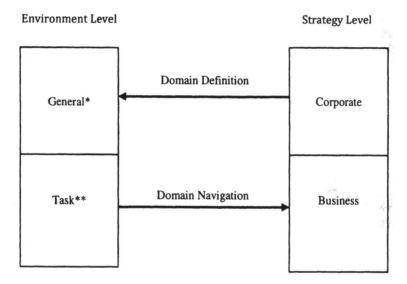

*General Environment: Is composed of multiple task environments; source of social, political, economic, technological, and demographic trends.

**Task Environment: Is composed of competitors, suppliers, customers, and regulatory bodies with whom the organization interacts and whose actions directly affect organizational goal attainment.

Source: Bourgeois (1980, p. 26)

Measures of performance such as profitability (return on investment), sales growth, and market share are the most commonly used, since they are quantifiable and, hence, considered to be objective. However, in certain cases where it is difficult to obtain objective measures, recent researchers (Dess and Robinson 1984; Pearce, Robbins, and Robinson 1987) have argued that subjective measures are an acceptable measure of performance. Dess and Robinson have suggested that, if objective measures are unavailable, a researcher might consider using subjective perceptual measures rather than removing performance from the research design. High Spearman correlations of subjective versus objective measures of performance were reported by Pearce, Robbins, and Robinson (1987), offering strong support for the subjective performance technique as a substitute for objective measures. Venkatraman and Ramanujam (1987) also lend their support:

> [I]t appears that perceptual data from senior managers, which tend to strongly correlate with secondary (objective) data, can be employed as acceptable operationalizations of BEP (Business Economic Performance). (p. 118)

This consensus, coupled with problems of disclosure often encountered in studies of multinational corporations (MNCs are not obligated to report financial data concerning their overseas subsidiaries), makes the adoption of subjective perceptual measures a compelling and viable alternative for the measurement of performance in such studies.

Note that the perception of performance is not a function of objective quantifiable measures only, but is also a function of other, sometimes non-quantifiable, measures. These include corporate goals and objectives; social responsibility; employee welfare; and personal values, ideals, and philosophies of individual managers (Drucker 1974; Child 1974a; Shetty 1979). These measures are sometimes fuzzy and sometimes conflict with one another (Yuchtman and Seashore 1967). Drucker (1974) suggested that to manage a business is to strike a balance on a variety of such goals and needs. Here the importance of power relations becomes salient not only within the top management team but also with suppliers, competitors, customers, and government (Pfeffer and Salancik 1978).

Also note that the present study is not a full-blown investigation of performance, but a study of how performance is related to environmental turbulence and strategic preferences. A host of pioneering researchers have undertaken in-depth analyses of performance, including Yuchtman and Seashore (1967), Child (1972, 1974b), Schoefler (1977), Wood and LaForge (1979), Lenz (1981), Dess and Robinson (1984), Frederickson and Mitchell (1984), Venkatraman and Ramanujam (1985), and Pearce, Robbins, and Robinson (1987).

Environment-Strategy-Performance

Planning versus Performance

Several studies have investigated the causal link between planning and organizational success. One stream of studies found in the literature addresses the relationship between planning and performance (Shrader, Taylor, and Dalton 1984; Leontiades and Tezel 1980; Malik and Karger 1975; Herold 1972; Thune and House 1970; Ansoff et al. 1970). Shrader, Taylor, and Dalton (1984) classified firms' formal planning practices and found that planners outperformed nonperformers. In a sample of 38 firms from six industries with sales of some $50 million to $500 million annually, Malik and Karger (1975) found that planners significantly outperformed nonplanners in nine out of thirteen financial performance variables. In an earlier study, Ansoff et al. reported that firms using formal planning systems significantly outperformed non-planners in all of the study's financial performance variables. Thune and House studied 36 firms in six industries, measuring performance in terms of sales growth, stock prices, earnings per share, return on equity, and return on capital. They concluded that formal planners were significantly more successful than non-planners. Herold validated the Thune and House study by adding a new variable (pretax profits) and arrived at the same conclusion. The general conclusion of studies from this stream of research is that planners outperform non-planners.

The problem with most of these studies is that they seem to draw the parsimonious conclusion that formal planning is the sole cause of high performance. This may be inaccurate, since some of the variation in the dependent variable (performance) might be explained by some extraneous factors. Examples include exogenous factors such as luck or technological breakthroughs; and endogenous factors such as the selection of good managers, the use of good development and training programs, compensation schemes, administration, and control. In other words, high performance may be a characteristic of a well-managed company. The generalizability of some of the findings (e.g., Herold 1972) has been further limited by small sample sizes. Another problem with studies from the first stream is the high correlation generally found between planning perception and actual planning (e.g., Leontiades and Tezel 1980). These scholars found that chief executive officers who rated planning highly spent more time planning. Such CEOs are likely to foster this belief down the corporate hierarchy with the consequence that the company will likely attribute any success to planning.

A different stream of research, which began with Child (1972), dealt with whether strategic planning or environmental influences had a greater impact on organizational performance. Strategic planning was conceptualized as activities and objectives resulting from managerial discretion. This stream of research, unlike the first, was inconclusive.

In a study to determine the relationship among the environment, organizational size, technology, and performance in 82 British companies, Child (1972) found that CEOs formulated objectives and plans in advance of achieved performance. He concluded that strategic planning was the ultimate determinant of a company's financial performance. Yet Grinyer, Yasai-Ardekani and Al-Bazzaz (1980) found that British firms perceived a less hostile environment when strategy and structure were logically linked, but could not conclude that their linkage led to superior performance.

In his study of the 64 largest companies in eight major, domestic manufacturing industries, Hall (1980) found that success is possible even in hostile environments, but is contingent upon the company's ability to align itself with its environment. Survival is possible for firms with the foresight to downsize their asset commitments into niches in their basic industry and that can invest their incremental capital in meaningful diversification. This line of reasoning is congruent with Porter's (1980) position that ultimate failure or perpetual subsidies would await companies that fail to achieve either the lowest-cost, the most differentiated, or a focused position in a unique market niche. He describes such firms as being "stuck in the middle" (Porter 1985: 16).

A general comment: Although many of the foregoing studies provide useful guidance for future research, they almost invariably explore strategy strictly at the business or domain navigational (Bourgeois 1980) level. The first research stream (i.e., planning and performance) treated the environment as static, an assumption that would be anathema in turbulent conditions.

CHAPTER 6

Business Corporations and Social Responsibility

Corporate social responsibility (CSR) is the expectation society has of corporations to engage in activities that go beyond their normal economic and legal obligations in order to contribute to greater societal benefit. Implied in this definition is the obligation by corporate management to take action to protect not only the economic and technical interests of the corporation but also the welfare of society as a whole (Carroll 1991; Davis and Blomstrom 1975; Wood 1991). A classic definition of CSR is offered by Davis (1973) as the firm's consideration of, and response to, issues beyond the narrow economic, technical, and legal requirements of the firm in order to accomplish social benefits along with the traditional economic gains which the firm seeks. Examples of CSR might include adopting environment-friendly manufacturing policies such as the use of recyclable or biodegradable packaging materials or embracing progressive human relations practices as in the advancement of women and previously excluded groups to positions of responsibility. The issue of CSR was brought to the forefront of public debate during the apartheid years with the call to withdraw investments in firms with business interests in South Africa (Polonsky and Grau 2008). The call was intended to force the White government to abandon the system of apartheid, and some analysts have credited this movement with assisting in the shift to a free and democratic society in South Africa (Malone and Goodin 1997).

By the 1980s, the continued presence of foreign multinational corporations (MNCs) in South Africa (SA) had become a hotly debated subject and one not without controversy. On one side of the debate were those who favored total disengagement from SA. Proponents of this view believed that the presence of overseas MNCs in SA gave moral legitimacy to the White minority government and created a vested overseas interest in the status quo, which, in turn, increased the desire to see the maintenance and stability of the existing political system. They proposed that economic sanctions, comprehensively applied against SA, would accelerate the dismantling of the racist system of government. On the other side were those who asserted that by liberalizing employment practices in SA, overseas MNCs set a positive example for other employers in the country. This would have the net impact of making everyone, regardless of color, economically well off in the long run. Thus, whereas the pro-investment group seemed to favor a "constructive engagement" approach to solving the apartheid problem, the pro-divestment group believed that application of economic pressure would hasten the elimination of apartheid.

Many believe that it was the pressure brought to bear on SA in the late 1980s, rather than a voluntary change of heart by the White government that precipitated some of the most momentous changes in the country's history. The major Black political organizations were unbanned, Nelson Mandela and other political prisoners were released, some of the key apartheid legislation was erased from the statutory books, and now the country is poised to have the first nonracial democratic elections in its history. What role did the MNC play in the socioeconomic transformation that took place in SA? This chapter discusses this role by analyzing the Sullivan codes of conduct for U.S. corporations in SA. It begins by providing a brief historical background of the situation and then concludes by echoing the notion that when repression has become pervasive in a social system and its coping capacity has reached the limits, only radical reforms can prevent the breakdown of social order. In the case of SA, the most effective contribution made by MNCs was targeted divestment.

Historical Background

There is a commonly held belief that the problems of SA are not just about Black and White but also about Black and gold. Indeed, any discussion of the problems of SA must begin with a clear understanding of the racial stratification of society there in the form of apartheid through which Blacks are exploited. But it must also delve into issues around the rich natural mining resources with which the country is endowed.

Early Settlement of South Africa

Recorded history on the settlement of SA typically begins in 1652 with the arrival of sailors of the Dutch East India Company. However, there are written accounts by Portuguese sailors who survived shipwrecks and landed on the SA coast more than 150 years prior to that date (Sparks 1990). Their description of the dress, way of life, and language of the inhabitants that they came across leaves no doubt that these were ancestors of the present-day SA Blacks. More recently, archaeological excavations and carbon-dating evidence suggest that certain areas of SA were occupied by the third century A.D. (Maylam 1986). This lays to rest the empty land myth that claims that the ancestors of the present day African people of SA migrated southwards across the Limpopo at the same time as Whites were first settling in the western Cape in the mid-seventieth century (Maylam 1986: 17). In fact, some writers have noted that human ancestors have lived in SA as long ago as 2 million years (Pascoe 1987).

Up until the 19th century, the SA economy was essentially a subsistence economy, with a large percentage of the population dependent on agriculture for a living. The roots of the present-day racial problems can be traced back to the arrival of the Dutch in 1652. Under the command of Jan van Riebeck, a halfway station was established at Table Bay with the aim of providing facilities for rest, refueling, and refreshments for the sailors on their long voyages to India. In the passage of time, the halfway station became a permanent settlement as more sailors settled at the Cape. European immigration to SA increased throughout the 18th century and 19th century -- with the arrival of the 1820 British settlers. Equally significant was the emergence of a class of Dutch farmers (the Boers) who resented being dominated by the British. As these groups gradually moved inland seeking better lands, they had several clashes with indigenous Africans, who felt tricked into openly welcoming the guests only to find themselves being subjugated and dispossessed of their lands. The classic encounters between the Bantu, the Boer, and the Briton are well documented in the history books (MacMillan 1963). These clashes were often both bloody and tragically uneven because of the superior technology of repeating rifles. Toward the end of the 19th century, perhaps the most decisive factor in the final demise of the indigenous African may well have been the invention and use in combat of the machine gun (Ellis 1975). With it in their armory, the Europeans, who were outnumbered by far, were able to scoff at the objections of the indigenous Africans and impose their control and domination, which was to last for more than a century (Ellis 1975). In fact, in the period between 1790 and 1890, the Europeans had fought no less than 10 wars with the indigenous people before ruthlessly crushing their resistance through rifle and machine gun power. After these encounters, the Europeans were able to consolidate their control over the vast tracts of land that became known as the "White" areas. Herein lies the foundation of the 1913 and 1936 Land Acts, which declared that all but 13 percent of the land be allocated to Whites. In the 19th century, for instance, an average Boer farm is reported to have been approximately 6,000 acres (Glennville-Grey 1985).

Industrialization and Labor Control

Earlier in the 19th century, there was little or no effort to systematically channel Black labor into the White-owned parts of SA, which were also still agrarian. The few commercial enterprises that existed then, such as wine growing, sugar production, wool, and so forth, still relied almost entirely on imported slaves from Malaysia and indentured labor from India. The situation took a drastic turn in the second half of the 19th century with the discovery of diamonds in 1867 and gold in 1885. Dreams of wealth generated by these discoveries enormously stimulated the acquisitive drive of many foreigners. Foreign, notably British, capital began to flow into SA. The process of industrialization took a serious turn and with it grew the need to bring Blacks into the labor force. An alliance was formed between the state governors and commercial interests, which resulted in a set of laws that regulated wages and working conditions of the Black labor force so as to minimize competition and, hence, costs.

The development of a strong White central government in 1910 created a structure whereby conditions that generated an unimpeded supply of cheap labor were made possible. Laws such as the Native Labor Relations Act of 1911 were passed, which made it impossible for Africans to strike (Hale 1985). In 1923, the Urban Areas Act was passed, which systematized control over the geographical movement of Africans in the country. Under the law, all African adult males had to carry passes that were to govern where they could live, work, or travel. Individuals could be directed to areas where their labor was needed and away from areas where their presence represented political or economic threat. Throughout this period of economic growth, however, the economy was dependent on migrant Black workers for unskilled positions, with the skilled and semiskilled positions being filled by trained European immigrants and poor Boers who had lost their land to commercial agriculture. The latter, feeling insecure that Blacks could be trained to do their jobs at lower wages, were protected from such a possibility in 1924 when the Industrial Conciliation Act became law. This law set up a collective bargaining system that only recognized White and "Colored" trade unions, thus effectively closing certain jobs to Blacks (Hale 1985).

U.S. Corporations in South Africa

In discussing the involvement of U.S. MNCs, two periods can be demarcated: the early infusion of capital from the turn of the century up to just before World War II and the period after World War II. Another significant factor about MNC involvement in SA is the areas of investment in which MNCs tended to make a difference in the functioning of apartheid.

Infusion of MNC Capital

Involvement of U.S. capital in SA dates back to the second half of the past century, initially in the form of entrepreneurs. These entrepreneurs ranged from insurance salesmen and diamond diggers to missionaries, merchants, and shipping agents. U.S. miners were lured by the riches they could get in SA, while missionaries prized the country for what it might eventually become. Several of the large U.S. corporations began to make their entry into the SA market in those early years. Among these were the automotive giants General Motors and Ford. In fact, by 1918, SA had become a major market for U.S. automobiles and stood in fifth place among all foreign buyers of U.S. automobiles (Hull 1990). The tire and rubber companies Firestone and Goodyear began business in SA in 1915 and 1916, respectively. In the 1930s, consumer goods corporations such as Johnson & Johnson, Colgate Palmolive, and Coca-Cola made their entry in SA, as did the financial services company Dunn & Bradstreet.

The Post-World War II Period

In the post-World War II period, several corporations entered SA. When rich gold fields were struck in the Orange Free State in the 1940s, Kennecott Copper loaned money to finance its extraction, and Dillon, Read, & Company (New York) negotiated a $10 million, 3-year revolving credit to the SA government from four U.S. banks. Banks such as Chase Manhattan entered SA in the 1940s, as did communications companies such as AT&T and RCA. In air transportation, World Airways of New York began a passenger service between SA and the United States in 1947, and 2 years later, Pan American Airways offered two flights a week between New York and Johannesburg. Other companies whose entry and presence is worth noting from that period are NCR and later IBM, and in the 1960s, Burroughs (Unisys), Control Data Corporation (Minneapolis), Hewlett-Packard in electronics; Polaroid and Kodak in instant cameras; and Xerox in copiers. By the

1960s, U.S. MNCs used the profits they generated to buy minority and majority interests in domestic firms. For example, Kimberly-Clark acquired a 38 percent share in Carlton Paper. ITT had shares in African Telephone Cables, and Newmont Mining had shares in Tsumeb Corporation of Namibia and Palaborwa Mining. SA also saw its introduction to U.S. popular culture through music and film in the early part of this century. Columbia Records, MGM, 20th Century Fox (merger between Fox Film Corp. and 20th Century Pictures) were among the first, followed by United Artists and Warner Bros. Interestingly, very little of SA could be found in the American cultural landscape until Alan Paton's Cry, the Beloved Country was staged as the Broadway musical Lost in the Stars (Paton 1948).

Attractiveness of South Africa

In the period following World War II, investors found SA to be a financially rewarding country. Among other things, SA's access to cheap, powerless labor made possible exaggerated rates of return in comparison with other geographic areas of foreign investment. For instance, according to the 1983 estimates, U.S. subsidiaries in SA earned an average of 18 percent after-tax return on manufacturing investment as opposed to an only 12 percent average elsewhere. For mining investment, the after-tax returns were 25 percent in SA and only 13.7 percent elsewhere (Leape, Baskin, & Underhill 1985; Schmidt 1985). These high rates of return can be assumed to be the main reason why U.S. and other foreign investors expanded their investments so rapidly in SA. Statistics show that between the years 1945 and 1975, U.S. direct investments in SA increased from $50 million to about $2 billion, an increase of 4,000 percent (Litvak, DeGrasse, & McTigue 1978; Schmidt 1985). By the end of 1981, U.S. direct investments in SA were reported to be $2.63 billion, reaching a high of $2.8 billion at the end of 1982. Since then, U.S. foreign direct investments have declined steadily to $2.3 billion in 1985 and $1.3 billion in 1986, with further declines in 1988. A slow upward trend was triggered in 1989 by the sweeping political reforms that were announced by President de Klerk and the lifting of U.S. sanctions announced by U.S. President Bush in 1991. Before the mass corporate exodus, the full extent of the financial involvement of the United States in SA reached beyond just direct investments: Approximately 6,000 U.S. companies did business in that country for a total financial involvement (both direct and indirect) of more than $14.6 billion (Litvak et al. 1978; Schmidt 1985). It is also interesting to note that at the same time as the U.S. direct investments were declining in SA, U.S. bank loans were increasing. Between 1981 and 1984—the year before SA declared a moratorium on debt repayment—U.S. loans had increased by 450 percent, reaching a high of more than $4.9 billion before declining to just less than $2.1 billion by 1988 (Hull 1990).

Key Points Industries

Of course, from the U.S. viewpoint, the SA involvement has always been small, accounting for about 1 percent of total U. S. foreign direct investments (Beaty & Harari 1987). But much of the U.S. corporate involvement in SA has been concentrated in certain key industries that require sophisticated technology such as the automotive industry, the oil refining industry, and the electronics industry (Conrad 1982; Omond 1986). Among the most dependent of these was the electronics or data processing industry. According to Conrad (1982), by 1982, U.S. data processing corporations controlled 75 percent of sales and 77 percent of rentals of computers in SA, generating up to $33 million per year in local taxes for the apartheid government. This sizable amount of support for the repressive regime attracted a number of critics against such investments. The criticism further intensified when it was revealed that, in terms of the National Key Points Act, some of the MNC facilities in the country could be converted into facilities for the manufacture of pro-government machinery and weaponry.

For their part, MNCs defended their involvement by stating that their presence in SA would serve as a "progressive" force for change: As foreign investments increased, so too would the strength of the SA economy. This would then have the advantage of creating more jobs, thus "trickling" down the benefits to the entire population. Some sources refuted the trickle-down theory noting that in 1980, 81 percent of the Blacks in the rural areas lived below the poverty datum line (Omond 1986; Schmidt 1985). There was abundant evidence that further negates the claim that the minority SA government would willingly bring about equality between Blacks and Whites. No two key areas of government involvement reveal this unwillingness to bring about accelerated equality of services to Blacks more than basic education and health care.

Basic Education

In the area of education (the key to the development of any society) as of 1989, the government was spending 7 times as much on a White child as it was spending on a Black child. The result was a grossly distorted illiteracy rate. This had the net effect of keeping the African population at the bottom rung of the economic hierarchy. Furthermore, a White child had 100 times as much chance of becoming a university graduate as did a Black child. Also, almost half of all White males had graduated from high school, compared to a mere 0.8 percent of African males (Smock 1983).

Health Care

In the area of health care, the per capita expenditure by the minority government was equally skewed. According to a study conducted by the Southern Labor and Development Unit of the University of Cape Town, there was 1 doctor for every 600 Whites and 1 for every 40,000 Blacks in the rural areas. The ideal doctor/ population ratio is considered to be 1/800 (Thomas 1981). The figure for Blacks was said to be comparable with figures found in the most underdeveloped countries of the world (Seedat 1987). The infant mortality rate among rural Blacks was 31 times as high as among Whites. In fact, in some parts of the Cape Province, the infant mortality rate was reported to be as high as 550 per 1,000 births in 1983 (Seedat 1987), and one half of all Black children in the rural areas were reported to die before they reached the age of 5 years. The major causes of these deaths were diseases of malnutrition such as marasmus, kwashiorkor, and other infectious diseases, which are regarded as diseases of poverty (Eberstadt 1988). The Black township of Soweto has only one hospital for more than 2 million people. The future hardly looked any brighter for Blacks, considering that of the 6,000 students registered in SA medical schools in 1978, only 494 were African. Of course, when the Black Medical University of Southern Africa (MEDUNSA), was opened, the output of Black physicians went up. However, the per capita figure still had a long way to go.

The Sullivan Principles

In early 1977, the Sullivan code of conduct was developed to monitor progress made by U.S. companies with subsidiaries in SA. The code was drafted by Reverend Sullivan, a Black Baptist minister and member of the board of directors of the General Motors Corporation. The original code had six principles that became known as the Sullivan Principles. They called for the desegregation of the workplace, fair employment practices for all employees, equal pay for equal work, job training and advancement of Blacks, increasing the number of Blacks in management, and the improvement of the quality of workers' lives outside of the workplace. In 1984, the code was amplified to include the use of influence to support the unrestricted rights of Black business to locate in the urban areas, influence other companies in SA to follow similar equal rights principles, and support the ending of all apartheid laws. In 1987, after Sullivan called for the withdrawal of U.S.

MNCs because of their failure to bring an end to apartheid, the codes were renamed the Statement of Principles and continued to be used as guidelines for corporations operating in SA.

Innocuous as these principles appeared to be, they were controversial from the beginning. For one thing, later additions contained in a 1986 letter to companies that had signed the principles began to challenge the apartheid government. Among other things, they called for signatory companies to practice corporate civil disobedience against all apartheid laws and to use the companies' financial and legal resources to assist Blacks in the equal use of public and private amenities (Crichton 1986). Nonetheless, critics charged that by putting a stamp of virtue on U.S. corporations doing business in SA, the principles stalled rather than accelerated progress to end apartheid. They were an IOU without a due date. This theory was put to the test when Sullivan issued an ultimatum in 1985 that he would call for the withdrawal of U.S. corporations if apartheid was not abolished by 1987. Indeed, when the 2-year period elapsed, Sullivan called upon all U.S. companies to pull out of SA, admitting that although the principles had made life better for some Blacks in SA, they had failed to produce change at a fast enough pace (Feder 1987). Many U.S. corporations began to withdraw from SA, heeding Sullivan's call, but many others cited the weakening economy of SA. Nonetheless, there were others that remained and continued to use the Statement of Principles as their guideline.

Impact of the Sullivan Principles

Although the Sullivan Principles made an impact on employment practices under apartheid, they fell short in that they did not offer the kind of solutions that were germane to the SA problem. They failed to address the major issues at the core of apartheid, that is, the fact that Blacks could not vote or own land in their own country. Instead, they focused essentially on Black employees of U.S. corporations, who only constituted less than 1 percent of the total number of economically active Blacks (Schmidt 1985). In addition, because they were only voluntary, the little impact they had was further diminished as borne by the number of companies that dropped out when the code was tightened. Several shortcomings have also been revealed in the reporting procedures of the signatory companies (Paul 1987), including the distortion of company progress through aggregation of data. For instance, it was reported that between the seventh and eighth reporting periods, non-White management positions went up from 6 percent to 15 percent. What was not revealed was that the figure for Africans was an increase from 3 percent to 5 percent (a 40 percent increase), whereas for Asians it went from 2 percent to 6 percent (a 66 percent increase), and for

"Coloreds" it went from 1 percent to 4 percent (a 75 percent increase). These differences tell a significant story when one bears in mind that Africans are 10 times as many as "Coloreds," and 25 times as many as Asians. As Paul (1987) notes, the systematic hiding of data through aggregation seems deliberate because if opportunities were being opened to Africans—the most disadvantaged group—the MNCs would have wanted the world to know.

The most critical inadequacy of the Sullivan Principles lay in the fact that even if they were fully enforced by every U.S. Corporation in South Africa, apartheid would still be far from being threatened. These principles could coexist with the disenfranchisement of Blacks; population controls; and removal, bannings, and detentions of people without trial. They seemed to be primarily aimed at correcting superficial inequities without addressing the root causes that support these inequities. A 1988 audit of the demographic comparison of Southern African population groups, which was published by *The Economist*, helps to drive the point home (David 1993). According to this report, on average, Black South Africans made $670 per capita in terms of gross domestic product (GDP), had a life expectancy of 57 years, had an adult functional literacy rate of 80 percent, and had an infant mortality rate of 57 out of every 1,000 children born. The figures for Botswana, a much less endowed neighboring country, were respectively 1,000 per capita GDP, 67 years life expectancy, 70 percent functional literacy, and 41 deaths per 1,000 children. Comparable figures for White South Africans show that they were enjoying one of the highest standards of living of any nation in the world: $6,500 per capita GDP, 73 years life expectancy, 100 percent adult literacy, and 13 percent deaths per 1,000 children.

If the continued presence of MNCs in South Africa helped to improve the quality of life, then the logical question to ask is why these disparities have continued to exist. Part of the answer may be that even if enlightened MNCs could press for more equitable wages between Blacks and Whites, they would eventually put themselves at a competitive disadvantage against rival firms. Furthermore, in the specific case of MNCs, the use of decentralized accounting techniques for performance evaluation emphasizes the need for each separate regional unit to show a profit. Failure to meet the required standards of return on investment will inevitably trigger capital flight. The principles that guide finance capital are clear and transparent: maximize return on investment with little regard to social and political consequences or national identity (Friedman 1970; Greidner 1997). It is within that context that the Sullivan and similar codes of corporate conduct should be understood and evaluated as a vehicle for bringing about social change.

Strategic Importance of South Africa

South Africa's strategic importance to the West arose during the Cold War era for two reasons. The first was the availability of several strategic minerals in the country, and the second was the alternative sea route access SA provided to the oil-rich Gulf of Persia.

Strategic Minerals

The primary importance of SA to the West in general, particularly the United States, lay in the fact that SA had a trove of strategic minerals essential to the functioning of U.S. industry. The United States obtained many of these minerals from abroad, mostly from SA. Heading the list were chromium, manganese, vanadium, and platinum, as shown on Table 6.1 (Norvall 1985; Thomas 1981). During the Cold War years, the fact that worried the West most was that together with the former Soviet Union, SA held more than 80 percent of the world's resources in most of these strategic minerals, as can be seen in Table 6.2. This table shows how the West would have been particularly vulnerable to a cartel formed between the two countries. Of course, the probability of this happening was substantially diminished with the end of the Cold War, the radical reforms that swept the former USSR, and the ultimate downfall of the apartheid government. But still, the fact remains that possession of strategic minerals gives a high amount of strategic leverage to SA in that, as a vice president of a steel company noted, without manganese it would be impossible to make steel (Thatcher 1980).

Alternative Sea Route

Another area of SA's strategic importance to the West has been the alternative Cape sea route to the East. In the early 1980s, some 2,300 ships traveled this route each month, delivering 57 percent of Western Europe's imported oil and 20 percent of U.S. imports. Some 70 percent of the strategic raw materials used by NATO countries were also imported via the Cape sea route (Thomas 1981). The Cape sea route has grown in strategic importance following such international conflicts as the invasion of Afghanistan by the former Soviet Union, the Iran-Iraq war, the invasion of Kuwait by Iraq and the subsequent gulf war, and the ever so volatile Israeli-Palestinian political situation. The extent of this strategic importance is such that it often gets referred to as the "choke point" of the south, or the "jugular vein" of the free world.

Table 6.1: Strategic Minerals Mined in South Africa as of the mid1980s

Mineral	Uses
Chromium	A key element in the manufacture of stainless steel, which is essential for the manufacture of a variety of implements, including hospital equipment, gun barrels, jet engines, and so forth. There is no known substitute for chromium and, according to experts, very little likelihood of finding one. The United States imports 30 percent of its needs, 50 percent from South Africa
Manganese	Vital for the production of steel alloys. American deposits that can be mined efficiently are negligible. The United States imported 98 percent of its needs, 33 percent from Africa.
Vanadium	Used to toughen steel and other alloys, this is the least worrisome of this group of metals. Although South Africa supplied the United States with 75 percent of its needs, the United States can meet more than half its needs from domestic mines that would boost production if the need arose.
Platinum	Vital as a catalyst in various industries such as oil refining industry, the platinum group metals are also a key element in the catalytic converters that limit pollutants in exhaust gases from automobiles. The United State's vulnerability was greatest in this group of metals in that it imported approximately 54 percent from South Africa and 42 percent from the Soviet Union in 1984. A crunch on this group would spark a scramble to find a substitute and/or to recycle.

Discussion

The foregoing discussion was an attempt to explain the factors that led to the socioeconomic dispensation that had been in existence until recently in SA and to put a perspective on the role played by multinational corporations in the workings of the apartheid system. From the arguments presented above, it is clear that the logic that a gradual improvement of the living conditions of the deprived majority through constructive engagement would eventually lead to the abolition of apartheid was faulted. As shown above, little of the country's economic growth that flowed from MNC investment was directed toward uplifting Black living standards in areas such as education, health care, housing, and civic protection. What was visible was the disproportionate spending of government revenues in the military (to be able to withstand a Black uprising) and the multiplication of services to accommodate the functioning of apartheid structure (e.g., the existence of 14 departments of education for the different ethnic groups). This might have been one of the most important reasons why some Blacks came to view foreign MNCs as instruments of their repression. The turning point in this perception might have been reached when large blocks of investors in the United States and other countries sent a clear message of condemnation of the human rights violations in SA by divesting their interests from SA-related stocks.

Table 6.2: Minerals Mined in South Africa and the Former USSR as of 1988

Metal	% of World Production
Platinum	99
Vanadium	97
Manganese	93
Chromium	93
Gold	71
Fluorite	50
Iron	46

The Paradoxes of Apartheid

One of the most intriguing paradoxes of the SA case—albeit one that this writer has often found hard to explain to international audiences—is the coexistence of strong industrial growth in the midst of worsening impoverishment of the vast majority of the population. The paradox is strikingly noticeable in the social, political, and economic spheres of life where the pigmentation of one's skin determines one's fate from the cradle to the grave, what some have called a pigmentocracy (Edmondson 1988). The question is why the international community remained tolerant of apartheid for such a long time. One explanation, although not complete, was given by the UN observer mission known as the Eminent Persons Group (EPG), which visited SA in 1986. Given the sophisticated way in which the Black areas had been separated from the rest of SA, the EPG noted how easy it was for a tourist in SA to be captivated by the natural beauty of the country and yet remain totally oblivious of the scale of human misery taking place.

The second paradox that is observed in SA has been the escalation conflict between the members of the Inkatha Freedom Party (IFP) and African
National Congress (ANC) followers, which claimed hundreds of lives. As
discussed elsewhere, the evidence pointed to initiatives by White military-
technocratic incumbents who were sponsoring this violence (Mangaliso
1992). And, of course, recent testimonies in front of the Truth and Reconciliation Commission (TRC) have verified this. Some security and military per-
sonnel of the apartheid regime had acted on the directives to disrupt, facilitate conflict among Blacks, and actually carry out acts of execution on certain individuals or groups deemed *personae non gratae* by the state. In spite
of all these problems, South Africans did elect its first democratic government in 1994, with Nelson Mandela being installed as president of the Government of National Unity (GNU). Over its early years, the new government
has had to deal with many of the disparities of the past as well as the pola-
rizing forces stemming from the apartheid era.

The Moral Obligation of MNCs

With their highly anticipated return to SA, MNCs have been expected to play
a major role not only in turning the economy around but also in issues concerning distributive justice through affirmative action and other on-the-job
training and skill-development programs primarily aimed at the Black labor
force. The existing challenges notwithstanding, they have tried to do this.
However, concerns about the propensity of MNCs to fulfill social obligations
have been raised. True enough, noted scholars such as Friedman (1970)
argue that the social responsibility of business is to maximize shareholders'
profits within the rules of the game. But in the case of apartheid SA, even
Friedman would agree that it was incumbent on MNCs to consider social
issues in that the "rules" had not been set democratically. In their book,
Global Reach, Barnet and Muller (1974) made the point that multinational
corporations are the most powerful human organization yet devised for
shaping the future. This great power can either enhance the possibility of
effecting great evil or enhance the possibility of effecting great good (as
would be possible in post apartheid South Africa). Indeed, it is from the latter perspective that many analysts including economist John K. Galbraith
saw the MNC as the most potent force for world peace (Donaldson 1989).
But, given the remoteness of the headquarters of many MNCs from their
host countries, they cannot be blindly expected to pursue their obligation to
do good, especially if doing good implies an erosion of profit margins. For
that reason, it is necessary that some code of conduct be in place to guide
the conduct of MNCs to assure their responsiveness to local conditions.

Moral Guidelines and Principles

One of the models for ensuring that MNCs do fulfill their obligations to society is suggested by Henry Mintzberg (1984). The Mintzberg model contains eight alternatives arranged in the form of a horseshoe. The alternatives range from "nationalize it" on the extreme left, to "trust it" in the center, to "restore it" on the extreme right. Which of the alternatives the corporation must be subjected to would depend on the shifting priorities of the country. This would require corporations to remain in touch with the evolving needs and priorities of the host nation. Another useful moral guideline would be what Donaldson (1989) has termed the "condition of business" principle. This principle states that, ceteris paribus, business transactions by B with A are impermissible when A is a systematic violator of fundamental human rights, unless those transactions serve to discourage the violation of human rights and either harm or, at a minimum, fail to benefit A in consequence of A's rights violation activity. Thus, in conducting business with countries that are potential violators of human rights, it would be worthwhile for corporate leaders to use the condition of business principle as a guideline as to whether it is appropriate to engage in business transactions with them or not.

Conclusion

The major lesson that comes out of the SA experience is that when evil and repression have become pervasive in a social system and when the limits of the social system's coping capacity have been reached, only drastic measures can prevent a complete collapse of that system. In the case of SA, it was the alignment of international condemnation, internal resistance, and corporate withdrawal – with all the hardships these entailed – that finally convinced the SA government that the human rights violations that apartheid embodied were not acceptable to the world community. It is perhaps one of the remarkable ironies of human existence that it was by their pulling out of SA that the MNCs proved that they could serve as agents for social change.

CHAPTER 7

Research Methodology

This chapter describes the study's methodology. The chapter comprises the following format: (1) research method, sample selection and data gathering; (2) measurement of variables, development of the research instrument; (3) generation of research hypotheses; (4) discussion of statistical methods of data analysis; (5) hypothesis testing; and (6) discussion of limitations of the research.

Research Method

Sample

The target sample for this study consisted of strategic-level executives from 120 U.S., 90 Canadian, and 100 South African companies. Huber and Power (1985) reported that the way to increase the accuracy of data obtained from strategic management questions is to use strategic-level managers as the key informants. In keeping with this recommendation, our target population consisted of executives with titles of Chairman; CEO; President; Vice President and Director of Overseas Operations. Our company selection criteria were as follows:

1. that the company must have (or must have had) a subsidiary in South Africa. Companies which had already divested were eligible for participation;
2. that the size of the company's operation in South Africa must be substantial, e.g., the number of employees must be more than 100; or the total assets must be greater than $500,000.

We obtained this information from sources such as the Dun and Brad-street's (1986) *Principal International Businesses*. U.S. firms were drawn from organizations listed in the *Fortune 500 Directory*, and the Canadian firms came from *Financial Post Industry's 500*. The South African firms were selected from organizations listed in the South African *Financial Mail*. The study was designed to stratify the Canadian responses into two categories, namely: Canadian companies, and Canadian subsidiaries of U.S. companies. However, because of the low response rate from the Canadian executives, the stratification was not feasible. The Canadian responses were thus combined with the U.S. responses to allow for meaningful inferences. The sample ended up being two-tiered: North American companies and South African companies.

Data gathering

A three-stage data-gathering procedure employed the following format: (1) personal interviews, (2) mail survey, and (3) document analysis. Ideas from semi-structured personal interviews with two executives from U.S. companies were incorporated into the design of the survey questionnaire. Some of the strategy-related statements were obtained by gleaning articles written by representatives of the target population in journals and periodicals such as the *Harvard Business Review, California Management Review, Business and Society Review, Fortune,* and *Forbes.*

Measurement of Variables

This section discusses the operationalization of the different variables utilized in the four sections of the questionnaire, i.e., perceived environmental turbulence, strategy preference, performance, and demographic variables. A summary of all the variables used in the study with their associated acronyms is presented in Appendix B.

Perceived Environmental Turbulence

Questions 1 through 21 (see Appendix A) constituted the Perceived Environmental Turbulence (PET) scale. The scale was an adaptation and combination of the instruments used by Duncan (1972), Khandwalla (1976), and Miller and Friesen (1983). Statements were randomly arranged to elicit the executives' view of *changes* in the environmental dimensions of dynamism, hostility, and heterogeneity of their firm in South Africa over the past five years. Respondents were asked to choose, on a five-point Likert-type scale, a rating that came "closest" to their "feelings about the matter." In general, the lower ratings indicated a dramatic increase and the higher ratings a substantial reduction in perceived turbulence. The Cronbach Alpha reliability for the overall PET scale was 0.81, indicating very good reliability. The correlation matrix of the items in this scale is presented in Appendix C.

Preferred Strategy

The preferred strategy scale consisted of questions 27 through 39. (See Appendix A.) These questions incorporated statements describing specific actions or strategies that a firm might take to help deal with issues that might arise in the South African business environment. These statements were then presented in the questionnaire, and each executive was asked to rate the extent to which he/she would adopt, or agree with, the propositions. This method of eliciting strategy preferences has been considered superior to presenting the respondents with previously conceptualized strategy typologies (Khandwalla 1985). The respondents' strategy preference was computed by averaging questions 27 through 39. The Cronbach Alpha statistic for the reliability of this scale was 0.24, which, according to Nunnally (1967), is below an acceptable range. Because of this relatively low reliability, we used responses to item 40—the item which directly prompted respondents to make a forced choice of their overall preferred strategy—as a measure of their strategy preferences. The correlation between this item and the computed average of items 27–39 was 0.36.

Perceived Performance

Performance was measured using five perceptual measures. (See questions 22 through 26.) Three of the measures—after-tax return on total assets (ATROTA), growth in sales (GROSA), and overall performance (OVERPER)—have been validated by Dess and Robinson (1984), who, as indicated earlier, had found high Spearman rank correlations between objective and subjective measures of these variables. The fourth measure, after-tax return on sales (ATROSA), was successfully validated by Pearce, Robbins, and Robinson (1987). Finally, public image and goodwill (PUBIG) is a measure of the executives' perception of their organizations' social contribution. That measure was considered important for this research, since Shetty (1979) had found that executives of large U.S. corporations rated this variable among their top five business goals.

Respondents were asked to estimate how their firms compared with similar firms in their industries, in South Africa, on each of the five items of the scale. Once again, we employed a five-point Likert-type scale, with the lowest number indicating the top 20 percent and the highest number indicating the lowest 20 percent. Reliability of this scale was very good (0.88). The correlation matrix of the items is presented in Appendix D.

A summary of the Cronbach Alpha statistics for the three scales—Perceived Environmental Turbulence, Strategy, and Performance—is presented in Appendix E.

Demographic Variables

The last ten questions of the questionnaire (questions 41 through 50) covered the demographic information of the respondents and their companies. The first six of these focused on the organization. For example, question 41 (a) and (b) measured the value of total assets employed (ASSETVA) and number of employees in South Africa (EMPLONO), which are used as indicators of the company's level of commitment. These questions allowed for the classification of companies into high and low commitment categories.

Questions 42, 43, 44, and 45 elicited information about the principal area of business in which the company was involved (PRINBUS), the type of business venture (INVESTYP), the number of years of corporate involvement in South Africa (YRSINSA), and the percentage of company sales coming from South Africa (PERCENT).

The variable YRSINSA was conveniently divided into five categories coinciding with some of the major events in South Africa. For example, the first category (0 through 10 years) coincided with the post-Soweto period.[8] The second category (11 though 25 years) covered the period between the declaration of the Republic of South Africa and the Soweto riots. The third category (26 through 43 years) coincided with the post-World War II era. The fourth category (44 through 60 years) covered the years between the two world wars. The last period (60 years or more) encompasses most of the period of industrialization of South Africa up to World War I.

Questions 46 through 50 presented the demographic profiles of the executive. These included job title (JOBTIT), highest level of education (LEVELED), major area of education (MAJORED), service in the company (SERVICE), and present age (AGE). At the end of the questionnaire, space was provided to allow the respondents an opportunity to add comments. At the very end they were asked to include their names if they wished to receive a summary of the findings.

Pilot Test

The questionnaire was pilot-tested on 28 MBA students who had had work experience in overseas subsidiaries of multinational corporations. According to Sudman (1976), a pilot sample of 20–50 cases is usually sufficient to discover major flaws in a questionnaire before they damage the main study. The choice of these MBAs was carefully considered in light of literature on the constitution of pilot-study respondents. Researchers are divided on how closely pilot-study subjects should resemble the respondents of the actual study. Some have suggested that pretest respondents be as similar as possible to the target population (Tull and Hawkins 1976; Zaltman and Burger 1975), whereas others have argued that this precaution is not always necessary (Galtung 1969; Brown and Beik 1969). These differences aside, the pilot study proved helpful in ensuring that the wording of the questionnaire was easily understood and that its timing was as estimated. To further enhance the content validity of the instrument, it was scrutinized by researchers on the management faculty at the University of Massachusetts.

The questionnaire was designed to tap the three constructs of (1) environmental turbulence; (2) strategy preference: and (3) perceived performance on a five-point Likert-type scale (Kerlinger 1973). The design also incorporated ideas from other researchers, notably; Pearce, Robbins, and Robinson (1987), Mascarenhas (1985), Smart and Vertinsky (1984), Miller and Friesen (1983), Bourgeois (1980), Khandwalla (1976), Downey and Slocum (1975), and Duncan (1972). The questionnaires were mailed to the Canadian and U.S. executives with a cover letter. The cover letters were individually typed on university letterhead, including each executive's address, an individualized salutation, altruistic wording, and handwritten signatures of both the researcher and his advisor, with their designations printed below the signatures.

Individualized, altruistically worded cover letters were adopted on the recommendation of researchers who have conducted mail surveys of the Fortune 500 companies (Gadeake and Tootelian 1976; Kerin and Harvey 1976). For example, in their study of the response patterns of the Fortune 500 Companies, Gaedeke and Tootelian found that individualized letters produced higher response rates than form letters. The same researchers found that an altruistic appeal generated a higher response than an egoistic appeal. Self-addressed return envelopes were also included in the mailing, with the U.S.—but not the Canadian—return envelopes bearing the "postage paid" markings. This, however, was not expected to cause any significant disparity in responses from the two groups, since earlier research had indicated that the availability of return postage had no statistically significant impact on response rates (Gaedeke and Tootelian 1976). Indeed, even some of the U.S. questionnaires were returned in a company envelope or in the supplied return envelope with company franking or postage marks.

The design of the questionnaire fulfilled most of the general principles espoused in the Total Design Method (TDM) suggested by Dillman (1978). The TDM consists of the following eight characteristics: (1) a cover letter, (2) a dated letterhead belonging to the sponsoring agency, (3) a personalized letter including the respondent's typed name and address and signed in ink by the researcher, (4) questionnaires stamped with an identification number, (5) the respondent's name on the envelope (never including an address label), (6) a follow-up postcard sent one week later, (7) a second cover letter and questionnaire mailed three weeks later to everyone who had not responded, and (8) another cover letter, complete with a replacement questionnaire sent seven weeks later by certified mail to those who had not responded. For an excellent discussion of the TDM, see Dillman (1978, 1983). Our study departed in several ways from Dillman's (1978) TDM. The first was the use of address labels on envelopes. Dillman had urged that address labels never be used. Presumably, with the growing acceptance of computing as a fact of life in many business organizations, address labels on envelopes are no longer perceived as discourteous. Indeed, in our study, no negative impact was discernible from their use. The second departure was that no identification numbers were used on the questionnaires to identify the respondents. This precaution was taken in the interest of anonymity, given the sensitivity of the research topic. Andreason (1970) alluded to the efficacy of anonymity when he asserted that under some circumstances the respondent may be more willing to reply if he/she thinks that his/her answers will be treated impersonally.

Three months after the first mailing, a personalized reminder was sent to the respondents with another copy of the questionnaire. The South African questionnaires were personally delivered to the director of a research organization in Johannesburg who had offered to coordinate their administration to the South African executives. The completed questionnaires were received from South Africa by the end of the fifth month, which signified the conclusion of the data-gathering phase of the research. Responses to the questionnaire and the accompanying discussion are covered in Chapter 6. Informal face-to-face and telephone discussions were conducted with a number of senior executives in South Africa in January 1988. Similar discussions were also conducted with North American executives.

Analysis

The hypotheses driving this research were presented in Chapter 2. They are restated in Table 7.1 for easy reference. The relationships are also depicted diagrammatically in Figure 7.1. To investigate the proposed sets of relation-ships, the present study employed contingency analysis (CROSSTABS). The CROSSTABS procedure is a joint frequency distribution of cases according to two or more classification variables. In this procedure, joint frequency distributions are statistically analyzed by certain tests of significance, such as the chi-square test or Fisher's (1950) exact test to determine whether or not the variables are statistically independent.

Table 7.1: Hypotheses

H1: Executives who perceive high turbulence prefer less risky strate-gies (i.e., hold, retrench, divest).

H2: Executives who perceive high performance will also perceive low turbulence.

H3: Executives who perceive high performance of their South African operations prefer "entrepreneurial"* strategies.

H4: In turbulent environments, the preferred strategy is related to the level of commitment in terms of assets, number of employees, profitability. The higher the level of commitment, the less risky is the strategy.

H5: Overseas-based top executives perceive the South African envi-ronment to be more turbulent than locally based top executives. This difference is also expected to occur between the sample of U.S. and Canadian top executives.

* The term "entrepreneurial" is used to denote expansion and oppor-tunistic growth.

Figure 7.1: Hypothesized Relationships

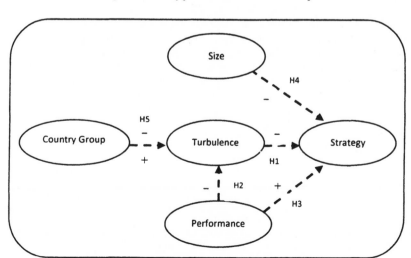

The formula for the Chi-Square test is:

$$\chi^2 = \Sigma \left[\frac{(O_i - E_i)^2}{E_i} \right]$$

Where:

χ^2 = the chi-square statistic
O_i = observed frequency of cell i
E_i = expected frequency of cell i

The χ^2 test is reliable when expected cell sizes are greater than five. When expected cell sizes are small, Yates's (1934) continuity correction is applied. In the specific case of 2x2 tables where expected cell sizes are less than five, Fisher's (1950) exact test is used in place of the chi-square test. These tests are available in the SPSS program. For more details, see Everitt (1977); and Nie et al. (1975). The chi-square formula reveals that the greater the difference between the observed and the expected frequencies, the larger the chi-square value, and the stronger the relationship between the variables given in the existing row and column totals. On the other hand, smaller chi-square values indicate statistical independence between row and column variables. In using the chi-square test of significance a word of caution is necessary. The test does not prove causality in the relationship between variables. Some scholars have argued that it is irrelevant for that purpose. However, this study did not intend to establish causality in the first place. Second, in their article entitled, "Proof? No. Evidence? Yes. The Significance of Tests of Significance," Winch and Campbell (1969) made the case that even though tests of significance may be irrelevant to interpret the cause of a difference, still they can prove useful in assessing the relative likelihood that a real difference exists and is worthy of interpretive attention. The five hypotheses in Table 6.1 were tested with the chi-squared statistic [along with?] a 95 percent confidence interval level for rejection of the null hypothesis of no relationship. The procedure for hypothesis testing is described in the next section.

Hypothesis Testing

Responses from each section of the questionnaire were grouped into low and high categories by combining the 1s, 2s, and 3s of the original scale into one category, and combining the 4s and 5s into another category. The end-product of this recoding was a bifurcated set of responses on all sections (except the demography section), with the higher category represented by 1s and the lower category represented by 0s. For instance, for the PET section (see questions 1 through 21 in Appendix A), the lower values represented *higher* environmental turbulence and were re-coded as 1s, while the higher values represented *lower* environmental turbulence and were recorded as 0s.

By using equal weighting of responses, a PET Index was calculated for each respondent. The same procedure was followed to derive a Strategy Index and a Performance Index. Consideration was given to other techniques for deriving indices which were not based on equal weighting of responses, e.g., principal component or factor analysis (Dillon and Goldstein 1984). They, however, proved to be unnecessary. Based on the recoded data and computed indices, the following comparisons were made:

1. Perceived Environmental Turbulence (PET) vs. Riskiness of Preferred Strategy.
2. Perceived Performance vs. PET
3. Performance vs. Preferred Strategy
4. PET vs. Level of Commitment
5. PET of North America–based executives vs. PET of SA–based executives.

The five hypotheses were tested using the CROSSTABS procedure card on the SPSS program of the University of Massachusetts Cyber 860 mainframe computer library. The results of the CROSSTABS tabulations are presented and discussed in the next chapter.

Limitations of the Research

An important limitation of this research stems from potential problems with the use of a mail questionnaire as the research instrument for obtaining information from key informants (Nunnally 1967; Phillips 1981). It is possible for the questionnaire to be incorrectly completed or to be completed by someone other than the intended respondent. The supplementary interviews were designed, in part, to help minimize such errors.

A second limitation generally associated with mail surveys is a nonresponse bias. It is well known that highly educated survey respondents tend to be more cooperative than less educated respondents. Furthermore, in a controversial issue more responses are likely to be obtained from those who are strongly for or against it than from those in the middle (Sudman 1976). Some respondents may perceive certain questions as potentially self-incriminating, or as giving away their strategic advantage. Given these considerations, there is a possibility that organizations whose executives did not respond had unique characteristics that differed from those whose executives who did.

Another important limitation of this research, especially from a positivist perspective, is that the study uses perceptual rather than objective measures. The positivist school of social science presupposes that the logic of the natural sciences can be extended into the realm of human behavior (Burrell and Morgan 1979). This school supports objective measures over subjective ones because they are more replicable and, therefore, more scientific (Starbuck 1976). The objectivist stance in social theory building has been under attack since its inception. For instance, some scholars totally reject it, reasoning that human actions are ad hoc in nature and thus cannot be detached from moral assessment. The determinism implied in positivism is seen as faulty owing to the impossibility of perceiving a phenomenon without making assumptions about its nature (Agger 1991). The most radical anti-positivist position asserts that there can be no such thing as a science of human behavior.

It was argued earlier that perceptual assessment allows one to obtain data in the required format. The trade-off is that this format also requires the respondent to make complex and difficult judgments (Phillips 1981). Evidence also suggests that such judgments may be inaccurate (Hoffman 1960; Slovic, 1969). The main source of the inaccuracies is the cognitive limitation of people as information processors (March and Simon 1958). Cognitive psychologists have found that people display predictable biases when responding to questions or confronting problems (Tversky and Kahnemann 1974). When dealing with complex problems, people often rely on heuristic principles and cognitive simplification processes (Schwenk 1984; Duhaime and Schwenk 1985). This does not mean that executives' cognitive propensities completely overwhelm reality, but it does indicate that their mental representations significantly bias their interpretation of the organization and its environment (Ireland et al. 1987). One example is the over-response to vivid or dramatic information that imbues it with a larger role in influencing opinion than justified by its objective content (Nisbett and Ross, 1980). Of greater importance to the present study is the notion of the availability of information to the respondent (Ireland et al. 1987). In the case of executives outside South Africa, the availability of information (or lack thereof) may introduce a systematic bias that may seriously affect their perceptions.

Another limitation of this research is that it is cross-sectional. It is well known that longitudinal studies are more powerful in capturing events as they evolve, particularly in dynamic settings such as the situation in South Africa (Van Vuuren et al. 1983). However, time limitations precluded the adoption of a longitudinal design. Finally, the loss of five survey questionnaires in the mail from South Africa may have limited the range of responses, especially if the lost responses differed from those that reached the United States.

Summary

In this chapter the methodology used in the research was outlined in some detail. Sample selection procedures, measurement of variables, and statistical methods of data analysis were discussed. Five hypotheses were reported, and the method of testing the hypotheses was presented. Finally, the limitations of the research design were outlined. The next chapter presents the results of the data analysis and discusses the findings of the study.

CHAPTER 8

Analysis

The results analyzed in this chapter represent tabulated information from the questionnaire, explanatory information from the interviews, and additional information from position and proxy statements from some of the respondents. In addition to some comparative statistical information, the chapter is arranged in the following order: (1) discussion of the response rate; (2) demographic data; (3) results of hypothesis testing; (4) interpretation of qualitative data; and (5) summary of the findings.

Response Rate

Summary statistics of responses received are presented in Table 8.1. This table indicates that of the 226 eligible questionnaires mailed to U.S. executives, 48 completed questionnaires were returned[9]. This represents a response rate of 21 percent, which is typical for Fortune 500 Companies (Gadeake and Tootelian 1976). Corresponding figures for South African executives were 24 completed questionnaires for a 17 percent response rate. In addition to the well-known difficulties associated with gaining access to senior executives of top companies (Hopkins 1978), the relatively low response rate can be explained in terms of two factors.

First and most important is the delicate nature of the study. Because of antiapartheid pressure and lobby groups, especially in the United States and Canada, corporate executives are careful about what they report about their operations in South Africa. A number of responses declining to participate in the study came not from the intended respondents, but from people with titles of Legal Advisor, Consumer Affairs Correspondent, Corporate Clearance and Editorial Review Manager, and so on. These individuals invariably adopted an unsympathetic, hard-line approach toward the study. Their typical response was that their company had a policy of not responding to any survey questionnaire unless it was required by law. The Canadian response rate was much smaller, for reasons to be discussed later. Responses from South Africa were much lower than anticipated. Again one can conjecture that confidentiality and anonymity issues may have played a role in reducing the response rate from this sample, given the sensitivity of the topic. The survey's origination from outside South Africa may have further accentuated the reluctance to cooperate.

Table 8.1: Analysis of Response Rates

CRITERION	U.S.	S.A.
Number of questionnaires mailed	273	140
Retired (US) = 14		
No operations in S.A. = 12		
No direct control of S.A. = 21		
Total ineligible responses = 47		
Eligible responses = 273 - 47	226	
Completed (N)	48	24
Not completed ...	16	5*
Declined participation due to fear of breach of confidentiality or loss of competitive advantage or has pulled out of South Africa		
Percentage of positive responses to eligible respondents	21	17
Percentage of usable responses to total possible responses	28	20
Total sample size (76)	52**	24

*The South African responses arrived in the United States in two batches. The first batch arrived with the following post office marks on the envelope: "Arrived Unsealed in Springfield Massachusetts." Five of the 16 completed questionnaires were missing. A telephone conversation with the originator of the mailing confirmed that a total of 16 completed questionnaires had been mailed.

** Includes 4 Canadian responses

The second factor that might have adversely affected the response rate is the unit of analysis. Because individual executives were chosen as that unit, two or more respondents were selected from each company. However, in every instance, only one response was returned from each company. In some cases, the second respondent declined to respond, by invoking the company policy of not responding to questionnaires and citing a variety of reasons.

Demographic Information

Demography has been defined as the scientific study of human populations, focusing primarily on their size, structure or composition, and development or change. It studies the determinants of population trends and the consequences of these trends, including problems resulting from them (Yaukey 1985). Table 8.2 summarizes the sample's demographic statistics.

Size of Commitment

Two measures for level of commitment used in this study were dollar figure of assets invested (ASSETVA) and number of employees (EMPLONO). Note that these two measures were used only as dimensions of size. Drucker (1974) indicated that size was a configuration rather than a single aspect of business. According to him, determining whether a company is big or small requires looking at a number of factors, e.g., employment, sales, value added (where applicable), complexity and diversity of its product range, and complexity of its technology. In keeping with this recommendation, this study considered these measures together in determining the size of commitment in South Africa.

Table 8.2 reveals that the companies for which U.S. executives worked had asset values ranging from $2 million to $1 billion, and an average of $45 million invested in South Africa. South African companies' assets ranged from $2.5 million to $5 billion, with an average of $160 million.[10] A salient feature in the responses to this variable is the number of missing cases from American respondents (50%). This seems to confirm that MNCs are sensitive to revealing information about the dollar value of their commitment in their overseas operations. All the South African respondents reported the asset value of their commitment.

Table 8.2: Summary of Demographic Information

VARIABLE	MEASURE	US/Canada	S. A.
Assetva (in S.A.)	Mean (Million)	45	160
	Range	2M – 1B	2.5M – 5B
Emplono	Mean	569	3791
	Range	9 – 10,000	9 – 24,000
Yrsinsa	Mean	37	35
	Range	5 – 94	5 – 125
Jobttl	Chairman/CEO	9	4
	President/MD*	9	11
	Vice President	13	0
	Director	10	7
	Other	5	1
Leveled	Some University	-	8
	Univ. Degree	19	7
	Graduate Degree	26	8
Majored	Business Related	31	13
	Social Sciences	4	5
	Natural Sciences	9	4
Service	Mean (years)	18	10
	Range	2 – 38	2 – 25
Age	Mean (years)	50	46
	Range	28 – 65	34 – 65

*MD = Managing Director

In comparison with ASSETVA, more American respondents gave information about their commitment in terms of number of employees
(EMPLONO) in South Africa. In this case only 13 (25%) North American
cases were missing. The North American sample employed an average of
569 employees versus an average of 3,790 employed by the sample of South
African corporations. A joint frequency distribution analysis on commitment level in terms of ASSETVA (see Table 8.3) revealed that more than
two-thirds (18) of the American companies fell in the low category of commitment, and less than one-third (8) fell in the high category of commitment. The corresponding figures for S.A. companies were a little over one-
third (8) in the low level of commitment, and almost two thirds (13) in the
high level of commitment. The figures for commitment by number of em-

ployees (EMPLONO) were found to be similarly distributed. Remember that, even though the information is anecdotal, that level of commitment might have differing strategic implications for a company in which the operation in question comprises only two percent compared with a company where the operation represents 100 percent of its total income. For the former, it may be a disposable entity; for to the latter, it would be a matter of survival. Also, the comparatively higher level of commitment by South African companies is likely to have different strategic implications than with overseas-based companies. (See the forthcoming section on hypothesis testing.)

Table 8.3: Cross-Tabs of Asset Value by Country Group

*ASSETVA

		LOW	HIGH	TOTAL
GROUP	North America	17	26	43
	South Africa	4	16	20
	TOTAL	21	42	63

Key:

*ASSETVA = Value of Assets Employed in South Africa.

In summary South African companies had a higher level of commitment on average in terms of both assets and number of employees. American respondents were reluctant to divulge the dollar value of their assets in South Africa, but were more willing to reveal their number of employees. South African respondents reported both their asset values and number of employees. Finally, most of the South African companies derived the bulk of their sales from the domestic market; in contrast, most of the American companies derived only about one percent of their sales from their South African operations.

Years in South Africa (YRSINSA)

The number of years of company involvement in South Africa was indicated by the approximate years that these companies had been operating in South Africa. Table 8.4 presents the number of American company start-ups in South Africa grouped into the five time periods discussed in chapter 3. In this table, the responses indicate that approximately two-fifths of the companies began their operations in South Africa during the 1960s.[11] That peak jibes with the literature on the growth of MNCs in South Africa, which reports that the major expansion in the secondary sector took place in the period subsequent to World War II (Seidman and Seidman 1979: 17). In fact, physical output as well as the value of output of the manufacturing sector doubled from 1966 to 1973.

Table 8.4: Corporate Start-ups of Sample Firms

PERIOD	SOUTH AFRICAN	NORTH AMERICAN
1977 – 1987	3	2
1961 – 1976	6	19
1945 – 1960	8	9
1920 – 1939	2	11
Pre–World War I	2	5
Not Reported	3	5
Total	24	51

Most of the companies in this study were involved in manufacturing, with a few exceptions in the South African sample. A majority of American companies began their operations in South Africa after World War II, and a significant percentage had their start-ups in the 1960s, when South African investments were yielding a high return in compared with similar investments in other parts of the world.

Other Demographic Variables

The typical American respondent held the title of Vice President, often in charge of overseas operations. He/she held a university degree in business or a related field; was approximately 50 years old; and had worked for her/his company for 18 years. Her/his corporation typically had a subsidiary in South Africa; was involved in manufacturing; and derived less than two percent of its worldwide sales from the country.

By comparison, the typical South African respondent held the title of Managing Director. He/she held a university degree or its equivalent; was approximately 46 years old; and had worked for her/his company for 10 years. Her/his South African company had majority ownership; was involved in manufacturing (although a few were in retailing); and derived most of its sales from South Africa.

These demographic variables reveal that both sets of respondents held positions close to, or at the top of their respective corporate ladders and were educationally well qualified. As indicated earlier, these two attributes are necessary in obtaining accurate information that is reliable for the analysis of strategic management issues (Huber and Power 1985). By comparison, the South African respondent was younger and had served his company for a shorter period. The most significant distinction was that South African companies depended on the local market for a much greater percentage of their profitability.

In analyzing the foregoing demographic information, remember that five questionnaires completed by South African executives were lost in the mail on the way to the United States. It is possible that their inclusion in the sample may have altered the overall demographic profile of the South African executives.

Hypothesis Testing

This section presents the results of the hypothesis tests. The five hypotheses were introduced in Chapter 7 and restated in Table 7.1. The primary method of testing the hypotheses was contingency table analysis—the chi-square method. In addition, multiple regression analysis and scatter plots were used to test the robustness of the findings. These methods confirmed the findings of the chi-square results.

Hypothesis 1

The first hypothesis of the study posited that executives who perceived high turbulence preferred the less risky strategies of hold, retrench, and divest. To test this hypothesis, a cross-tabulation table was constructed for perceived environmental turbulence (PET) and preferred strategy. As noted in chapter 3, PET is an index that was developed by computing a simple average of the 21 environmental turbulence items. Since the strategy scale had marginal reliability, it was decided to use the response to question 40 (see Appendix A) for strategy preference. Both variables were bifurcated, thereby producing a 2x2 cross-tabulation table for this comparison[12]. The test for cross-tabulation of PET and strategy riskiness indicated no significant difference between these variables for the sample (N = 63). The results were: chi-square = 1.55; d. f. = 1; p = 0.21. (See Table 8.5). Even when each of the strategy preference statements was cross-tabulated with PET, none of them indicated a significant relationship, which provides further evidence for rejecting the hypothesis. For this sample of respondents, the results indicate that the null hypothesis—i.e., that no significant relationship exists between perceived environmental turbulence (PET) and strategy riskiness—cannot be rejected. It can thus be concluded that there is no relationship between perceived environmental turbulence and strategy.

Table 8.5: Cross-Tabs of Environmental Turbulence by Strategy

GRDSTRA

		LOW	HIGH	TOTAL
*PET	LOW	17	26	43
	HIGH	4	16	20
	TOTAL	21	42	63

$$\chi^2 = 1.5; \text{d.f.} = 1; p = .21$$

Key:
*PET= Perceived Environmental Turbulence
**GRSTRA = Grand Strategy Preference

Hypothesis 2

The second hypothesis proposed that executives who perceive high performance of their company will also perceive low environmental turbulence. In this case, we used the composite index of performance (AVPER) computed from the five performance measures—after tax return on total assets (ATROTA), after tax return on sales (ATROSA), growth of sales (GROSA), public image and goodwill (PUBIG), and overall performance (OVERPER). This index was cross-tabulated with PET, resulting in the matrix shown in Table 8.6.

Once again, the chi-square statistic for this cross-tabulation revealed no significant relationship between these two measures (chi-square = 0.025, d. f. = 1, p = 88). This means, therefore, that the null hypothesis of no significant relationship between perception of performance and environmental turbulence cannot be rejected for this sample of respondents. This leads to the conclusion that no relationship exists between perception of performance and perception of environmental turbulence.

Table 8.6: Cross-Tabs of Performance by Environmental Turbulence

**AVPER

		LOW	HIGH	TOTAL
*PET	LOW	10	31	41
	HIGH	6	14	20
	TOTAL	16	45	61

$\chi^2 = 0.025$; d.f. = 1; p = .88

Key: *PET = Perceived Environmental Turbulence
**AVPER = Average Performance of the SA Subsidiary

Hypothesis 3

The third hypothesis was that executives who perceive high performance of their South African operations prefer "entrepreneurial" strategies. To test this hypothesis, the performance index AVPER was cross-tabulated with the grand strategy chosen (GRDSTRA), resulting in a 2x2 contingency table. (See Table 8.7.) As can be seen, the chi-square test indicates that the variables AVPER and GRDSTRA are not independent; a significant relationship does exist between these two measures (chi-square = 4.81; d. f. = 1, p = .03 In the case of hypothesis 3; therefore, the null hypothesis that no relationship exists between perception of company performance and strategy riskiness was rejected for this sample. It can, thus, be concluded that a relationship does exist between perception of performance and strategy. In other words, respondents who perceived high levels of performance of their companies preferred entrepreneurial strategies.

Table 8.7: Cross-Tabs of Strategy by Average Performance

**GRDSTRA

		LOW	HIGH	TOTAL
*AVPER	LOW	10	7	17
	HIGH	11	33	44
	TOTAL	21	40	61

$\chi^2 = 4.81$; d. f. = 1; p = .03

Key: *AVPER = Average Performance of the SA Subsidiary
**GRDSTRA = Grand Strategy Preference

Hypothesis 4

According to this hypothesis, it is expected that among executives who perceive high turbulence, the higher the level of commitment, the less risky the preferred strategy. To test this hypothesis, only the executives who perceived high turbulence were selected. Their strategy preferences were cross-tabulated with each of the commitment measures (i.e., assets employed and number of employees). As with the previous tests, the measures were bifurcated to produce 2x2 tables. In this case, however, since two of the cells had frequencies below five, Fisher's (1950) exact test was used. The results of the cross-tabulations can be seen in Tables 8.8 and 8.9. The results of Fisher's test are: $p = .85$ for ASSETVA and $P = .50$ for EMPLONO. In both cases, therefore, the data show no evidence that a significant relationship exists between perception of environmental turbulence and commitment level.

Table 8.8: Cross-Tabs of Strategy by Value of Asset

**ASSETVA

		LOW	HIGH	TOTAL
*GRDSTRA	LOW	10	7	17
	HIGH	11	33	44
	TOTAL	21	40	61

Fisher's Exact Test: p = 0.85

Key: * GRDSTRA = Grand Strategy Preference
** ASSETVA = Value of Assets Employed (in SA)

From the above, it follows that the null hypothesis that no relationship exists between level of commitment and strategy preference cannot be rejected. This leads to the conclusion that in turbulent environments (i.e., where high turbulence is perceived) no relationship exists between strategy choice and level of commitment.

Hypothesis 5

The final hypothesis stated that overseas-based executives perceived the South African environment to be more turbulent than locally based executives. In this case, PET indices of the two subsamples were compared by

Table 8.9: Cross-Tabs of Strategy by Number of Employees

**EMPLONO

		LOW	HIGH	TOTAL
*GRDSTRA	LOW	2	1	3
	HIGH	7	8	15
	TOTAL	9	9	18

Fisher's Exact Test: p = 0.50
Key: * GRDSTRA = Grand Strategy Preference
** EMPLONO = Number of Employees (in SA)

cross-tabulating them against each other. The results are presented in Table 8.10. This table demonstrates a significant difference between American-based executives and South African–based executives in their perceptions of environmental turbulence (chi-square = 4.77; d. f. = 1; p < .03). These results strongly indicate that the null hypothesis of no significant difference between the perceptions of these two groups should be rejected. Further inspection of the joint distribution between the two subpopulations indicates that American executives perceived the South African operating environment to be *less* turbulent than their South African counterparts—the opposite of what was hypothesized.

Table 8.10: Cross-Tabs of Environmental Turbulence by Country

COUNTRY GROUP

		USA	RSA	TOTAL
*PET	LOW	34	12	46
	HIGH	9	12	21
	TOTAL	43	24	67

$\chi^2 = 4.77$; d.f. = 1; p = 0.03
Key: *PET = Perceived Environmental Turbulence

To further investigate the specific area of difference between the two groups of executives (i.e., Americans and South Africans), responses to the

21 perceived environmental turbulence elements of the questionnaire were analyzed by group. Table 8.11 presents the chi-square values and the probability level of making a type 1 error. All the chi-square values had one degree of freedom. The items are presented in order from the lowest probability to the highest. Five variables, when cross-tabulated with PET, produced chi-square values that are significant at $p = 0.02$. Specifically, DIVMETH (needed diversity in production and marketing tactics to cater to different customers) and MATSUPL (availability of material supplier) are highly significant ($p = 0.0001$ and 0.0003, respectively).

DIVMETH: This element is based upon question 19. (See Appendix A.) The question asked the respondents, "In general what would you say about the environment of your organization in South Africa: the number of components in the environment which are important for decision-making has 'become smaller' and components are similar, has 'remained unchanged', or has 'become larger' and components have become more diverse?" Of the American respondents, 37 (80 percent) answered that the number of components had remained unchanged or decreased and only nine (20 percent) responded that the number had actually increased. By contrast, only seven (29 percent) of the South African respondents answered that the number of components had remained unchanged or decreased, while 17 (71 percent) thought that the number had increased. The high significance level of the difference—0.0001—is noteworthy. Clearly, this sample of American and South African executives perceived diversity in the South African environment differently.

MATSUPL: On the question of whether material supplies had "become very scarce," availability had not changed, or they had "become quite plentiful," these two groups differed substantially. An overwhelming number of the American executives, 44 (96 percent), thought that this resource either had remained unchanged or had become more plentiful, while only two (4 percent) thought the resource had become very scarce. The South African respondents were about evenly divided on this question, with 14 (58 percent) thinking that the resource had remained at the same level of availability or had become more plentiful, while 20 (42 percent) thought material supplies had become very scarce.

MKTHOST: On the question of whether marketing activities of key competitors had become far more hostile, had remained the same, or had become far less hostile (see question 7 – Appendix A), 36 (75 percent) of the American executives thought that marketing activities of key competitors had remained unchanged or had even become less hostile, while 12 (25 percent) thought that the marketing activities of key competitors had become far more hostile. The South African respondents thought, by a 2:1 margin, that marketing activities of key competitors had become much more hostile. This reflects how very differently these two groups of executives perceived the South African environment. The last two questions where North American and South African executives showed significant differences dealt with human resource needs. These were availability of top and middle-level managers and availability of skilled labor and first-line supervisors.

TOPMOST: In their responses to the first question, North American and South African respondents differed on the extent that top and middle-level managerial talent were available or scarce.(See Appendix A, question 16.) American respondents were about evenly divided on the issue with 27 (59 percent) responding that the resource had remained unchanged or had become more plentiful, while 19 (41 percent) thought that it had become very scarce. In contrast, the South African executives indicated by a margin of 20 (83 percent) to 4 (17 percent) that top and middle management talent had become very scarce.

SKILDLA: The executive responses also differed significantly on the question about the extent to which skilled labor and first-line supervisors had become scarce or plentiful. (See Appendix A, Question 14.) More North American respondents—34 (74 percent) versus 12 (26 percent)— responded that these resources had remained unchanged or had become more plentiful. South African respondents, on the other hand, were split two ways, with 10 (42 percent) responding that these resources had remained the same or had become more plentiful and 14 (58 percent) indicating that they had become scarcer over the last five years.

The findings of hypothesis 5 can thus be summarized as follows: Stated in its null form, the hypothesis maintained that no significant difference existed in the perception of environmental turbulence among executives whether they were based overseas or based on site in South Africa. The null hypothesis was rejected by this sample. From the above it can thus be concluded—contrary to expectations—that South African executives perceive the South African environment as different and, in fact, more turbulent than North American executives do. Furthermore, these respondents differed significantly on five of the variables used to measure turbulence.

The above analysis of the South African environment suggests the following enigma: If executives based at overseas-based corporate headquarters get their information about their subsidiaries through normal reporting channels in the chain of command, why should perceptions of the same situation be so different? An explanation may lie in the different national cultures of the two sample groups. As discussed earlier, differences in the grooming of the respondents—a product of their national cultures—would account for some of the explanation for this question.

Table 8.11: Chi-Square Test of Each Element of PET Cross-Tabulated
with Country Group & Ranked in Order of Significance Level

ELEMENT	N	χ^2	SIGNIFICANCE LEVEL
DIVMETH**	70	15.63*	0.0001
MATSUPL**	70	12.95	0.0003
MKTHOST**	72	10.00	0.0016
TOPMMGT**	70	9.65	0.0019
SKILDLA**	70	5.71	0.0169
LABDIS	72	3.27	0.0707
INFLAT	72	3.08	0.0791
MKTPRED	72	2.51	0.1138
TRBAR	72	2.01	0.1559
FISCHA	72	2.01	0.1564
INDFLCT	73	1.78	0.1818
DIVSEN	69	1.76	0.1846
STABENV	70	0.54	0.4611
PUBATT	73	0.49	0.4853
POLSTAB	73	0.21	0.6470
PRIMRA	72	0.18	0.6710
CAPITAL	70	0.00	1.0000
GOVCONT	70	0.00	1.0000
HASFA	70	0.00	1.0000
PRICO	72	0.00	1.0000
THRTSUV	73	0.00	1.0000

* Corrected chi-square figures (with 1^0 F).
** Significant at $p < 0.02$

Key: DIVMETH = Needed diversity to compete
        MATSUPL = Availability of material supplies
        MKTHOST = Hostility of competitors' activities
        TOPMMGT = Availability of top and middle managers
        SKILDLA   = Availability of skilled labor

For quick reference, a recapitulation of the results of the hypothesis tests is summarized in Table 8.12. The next section discusses the regression results. The results then follow, which incorporate the respondents' notes and comments, both on their questionnaires and in personal interviews.

Table 8.12: Summary Results of Hypothesis Tests

RELATIONSHIP	SIGNIFICANCE
Pet vs. GRDSTRA	Not significant
PERFORMANCE vs. PET	Not significant
PERFORMANCE vs. GRDSTRA	Significant (p. < .03)
GRDSTRA vs. COMMITMENT	Not significant
N.A. vs. S.A. (on PET)	Significant (p. < .03), in opposite direction to prediction

Key:

PET   = Perceived Environmental Turbulence
GRDSTRA = Strategy preference (for high PET)
N.A.   = North American Executives
S.A.   = South African Executives

Regression Results

To test the robustness of the above findings, multiple regression analysis was performed on the data, by defining two functional relationships of environmental turbulence (PET), strategy preference (GRDSTRA), performance (AVPER), country of origin (GRP), and level of commitment (ASSETVA and EMPLONO) as follows:

(1) PET = f (AVPER, GRP) H2; H5
(2) GRDSTRA = f (PET, AVPER, ASSETVA, EMPLONO) H1; H3; H4

The results of the regression analyses appear in Appendix E. In general, the regression results were consistent with the chi-square test results. In particular, the regressions supported the findings of hypotheses H1, H2, and H4. Support for the hypotheses H3 and H5 was not strong. Also, when the regression analyses were conducted separately for each group of executives, the same results were obtained.

Interpretation of Qualitative Data

This section reflects on the study's findings in a broader perspective. For example, what salient issues have emerged from the results? The section explores these factors and analyzes the information obtained from interviews and additional comments by respondents on the questionnaire.

Perception of Environmental Turbulence

On the whole, most of the respondents in South Africa and North America perceived the South African environment to be changing and believed that more change was needed. Some commented that the environment itself was relatively stable—that the government was in full control—but that the underlying factors were destabilizing and, therefore, creating greater turbulence in the environment. As one North American executive stated on his questionnaire:

> It is clear that they (the S.A. government) have the strength and resolve to maintain control. They have become more repressive and have cancelled or curtailed progressive moves initiated before sanctions.
>
> (Respondent No. 16)

However, this increased control had a disadvantage, which was observed by one of the executives in an interview in South Africa. He perceived that stringent government control—as manifested in the state of emergency regulations and the intervention of the police and military, especially in the townships—actually intensified the existing hostilities. He added that the township unrest had an impact at the workplace and on business in general.

The impact of the turbulence was felt by some who stated that the "hassle factor" had increased to a level that made it economically untenable to continue operations in the country. For instance, according to some reports (Orkin 1986), executives of some American companies complained that problems with their South African subsidiary which had once occupied one day a month occupied one week a month in 1985. One executive remarked that his company was procuring ten percent of its profits from South Africa but that the subsidiary was taking up 50 percent of the firm's boardroom time.

Another issue that emerged from the questionnaire responses and even more strongly from the executives' additional comments was the great concern about the well-being of company employees and their relatives. It has been asserted by others that managers have a "natural" tendency to pursue profits single-handedly, and only modify that aim when they perceive it to be in conflict with what society expects of them (Orpen 1987). In fact, Milton Friedman (1962, 1970) stressed that the only social responsibility of business is to maximize profits "within the rules of the game." The following sampling of comments by North American respondents seems to indicate a departure from Friedman's line of thinking:

> Business has a long-term responsibility to its faithful employees.
> (Respondent R12)

> When we owned the company, our company had many Black employees and there was a 50% Black employment. Now only one Black [employee] remains.
> (Respondent R30)

> Withdrawal would abandon the people we are trying to help and would reduce the pressure on the government for reform. ...
> (Respondent R31)

The picture that seems to emerge from the comments is that many of the respondents perceived the role of business as transcending the "bottom line" to encompass issues beyond the workplace. However, from analyzing the data and inspecting the historical record of the corporations in this study, the conclusion that emerged was that if the elimination of apartheid was the goal, something more needed to be done than the initiatives undertaken by the MNCs up to the time of this research.[13]

The analysis of the data revealed that both groups of executives perceived a shortage of qualified human resources, although Americans perceived the need to be less acute than the South Africans. From their responses, the South African respondents seem to be welcoming the opening up of the economy to Blacks. In particular, one senior executive of a large South African company commented that Blacks themselves had adapted well to the collective bargaining process[14]. In his words, they had taken to union negotiation as "ducks take to water." He did state, however, that some of the highly politicized unions tended to be more hostile.

To sum up, the South African business environment was perceived to be turbulent (potentially, at least) by a majority of the respondents. Many commented that the hostility dimension of turbulence, e.g., the "hassle factor," was on the increase. As for the heterogeneity dimension, it was not surprising that heterogeneity was also perceived to be increasing. South Africans are not a monolithic. As the various groups—each with its own idiosyncratic needs—enter the sociopolitical and economic mainstream, heterogeneity can be expected to increase.

Preferred Strategies

In their views on preferred strategies, both groups gave similar responses. Beyond the items on the questionnaire, a certain measure of anger and frustration could be discerned from the responses of American executives. It appeared that their agenda for the "right strategy for effecting change in South Africa" had been torpedoed. They had been forced into the decision to divest. Most of them preferred strategies of growth and expansion (Rothschild 1979; Harrigan 1985b), but indicated on the questionnaire that their company had been forced to adopt the withdrawal strategy. Most felt that economic stability was a precondition for the elimination of sociopolitical turbulence and were disdainful that they had been compelled to withdraw. One senior executive of a giant corporation which had withdrawn echoed this frustration:

> I had direct access to all top executives in the South African Government, including (President) Botha and a high degree of influence to bring about change. We foreclosed our ability to bring about change when we divested.
>
> (Respondent R16)

In a rare comment, one of the South African respondents asserted that overseas pressure was necessary to fuel reform domestically, stating that if the pressure were removed, reform would stop. A majority of the South African respondents indicated both on the questionnaire and in interviews that they strongly preferred that the MNCs remain in South Africa, since they would strengthen the economy and catalyze change.

What emerged from the analysis of the comments made by this sample of executives and from the interviews conducted was a sense of their commitment to remain in South Africa. Most had aspirations of helping to bring about the demise of apartheid and of empowering Blacks. On face value, these goals may sound good. An important question, however, is whether they were consistent with what the Blacks—the recipients of this help—were asking for. Several surveys have indicated that an overwhelming proportion of Blacks preferred that MNCs begin withdrawing from South Africa. (See Orkin 1986, and Beaty and Harari 1987.) Many corporations recognized this, reality and embarked on all sorts of innovative withdrawal strategies while exiting the South African market.

The next section describes how two MNCs tried to comply with the pressure to withdraw from South Africa, but, at the same time, left a door open for re-entry should the turbulent conditions subside.

Corporate Exodus from South Africa

According to Battersby (1987), 1332 U.S. companies had pulled out of S.A. by mid 1987. The textbook definition of the withdrawal (or disinvestment) strategy has been given as the process whereby a company pulls out its investment from the area where the company has deemed it not desirable to continue investing (Harrigan 1985b; Rothschild 1979). The company that followed this definition to the fullest was Eastman Kodak. When the Rochester, N.Y.–based company announced its pull-out in July 1987, it also announced that it planned to prohibit the distribution of its products. It is should be added parenthetically that Kodak's products—as was the case with the products of many of the other companies that had withdrawn from South Africa—were still available through local companies, which purchased them from third parties (Battersby 1987).

The corporate exodus from South Africa and the manner by which corporations responded to the pressure to divest has been documented in several recently conducted studies (Mangaliso 1999; Mthombeni 2006; Spivey 2008). It is noteworthy that because of the complex nature of the logistics of withdrawal from South Africa, many U.S. companies came up with several creative ways of complying with pressure to disinvest from South Africa while, at the same time, not completely abandoning the S.A. market. Of the companies that left, the vast majority sold to local managements of local companies. In a number of cases, this was done by creating new companies for the sole purpose of selling the subsidiary. Some of the companies that sold to local management either sold to the highest bidder following the 'maximin' strategy of maximizing the minimum gain possible under conditions of extreme pressure. There were also those that had specific black empowerment objectives of selling to buyers who demonstrated a commitment to increasing the number of Blacks in their management ranks. Others left by selling to third nations.

In a more innovative withdrawal strategy, an overseas multinational company sold its shares in a local company to a trust established for the purpose of continuing the operation. This strategy of disinvestment was adopted by companies that desired to have an appearance of "clean hands" to their American customers but who also wished to have the option to re-enter the South African market in the short to medium term (Battersby 1987; Kneale 1987). Many of the trusts thus established contained built in reacquisition clauses. Other MNCs chose to move their manufacturing bases to adjacent countries such as Swaziland (Thurow 1987), but continued to service the South African market, as will be seen from the examples that follow. A graphical schema of the strategic choices made by the various U.S. corporations when faced with the pressure to divest is shown in Figure 8.1 below.

Figure 8.1: Strategic Choices Faced by MNCs in South Africa

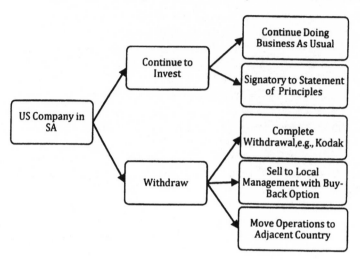

Two Cases of Withdrawal

Among the respondents who declined participation via the survey questionnaire and, instead, chose to send in information about their activities related to South Africa, were those who worked for Coca-Cola Co. and Ford Motor Company[15].

Coca-Cola Company

Coca-Cola Company (hereinafter: Coke) accomplished its withdrawal in November 1986, through a complex arrangement that allowed it to continue selling its product in South Africa. Coke sold its South African subsidiaries to local management through a leveraged buyout. Coke's equity in Coca-Cola Export Corp., Amalgamated Beverage Industries, and Amalgamated Beverage Canners was sold to a newly created company, National Beverage Service Industries (NBS). It relocated its syrup plant to Swaziland, a neighboring country almost totally surrounded by South Africa. The Coke divestiture strategy created multi-equity participation in both Amalgamated Beverage Industries and Amalgamated Beverage Canners by stipulating in the terms of the sale of NBS that part of its interests should be sold to African investors. The *Race Relations Survey, 1986* (Cooper et al. 1987) observed that Coke had recognized that it would make business sense to involve African entrepreneurs because about 76 percent of Coke sales were to African consumers.

Through this arrangement Coke would technically have divested from South Africa. However, the owners of the new company, NBS, were the former management of the South African branch of Coke. NBS was created to buy the Coke assets, monitor and control the quality and use of the Coke trademark, and insure strict adherence to the Sullivan principles[16]. A recently completed study that investigated the actions of Coke and Pepsi in South Africa during the anti-apartheid years and since has made some interesting observations (Spivey 2008). Both Coke and Pepsi placed far more importance on their profitability than on the well-being of the Black African workers who produced, delivered, or consumed their products. But beyond their common commitment to profitability, each responded differently to the pressure from the divestment movement. Coke, which never signed the Sullivan Principles, only announced their intention to withdraw much later in the game, close to the time of the passage of the 1986 Comprehensive Anti Apartheid Act by the U.S. Congress. An early signatory of the Sullivan Principles, Pepsi was one of the first companies to pull out of South Africa (second only to Polaroid) in the 1970s. When they did, they made provision to support the empowerment of Blacks through their contributions to scholarship funds administered by the South African Institute of Race Relations. Thus, when confronted by the divestment campaign, Pepsi seems to have hearkened to the social mandates in their exit strategy. The Coke announcement to withdraw, on the other hand might, at best, be interpreted as contrived—the company was averse to bowing to the pressure to withdraw and remained in the country. The paradox is that when apartheid ended and many MNCs returned, Pepsi found it extremely difficult to compete against Coke because of the dominant market presence it had gained in the absence of competitors such as Pepsi, which goes to show how differently the strategic choices made in the uncertainties of the 1980s affected the companies after the uncertainty (in this case apartheid) was removed.

Ford Motor Company (FMC)

FMC held a 42 percent stake in SAMCOR, one of the biggest South African automobile-manufacturing companies. In 1986, FMC announced that it was withdrawing from South Africa primarily because the operation was losing money, but also because FMC's senior management was disillusioned with the pace of change. When FMC announced that it would withdraw from South Africa, it negotiated the transfer of a major share of its holding in this company to a trust for the benefit of its Black employees. FMC announced that it would continue to supply SAMCOR with components and allow for the continuation of the Ford logotype, which had been in use in the country for over half a century. FMC would also continue to have financial and technical links to locally owned producers. The main feature of the FMC withdrawal was the donation of a major part of its investment in South Africa to a trust for the benefit of its Black employees. After the FMC move, many other major corporations established trust funds as part of their withdrawal strategies.[17] Many indicated their strong desire to re-enter the South African market if the sociopolitical climate returned to normal. (Smith 1986) expressed the frustration of many corporate executives over the slow pace of change in South Africa when he stated:

> But it soon became clear that too little was happening too late. South Africa still lagged behind world opinion and unfolding events, and the country seemed unable to generate the momentum needed to produce the progress the times require.

Note that for a long time, Smith had been a staunch proponent of remaining in South Africa. Along with Blumenthal of Burroughs (now UNISYS), he co-founded a joint organization of American companies with businesses in South Africa to strengthen their bargaining position. It is not surprising that soon after Smith made the above statement, more U.S. corporations announced their plans to withdraw from South Africa (Battersby 1987). Their perception was that environmental turbulence was not being reduced but was, indeed, intensifying.

Summary of the Findings

In this chapter the results of the survey questionnaire were presented and analyzed. The postulated relationships among the variables were explored using cross-tabulations and regression analysis. Comparisons between the perceptions of North American and South African corporate executives yielded some significant differences. The demographic information revealed that South African companies had significantly higher levels of commitment both in terms of number of employees (EMPLONO) and asset value (ASSETVA). Due to the high number of nonresponses to the variable ASSETVA, however, it became difficult to determine the extent to which the two groups differed on this variable, although North American companies inclined toward higher capital-intensity than South African companies. In both cases there were more company start-ups in the 1960s than in any other period. This finding was not surprising, as South Africa experienced an economic boom during that period.

The most significant findings about the respondents themselves were that on average South African executives were five years younger and had a shorter tenure with their companies than their North American counterparts. It is conceivable that these two factors might have had an impact on the way these executives perceived their environment and their strategy choices. As for the hypothesis tests, the results can be recapitulated as follows: Hypothesis 1—that there was a positive relationship between perceived environmental turbulence and strategy preference—was rejected. This was true even when responses from each of the groups were analyzed separately. Hypothesis 2—that there was a positive relationship between perception of turbulence and performance—was also rejected. Also, even when North American and South African responses were analyzed separately, these findings still held true. Hypothesis 3—that perception of high performance was related to strategy preference—was supported by the sample. By implication, this meant that a significant relationship exists between performance and strategy preference. Hypothesis 4—that there was a relationship between strategy preference and level of commitment in terms of either employee numbers or assets—yielded no significant results.

Hypothesis 5—that executives based overseas perceived the South African environment to be more turbulent than did locally based executives—not only was rejected but the results were the opposite of the predicted outcome. In particular, the two sets of executives differed significantly in the how they perceived factors such as the shortage of skilled labor, top and middle-management talent, material supplies and needed diversity in methods of competing. In most of these cases, North American executives, compared with their local counterparts, underestimated the gravity of the problems. The next chapter discusses the implications of these observations and findings for management theory and practice.

CHAPTER 9

Implications of the Study Findings

This chapter summarizes the preceding four chapters and discusses the major finding of the study. The chapter concludes with an overview of the study's implications both for theory and practice and offers suggestions for future research.

Summary

A Recap of the Study's Objectives

The study investigated the relationship among environmental turbulence, strategy preference, and performance. All data were obtained from two groups of corporate executives: one based in South Africa and the other in North America. Respondents were asked to state their views on the environment of their subsidiaries in South Africa. To this researcher's knowledge, no other study had conducted a similar comparative analysis in strategic management beyond North America. The basic tenet of the study was that the propensity of executives to adopt a given strategy was a function of, among other things, their perceptions of the environment and their companies' performance. This tenet was informed by the following questions, which the research sought to answer.

1. Are there significant differences in strategy preference between executives who perceive high turbulence and those who perceive low turbulence?

2. Are there significant differences in the perception of environmental turbulence between executives based in loco at the overseas subsidiary compared with those based at corporate headquarters?

3. Is strategy preference a function of performance, and/or level of commitment?

The questions were restated in the form of five hypotheses, which were tested on the samples of executives in South Africa and in North America. In general, the answer to question (1) was no; to question (2) a strong yes; and to question (3) yes to performance but no to commitment.

Most Important Findings

Within the limitations of the study sample, the results did not support the hypothesis that perceived environmental turbulence is related to strategy preference. This finding is consistent with Anderson and Zeithaml's (1981) conclusion that environmental factors have little impact on strategy preference. It also corroborates Carter's (1987) observation of no solid link between turbulence and decision makers' preferences for plans. This finding, by itself, provides the significant observation that theoretical notions, in this case the relationship between strategy and environment, can be exported across international borders. A cautionary word is advisable, however, since South African managers have been found to have managerial preferences that more closely resemble those of Canadian and U.S. managers (Hofstede 1980).

The findings also demonstrated no significant relationship between strategy and either perceived environmental turbulence or level of commitment. A caveat concerning the latter relationship: the great number of nonresponses to the question of commitment in terms of net assets employed precluded reaching any meaningful conclusion from the test results on that performance indicator.

An important observation from this study is that even in highly turbulent environments, laws of economics still hold. The reference here is to the significant relationship between the perception of performance and strategic choice. This hypothesis test showed that higher performers preferred strategies of growth or opportunistic expansion.

The most revealing finding of this research was that although both groups acknowledged that the environment had become more turbulent, they differed over the degree of that perceived turbulence. Even more surprising, the results reversed the hypothesized relationships. The South African executives rated the environment as more turbulent than did the American executives. The expectation going into the research had been that American executives would have more amplified rather than attenuated perceptions. Since the outbreak of the sustained violence in South Africa in mid-1984, the U.S. media coverage of South Africa had been consistent in its graphic presentation of the violence in the strife-torn country. After the White South African government instituted a news blackout in 1985, U.S. coverage of news from South Africa greatly diminished. Whether the American respondents had been desensitized to the gravity of the situation by reduced media coverage is open to speculation. But the diminished perceptions could be seen in their underestimation of change in the environment—items such as the level of diversity needed to cater to customers; the availability of material supplies; the degree to which market hostility had increased; and the availability of top- and middle-management talent.

The comments and writings of the respondents revealed a passionate sense of helplessness in their inability to influence the source of turbulence. (See Appendix F.) Most of the executives appeared to perceive the involvement of their corporations in South Africa as not solely profit motivated, but also as vehicles for social change and reform. Even though Rev. Sullivan had given up on his Principles as ideal, many others still fervently viewed the Statement of Principles as evidence that they could make a difference, particularly the 7th principle, which encouraged corporations to disobey all apartheid laws. More and more corporations, however, came to terms with the reality that international opinion had become highly critical of apartheid and its accompanying turbulence. Most U.S. companies had to choose between remaining in South Africa or contending with losses in domestic markets.

Implications of the Study

More than thirty years ago, Child (1972) wrote that a distinction must be made between characteristics of environments and the perception and evaluation of those characteristics by members of organizations. Aldrich (1979) later added that the distinction was important for strategic choiceIf people do not always accurately perceive environmental characteristics, and if perceptions are the intervening link between the environment and organizational activities, then the dominant coalition's view looms larger. Earlier it was posited that corporations perceive their environments through their managements, and that elements of the environment that go unperceived are not intentionally factored in strategic plans. The importance of accurate and early perception of warning signals of environmental turbulence thus becomes critical in strategic choice (Child 1972; Ansoff 1984). The differences uncovered by this research between the two groups of managers have several implications for management theory and practice.

Implications for the practice of management

Although South Africa poses unique circumstances for foreign business, MNC experiences in the South Africa of the 1980s can shed light on doing business in other countries with high levels of turbulence. Lessons from South Africa would be most useful in countries poised for social change. We now turn to a discussion of those implications.

Talk to all parties

According to Kobrin (1982), managers do not rigorously and systematically evaluate the impact of politics on operations. By broadening their contacts, and engaging in discussions with the key players on all sides, managers can insure that their strategy choices will bring about optimal utility in any politicized environment. Some scholars have implored business leaders to be politically informed without taking sides (Austin and Ickis 1987). The preemptive move by a group of senior executives of South African companies to meet with leaders of the exiled African National Congress in Lusaka, Zambia (Bloom 1987) was both prudent and informative for the business community. In adapting its divestiture strategy, Coca-Cola also held talks with key Blacks. A well-intended strategy, though—however carefully thought out-- may be subject to misinterpretation if key, representatives of involved parties fail to participate in the early stages of its formulation. A good example is the strong criticism that the Ford withdrawal plan drew from its workforce and from some South African black trade unions, which accused Ford of being paternalistic. In this instance, Ford had taken the precaution of consulting with worker representatives who unfortunately lacked the mandate of the broader workforce.

In a politically turbulent environment, talking to existing powers may be a necessary but not a sufficient condition for success if the organization considers itself as an ongoing concern. This, unfortunately, seems to be the stance adopted by some organizational leaders, especially if the opposing party holds antagonistic views toward the "free enterprise" system. As observed in Austin and Ickis' (1987) study of forty MNCs in Nicaragua, ideological differences often need not translate to hostility toward business. The political and social reforms—known as *glasnost* and *perestroika* respectively—that were introduced in the former Union of Soviet Socialist Republics under Mikhail Gorbachev signaled the extent to which a system so different from the market economic system was willing to try its hand at it.

Redefine strategy priorities

First, it is important to recognize turbulence when it exists. Denying its presence when all signs indicate otherwise invariably leads to inappropriate strategic choices. A turbulent environment does require a special effort by strategic decision makers, an ability to redefine strategies and foster new relationships with such key players as the government, employees, suppliers, and competitors. This may even mean redefining the markets served to ensure a proper fit with emerging trends. In their study, Austin and Ickis (1987) found that by redefining their strategies, the MNCs in their study continued to generate profits in spite of a widely regarded "hostile" regime and foreign exchange shortages.

Improve environmental scanning capabilities

The importance of environmental scanning, which was advocated by Aguilar (1967), becomes more critical under conditions of turbulence. This means that organizations must equip themselves with the most efficacious methods of environmental scanning to anticipate events before they bring irreparable harm to the organization. The rigid numbers-based analytical techniques that many organizations seem to be imposing on their general managers (Kotter 1982) may hinder strategic thinking. In fact, in their article, "Managing Our Way to Economic Decline," Hayes and Abernathy (1980) castigated the over-reliance by American managers on analytical techniques and their methodological elegance to the exclusion of interpretive, experiential insights, which can shed light on today's complex organizations. Even such qualitative techniques as scenario building and political mapping, if not carefully constructed to draw on fruitful judgments and insights, can offer little more than conjectures about causal relationships (Das 1986). The implication here is that organizations need to exercise great discretion in deciding on any scenario.

Develop a strong management team

It is now almost axiomatic that the most important assets of any organization are its human resources. If a strong management team is a prerequisite for a successful organization, then it becomes crucial in turbulent times. While many corporate leaders recognize this, in reality this fact, unfortunately, gets overshadowed by other, more pressing, needs such as short-term profitability. As Drucker (1974) stated, management development is a slow process with a relatively long gestation period. Achieving short-term profitability at the expense of developing a strong management team may weaken a company's long-term competitiveness. With this in mind, recruiting the management team from local talent, where practicable, will keep misperceptions based on cultural differences to a minimum.

Managers from corporate headquarters assigned to overseas subsidiaries that are experiencing turbulent environmental conditions should be chosen from those best prepared for the task. The merits of deploying managers with the best strategic fit have been reported in the strategy literature (*Business Week* 1980; Leontiades 1982; Tung 1987; Kobrin 1988). Managers should have considerable cultural, social, and political sensitivity; commitment; and creativity. Above all, the success of any chosen strategy hinges on the personal style and credibility of the manager who interfaces with the local people. The best-designed strategies will go astray if placed in the hands of individuals who cannot develop credibility with the local community.

Improve relations with the workforce

In social restructuring, workers bargaining power—as was the case in Nicaragua, Iran, and Zimbabwe—can rise to unprecedented levels. At the same time, managers may perceive their own power as eroding. This mindset is counterproductive and management must be prepared for *quid-pro-quo* bargaining failing which the results might be costly as the following example demonstrates. In 1987 a strike was called by the National Union of Mine Workers (NUM) consisting of 200,000 Black miners at 46 of South Africa's gold and coal mines over a dispute with the Chamber of Mines. The strike was instructive in terms of lost revenues, productivity, and jobs. That strike resulted in the firing of 45,000 men and losses of $50 million. When work finally resumed, productivity was hampered by the serious underground rock convergence and other impediments that had taken place during the 21 days of the strike. Six months after the strike was over, production levels had still not reached the pre-strike levels (Burns 1988). It is essential that workers also reap the benefits of the market system otherwise disillusionment might drive them to more radical political solutions where there are no winners.

Implications for theory

Although the implications of research are conventionally separated into those for practice and those for theory, both areas are very closely related in the field of management. This research, however, does offer implications for management theory.

The first is that management cannot be considered to be value-free; it has a value system that is grounded in the ideology of each national and/or cultural group. With more business taking place across cultural and geographic borders, many theories originating in the West will need local validation before they earn universal acceptance. A related issue is the role of political, geographic, and social distance in determining perceptions from events in other countries, in another region of one's own country, or in socio-cultural settings other than one's own. In this research, managers based at a local operation consistently perceived greater turbulence (hypothesis 5).

Although they might be preliminary and limited by the sample size, the findings from testing the hypotheses here added new light to the study of strategic management under conditions of turbulence. For example, the finding that there is no relationship between the perception of environmental turbulence and strategy preference, but that there is a relationship between performance perceptions and strategy preference has implications for strategy theory. Indeed, it supports the contention that firms tend to maximize at the individual rather than at the collective level. And it further strengthens the argument that under conditions of turbulence, what is individually rational is collectively irrational. The finding from hypothesis 4—that in a turbulent environment there is no relationship between strategy preference and the level of commitment—merits further investigation with a large sample.

Finally, researchers need to win the confidence of respondents when a study entails this level of sensitivity. Several respondents, either in their letters or in telephone conversations, appeared reluctant to answer specific questions until rapport had been established with the researcher. The low response rate, especially from Canada, may have resulted from this problem. The Canadian response rate was further reduced by two factors: many of their South African holdings were controlled by a U.S. parent company, and strong anti-apartheid policies had been adopted by the government of Canada.

Suggestions for Future Research

The first suggestion for future research is to use the insights from this study to develop an instrument for measuring strategies more appropriate for turbulent environments. The instrument used in the present study was adapted from the works of Duncan (1972), Khandwalla (1976), and Miller and Friesen (1983); the strategy options were adapted from the works of Harrigan (1985b) and Rothschild (1979). Although the instrument was adequate for the present exploratory study, it would need further development to assure increased methodological rigor. For the present study, the results were interesting enough to justify investment in the development of a more appropriate instrument.

Next is the issue of causality among the variables of environment, strategy, and performance. By design, the present study precluded the determination of causality. However, the study found no relationship between environment and either performance or strategy choice. This confirms Lenz's (1981) position that the relationship is neither direct nor unidirectional. It is possible that some intervening variables are in play. The role of confounding variables—especially given the subjective nature of the design—cannot be overruled. Employing more sophisticated instrumentation and using a longitudinal study might bring additional insight to the causality relationship among the variables.

A third line of research that would cast more light on the environment-strategy–performance interface would be to compare the perceptions of top executives in privately held companies with those of companies whose stocks are traded publicly. Are organizations with greater exposure to public scrutiny and accountability more responsive to public political action? This research might be designed to test the degree to which public accountability translates to strategy choices. Another interesting line of research, although tangential to this study, would be to investigate the degree to which personal characteristics such as the age and educational and functional background of the respondents influenced their strategic choices and perceptions of the environment. This study provides evidence that these factors might well have played a part.

A related undertaking might be to determine who actually responds to surveys intended for top executives. In a few responses, another officer answered the questionnaire on behalf of the intended senior executive. This might result in the loss of the panoramic view referred to and hence might introduce artifacts. Furthermore, many of the substitute respondents might be disposed toward reporting the organization in a good light to outsiders. Such issues need to be researched. Finally, replicating the study, but with culturally dissimilar respondents, e.g., American managers (who uphold essentially Western, capitalistic ideals) and indigenous African managers might yield interesting findings. Such a study would have significant implications for the management of multinational corporations.

A disconcerting feature of the study was the exceeding difficulty of obtaining responses from the CEOs of large companies. In many instances corporations appeared to shun the investigation, and to consider information about their operation as private and confidential. Hopkins (1978) stated that surveying top officials, especially those involved in domestic and international policy decisions, tends to be hard, and that such officials tend to be reluctant to discuss their personal roles. Methods need to be developed to insure that scholars of strategy tap the riches of such people's knowledge.

Summary and Conclusion

As powerful international social agents, multinational corporations will continue to play a key role in the social, economic, and political changes in countries in which they operate (Dicken 1998). Strategic decisions by corporate executives will therefore have important consequences for the citizens of those countries. At the same time, the long-term viability of MNCs will depend on the wisdom of the strategic choices by their top management teams. In an increasingly interconnected information-driven global economy, these strategic choices will be made in rapidly changing, turbulent conditions.

Turbulent environments will persist in different parts of the world, each with its own characteristics and each posing different challenges for the corporation. By studying each of these situations and learning from those who have experienced them, corporate leaders might be better equipped to deal with environmental turbulence. Thompson's (1967) question is relevant here: Is there any such thing as the right strategy? This can be re-phrased here in terms of high velocity, turbulent environments: Is there any such thing as the right strategy for turbulent environments? In the same sense, some scholars stated that turbulence lies in the eye of the beholder, the "right" strategy will really depend on how appropriately the situation is defined by the key executives (Woodward 1982; Mintzberg 1990). This research deliberately employed a subjective approach and sought top executives as key informants because too much emphasis has been placed on the so-called "objective" approaches, which only serves to perpetuate the old corporate rain-dance ritual. That rain dance, as Ackoff (1981) suggests, improves the dancing but produces no effect on the weather.

CHAPTER 10

Epilogue: Conditions in the Post-Apartheid Era*

Many years ago, in his conviction that political independence was the key to the overall improvement of the quality of life, Kwame Nkrumah paraphrased the biblical adage (Matthew 6:3) by imploring Africans to "seek ye first the political kingdom and its righteousness and all these things shall be added unto thee." But effecting the vision entailed in this imperative has proved to be highly elusive for most African countries because of the missing element in the adage: economic power. The dream that the abolition of apartheid would bring prosperity to a majority of South Africans has proven to be equally elusive. Democracy did deliver the much anticipated universal franchise—the "political kingdom"—to all, but by any measure, economic power still largely remains concentrated in the hands of those who were in control before. Even worse, the traditional disparities between the 'haves' and 'have-nots' appear to be increasing. What lessons can be learned from the experiences of sanctions and divestment from South Africa as an instrument for socio-economic transformation? In this chapter we assess the merits of the divestment strategy, offer our observations about current disparities in post-apartheid South Africa, and comment on the programs that have been implemented to deal with them. We close the chapter with some final thoughts and reflections.

Sagacity of the Divestment Strategy

Analysts have studied the impact of sanctions on South Africa, as well as the impact of performance on the strategic decisions by companies to divest

---

* This chapter is coauthored with Dr. Zengie Mangaliso of Westfield State University, Westfield, Massachusetts.

their business operations from South Africa (Crawford and Klotz 1997; Meznar, Nigh and Kwok 1994; Wright and Ferris 1997; Ngassam 1992; Posnikoff 1997; McWilliams, Siegel and Teoh (1999). Meznar et al. (1994) looked at the impact of the announcement of withdrawal on stockholder wealth using event study methodology. They found that such announcements were associated with a significant drop in the withdrawing firm's stock value. A similar study by Wright and Ferris (1997) also using event study methodology, found that the announcements were associated with significant high negative stock returns. One explanation was that agency problems may have played a role because senior corporate executives may have acted in their own self-interest rather than in the interests of stockholders, the owners of the corporations. Another study by Ngassam (1992) using event study methodology also concluded that divestment hurt the firm's stock price and that the larger the firm, the greater was the impact of the loss.

But a study by Posnikoff (1997) using standard event study methodology yielded a different conclusion. It found that, with one exception, "U.S. firms that made a public announcement of plans to withdraw from South Africa experienced a positive and significant increase in returns in the period immediately surrounding the announcement of disinvestment" (Posnikoff 1997:84). In this study, the positive and significant increase in returns for the two-to-three day period surrounding the published announcement of plans to withdraw from South Africa seems consistent with the predictions of the voluntary sell-off literature where the announcement of the sale of a corporate subsidiary leads to an increase in returns (Alexander et al. 1984; Jain 1985; Klein 1986).

From looking at the situation in South Africa through the studies reported above, McWilliams, Siegel and Teoh (1999: 360) conclude that the lack of consensus found in these studies is attributable to differences in how researchers address critical research design and methodological issues. These authors go one step further, making the poignant point that any additional analysis of the stock price effects of divestment, based on event studies, is not fruitful since it will not improve our understanding of the impact of corporate social responsibility. Judged from the conclusion of a majority of the studies cited above, the withdrawal decision can be said to be neutral to, or to have an attenuation effect on, corporate wealth as judged by the stock price of the withdrawing firms. But for the most part, these studies focus on the interests of only one group of stakeholders—the shareholders. Moreover, they look at the short-run effects of the withdrawal decisions. Furthermore, because of their short window of observation, event studies do not accurately capture the economic impact of complex strategic decisions especially under conditions of great flux (Oler, Harrison and Allen 2008). But, by definition, strategic decisions require a much longer-term view as well as consideration of the interests of a much broader group of stakeholders—defined as "any group or individual who can affect or is affected by the achievement of the organization's objectives" (Freeman 1984: 46; Chandler 1962; Andrews 1971; Goodpaster 1991).

This brings the discussion full circle to the larger question of the role of business corporations in society. Should business corporations be viewed as mechanisms for maximizing shareholder wealth or should they be seen as instruments which, while bringing a healthy return to investors, also serve to promote greater societal good? In other words, does doing good lead to doing well? What is the appropriate thing to do when the interests of the stakeholders, broadly defined, seem to signal a direction that diverges from the classical business goal of maximizing shareholder profit? This question lies at the heart of the divestment debate. Unfortunately, the corporate social responsibility literature is divided on this issue (Friedman 1970; Waddock and Graves 1999; Carroll 1984; Wood 1991).

We believe that divestment was, in many respects, a socially responsible strategic choice given the reprehensible conditions in apartheid South Africa. The argument that divestment would hurt Blacks lacks credibility when one considers that the most authentic black leaders, including Nobel Laureates Archbishop Desmond Tutu and Nelson Mandela, as well as organizations such as the ANC, had taken a firm position in favor of it. These and other leaders in the mass democratic movement both inside and outside the country had stated unequivocally that the continuation of investments by MNCs would serve to prolong, not shorten, apartheid rule. In their view, sanctions and the withdrawal of MNCs from South Africa were the surest means of bringing down apartheid. The suffering that would come with sanctions was a price they were willing to pay. The alternative—armed warfare—was too ghastly to contemplate. Most of them had taken the position that the social pay-off from the combination of economic sanctions, corporate divestment, and the popular resistance movement was much greater than the social costs. In recalling the historical struggles against oppression, Archbishop Desmond Tutu recently remarked that the end of apartheid stood as one of the crowning accomplishments of the past century. But he also noted that the victory might not have been possible without international pressure—in particular the divestment movement of the 1980s.

Socio-Economic Disparities

Reports by the Human Sciences Research Council (HSRC) indicate that the proportion of people living in poverty in South Africa did not appear to have changed significantly in the years following the attainment of democratic rule (HSRC 2004). Instead, households living in poverty seem to have sunk deeper into poverty, and the gap between rich and poor appears to have widened. That the disparity gap has grown faster than the economy indicates that poor households have not shared in the benefits of economic growth. In 1996 the total poverty gap was equivalent to about 6.7 percent of gross domestic product (GDP); by 2001 it had risen to 8.3 percent. At the same time, poorer households have not shared in the proceeds of economic growth—another manifestation of the rise in inequality between rich and poor. A popular measure of inequality, first introduced by Italian statistician and demographer Corrado Gini, is the Gini coefficient (Söderblom 2005). The Gini Coefficient ranges from zero where no income inequality exist and each member of society receives the same income (i.e., 0.0 = no inequality); to one where only one citizen receives all the income and the rest of society gets nothing (i.e., 1.0 = maximum inequality). With its inherited legacy of apartheid, South Africa has competed for the most skewed income distribution in the world along with other developing countries such as Brazil. But since the abolition of apartheid inequality, the Gini coefficient for South Africa rose from 0.68 in 1991 to 0.77 in 2001. By comparison, the Gini coefficient for Brazil dropped from 0.57 in 1995 to about 0.55 in 2002 (Arvigan 2006). Corresponding figures for the more developed nations such as Germany, Sweden, and Finland indicate relatively low Gini coefficients of around 0.25 in 2000.

A more intriguing observation is revealed in the Gini coefficients within each of the four major racial groups of South Africa, as shown in Table 8.1. In the past, inequality was largely defined along race lines; in post-apartheid South Africa it is becoming defined increasingly by inequality within population groups as the gap between rich and poor within each group has increased substantially. Between 1991 and 2001 the Gini coefficient for the African population rose from 0.62 to 0.72. That degree of inequality is comparable with the World's most unequal. The White population had a Gini coefficient of 0.60, which is extremely high for a group whose education and occupational profile matches that of societies in highly industrialized countries.

At first glance, therefore, it appears that democratic rule has truly taken hold in South Africa. In a short space of time, the government has taken on more responsibility in bringing about equity. For instance, unlike the constitutions of most countries, which confer only civil and political rights upon their citizens, the 1996 South African Constitution also ensured justifiable socio-economic rights for all of its citizens. Clauses in the Bill of Rights detail the obligations that ensure the citizen's rights to housing, health care, food, water, social security and education (Ajam & Aron 2007).

Table 8.1: Gini Coefficient

	1991	1996	2001
African	0.62	0.66	0.72
White	0.46	0.50	0.60
Colored	0.52	0.56	0.64
Asian	0.49	0.52	0.60
Overall	0.68	0.69	0.77

Source: Human Sciences Research Council 2004

But upon further scrutiny these lofty goals prove easier said (or written) than done, which the evidence from many regions of the country makes abundantly clear. The Gini coefficient figures above show that for many previously disadvantaged South Africans the picture has changed but little. Inequalities persist and, for some, the situation has become worse that before. This may be less than surprising since from ancient times democracy has always been partial and incomplete, favoring some and often bringing privilege to a smaller part of the population (Deetz 1992). Table 8.2 shows the extent of the discrepancies that persist in the quality of life among the different race groups in South Africa.

Public Health Issues and Attendant Problems

One of the World's and South Africa's most vexing problems has been the HIV/AIDS pandemic that emerged in the 1980s. According to the UNAIDS global report 33.8 million to 46 million people worldwide were living with HIV/AIDS infections worldwide in 2005 (UNAIDS 2006). Approximately 25 million people living with the virus were on the African continent, with approximately 5.5 million of them in South Africa, where 20 percent of the adult population is reported to be HIV-positive (Mogotlane 2009). The impact on country's demographics has been devastating. According to the World Bank, life expectancy in South Africa has fallen from 62 years in 1990 to 48 in 1999 because of HIV/AIDS (World Bank 2002). The number of AIDS orphans—defined as children under the age of 15 years who have lost their mother or both parents to HIV/AIDS—has grown exponentially. According to UNAIDS, in 1999 there were 371,000 AIDS orphans and another 500,000 children who died of the disease. The Center for the Study of AIDS at the University of Pretoria projected the number of AIDS orphans to reach 1.1 million in the mid-2000s and forecasts the number to grow to 2 million AIDS orphans by 2010 (Mogotlane 2009; Woolard 2002; Whiteside and Sunter 2000). Because of the premature deaths due to HIV, it is not unusual to find child-headed households with the misery that the situation brings to these children. The added strain on the country's already overburdened social services budget has resulted in the Health Care System's characterization as the AIDS Care System.

Table 8.2: Inequality in South Africa: Selected Social Indicators

SOCIAL INDICATOR	BLACK	"COLORED"	ASIAN	WHITE
Infant mortality (per 1000 births)	54.3	36.6	9.9	7.3
Female life expectancy (year)	67	65	70	76
Human development Index	0.50	0.66	0.84	0.90
Mean household income (R '000)	17.9	22.6	40.9	59.8
Poverty rate (%)	60.7	38.2	5.4	1.0
Unemployment rate (%)	41	23	17	6
Access to piped water (%)	33	72	97	97
Access to public electricity (%)	51	84	99	99
Access to telephone at home (%)	14	38	74	85

Source: Moller (1999), DOJ&CD (1997)

Post-apartheid South Africa also suffers from mounting crime and violence. The most vulnerable targets have been women and children with rape—one of the most grievous human rights violations and serious public health issues—occurring with regularity in South Africa. Police records indicate that 54,000 rapes or 150 per day were reported in 2006. According to the Medical Research Council of South Africa, most of the victims were young women between 16 and 25 years (Christofides, et al. 2006). But this seriously understates the problem as many incidents go unreported. One of apartheid's most deleterious effects of apartheid is that men felt emasculated and humiliated. They would take out their frustrations on the weakest victims—women and children. That trend seems to have continued into post-apartheid South Africa, where one unfortunate public health consequence of rape is an opportunity for the direct transmission of HIV.

New Government Programs to Restore Equity

The social and economic inequalities that had characterized the apartheid era have continued to dog South Africa in the post-apartheid era as well. At the onset of democratic rule in 1994 the country adopted an interim constitution, made permanent in 1996, that emphasized fiscal prudence, accountability and transparency within all three branches of government. The Public Finance Management Act (PFMA) of 1999 to gave voice to the constitutional imperatives of budgetary efficiency and fiscal transparency. A key characteristic of the PFMA was the institution of the Medium Term Expenditure Framework (MTEF) with its provision for three-year rolling budgets to guide and monitor the responses to priorities with greater timeliness and responsiveness. With the passage of the PFMA, the emphasis shifted from an input-output oriented system towards a more outcome- and impact-oriented system (Ajam and Aron 2007). Soon after the election, the new ANC-led Government of National Unity (GNU) introduced its first program of reform, the Reconstruction and Development Program (RDP). Released in 1994, the document pledged to meet the country's basic needs in a consultative, people-driven manner with an emphasis on Keynesian-type redistribution and economic growth. It represented tangible evidence that the GNU was serious about redressing past injustices and inequalities and eradicating the poverty afflicting a significant number of the 40 million Blacks who constituted the majority of South Africa's population (Hart 2002). To ensure its effectiveness, an RDP Office established within the Office of the President held responsibility for coordinating RDP-related activities across the country.

But in early 1996, amid much public debate over what the program meant for economic policy, the RDP Office was closed down and its staff redeployed to other government departments. At about the same time, the government introduced a new, neo-liberal initiative called the Growth, Employment, and Redistribution (GEAR) program. The business community applauded the program because of its emphasis on fiscal restraint, its expressed commitment to controlling inflation and interest rates, and the promise of relaxed foreign exchange controls. Philosophically, GEAR uncomfortably sat astride the emancipatory promises of the liberation struggle on the one hand, and the material hopes, aspirations, and rights of the Black majority on the other (Hart 2002). And according to some analysts, because of its neo-market-oriented policy, GEAR seemed to serve the interests of those who already had the wherewithal to take advantage of the lucrative opportunities in place for procuring government contracts (Avirgan 2006). GEAR is thus seen to benefit only a few Blacks, while offering little or nothing to a large majority.

Another government initiative that addressed the wealth distribution problem was the Black Economic Empowerment (BEE) program. BEE was a flagship program intended to accelerate the participation rate of Blacks in the country's economy without disturbing the fundamentals of the market enterprise system. As a form of affirmative action, BEE was seen as the best hope for compensating for apartheid's negative legacy, thereby accomplishing ownership and employment equity in the workplace (McFarlin et al. 1999). True enough, some progress has ensued in the form of a steady rise in both the number and size of corporations owned or controlled by Blacks since the mid-1990s. For instance, through mergers and acquisitions, Metlife became the largest black empowerment investment in the financial services sector as of 1999, making it the 26th largest company on the Johannesburg Stock Exchange (Southall 2004). Various sectors of the economy— media, forestry and paper pulp, food and beverages, or fishing—have all attracted large-scale black investments (Carter, 1999). In spite of these indications of success, progress made has been modest, uneven and difficult to quantify. Of concern, a significant number of South Africans have remained skeptical of BEE, viewing it as problematic with some going as far as calling it discrimination, or reverse racism. To complicate matters, BEE, in its implementation became mired in problems that resulted in the slow growth of genuinely entrepreneurial Blacks. Accompanying problems included a lack of start-up capital, the closed nature of business fraternities, fronting, and corruption. Unfortunately the program has drawn into the economic mainstream only a handful of politically connected Blacks who, in a short space of time, have become remarkably wealthy (Southall 2004). Below Randall (1996: 662) cites some of the more prominent voices that have been critical of the emerging class of Black capitalists in South Africa.

> The rise (of the Black capitalist class) is perceived to be part of 'a cosmetic attempt to dress up old apartheid structures of power and priviledge,' so as to 'maintain the status quo, lipsticked and pretified. The result, the argument goes, is that Black capitalists are not genuine capitalists, having 'nothing more than a press-release understanding of the company,' surrounding themselves with White advisors and consultants who then run the company by remote control while they are left to indulge in the life of the 'nouveau riche.' Senior Black managers are 'hired for their compliance and for their smiling faces in our corporate brochures,' or to act as 'the gopher: get the business in, smile, shake hands, and then leave it to us to get on with the job.' Whites, it is asserted, have assured at all costs that their black lackeys 'don't ever get involved in our core business issues.'

From these observations, the BEE program appeared to be headed towards GEAR's unhappy fate. To mitigate this, the program was revised and expanded to draw in community groups and employee trusts as participants in the preferential contract procurement framework. The revised program was codified into law as the Broad Based Black Economic Empowerment Act (BBBEE) of 2003. The jury is still out over whether the new BBBEE program will yield the desired outcomes.

Final Thoughts and Reflections

The tidal wave that goaded MNCs into the divestment decision provides compelling evidence that it is possible for corporations to take an objective view, focused mainly on their economic interests, even in countries with totalitarian regimes. This was certainly true in South Africa until the pressure to divest escalated to a tipping point in the late 1980s. Business can influence the country towards democracy as well as prosperity within the confines of the firm's constraints. True enough, many U.S. MNCs used their resources to challenge the system beyond the normal functioning of their businesses. They built integrated residential areas, improved wages and related social benefits, and provided training and education programs for Blacks in the late 1980s, even those not employed by them. But they faced ongoing tensions between the political priority of improving the conditions of life for Blacks and the economic imperative of stabilizing the economy to ensure the profitability of their enterprises. These tensions will persist and the challenges of the divestment movement will likely reemerge in some other form in the future.

CHRONOLOGY OF EVENTS IN SOUTH AFRICA

270 .A.D.   Archeological sites uncovered at Silver Lakes near Tzaneen, and at Mzonjani 15 kilometers north of Durban indicate this date as the earliest date recorded for the occupation of South Africa by Early Iron Age people.

1488   Portuguese explorer Bartholomeu Diaz 'discovers' the Cape of Good Hope when he landed in Mossel Bay, and sailed as far north as the Great Fish River.

1497   Portuguese explorer, Vasco da Gama and his crew sailed around Southern Africa, landing in some ports for rest and recuperation on their way to India.

1652   Arrival of Dutch sailors. A half-way station is established in Cape Town, which eventually became a permanent settlement.

1820   The Arrival of British settlers marks a period of massive European immigration and the emergence of a class of Dutch farmers, the Boers, who resisted British rule. The Dutch establish new colonies in the Orange Free State and Transvaal. They remained agrarian and used slaves from Malaysia or indentured labor from India to work their farms.

1800s   An increase in the influx of Europeans leads to clashes with several wars with the indigenous African population. In most cases the Europeans won with the use of superior rifles and machine guns. This eventually led to White control of land.

1867   Diamonds are discovered in the area around the city of Kimberley.

1885   A large vein of gold is discovered in the Transvaal. Enormous
            influx of foreigners flows into the territory. The Boers them-
            selves remain agricultural and want to be left alone. They levy
            taxes on the miners, but do not allow the *uitlanders* to have a
            say in government. Industrialization begins. Black labor force
            is needed for mining so laws are enacted to regulate the wages
            and working conditions of Blacks.

1899   Anglo-Boer War breaks out. The British side is represented by
            the two British-majority colonies—Cape Colony and Natal. The
            Boer side is represented by the two Boer Republics—the
            Orange Free State and the Transvaal Republic. The war was
            largely a result of Cecil Rhode's interference in the region, and
            his passionate insistence that a unified South Africa was im-
            perative for British interests.

1902   Anglo-Boer War comes to an end with a victory for the British.
            The Treaty of Vereeniging is signed. The two Boer republics
            agree to come under British sovereignty, with the promise of
            eventual self-government. Work begins on the consolidation of
            the four provinces and drafting of a constitution for the Union
            of South Africa. The political future of Black Africans is left in
            abeyance.

1909   The final draft constitution is sent to Britain for the approval of
            the imperial Parliament. Representatives of South Africa's
            Blacks, along with a few South African Whites, send delega-
            tions to London to object to the Whites-only system. However,
            the British parliament approves the South African Act over-
            whelmingly in September.

1910   On May 31 the Union of South Africa, consisting of the afore-
            mentioned four provinces, becomes a legal entity with domi-
            nion status within the British Empire. Louis Botha—who had,
            ironically, fought the British on the battlefield—is chosen as
            the first Prime Minister.

1913   Natives Land Act is passed to prevent the 'encroachment' of
            Blacks into White lands. Blacks, who constitute four fifths of
            the population, are no longer able to own or rent land outside
            of designated reserves which amounted to 7 percent (later in-
            creased to 13 percent) of the most arid parts of the country, or
            the 'homelands.' The act also ends a sharecropping practice
            under which Black farmers are able to cultivate White-owned

land with their own implements and to receive half of the crop. Furthermore, it stipulates that Blacks can only live outside the reserves if they can prove that they are in White employment.

1915+   Initial entry of U.S. corporations into South Africa. Among the early arrivals are Ford, General Motors, Goodyear, and Firestone.

1923   Urban areas Act is passed, which sets up a systemized control of the movement of Blacks within the country. All adult African males are required to carry identification "pass books" containing fingerprints, photo, and other information with them at all times. The system can move Blacks anywhere their labor is needed.

1924   Industrial Conciliation Act is passed. It sets up a collective bargaining system that only recognizes White and Colored trade unions. Blacks are excluded, which effectively closes a number of job categories to them.

1936   The provisions of the 1913 Natives Land Act are extended to deny Blacks the right to own land even in Cape Province, where it was legally not applied up to this time. By way of compensation, the government offers, through the Development Trust and Land Act, to increase the amount of land reserved for Blacks to 13 percent of the country's total land holdings.

WWII+   Other industries begin to enter SA attracted by ROI made possible by abundant, cheap and non-unionized labor. Areas of investments include financial services (Chase Manhattan Bank); communication (AT&T); airlines (Pan American, World Airways); and computers (NCR, IBM).

1948   Universal Declaration of Human Rights by the United Nations General Assembly's set forth that all human beings are entitled to universal rights and freedoms without distinction of race, color, sex, language, religion, political or other opinion, national or social origin, property, birth or other status.

1948   The National Party, controlled by Afrikaners, defeats the United Party and begins to implement serious apartheid reforms. The philosophy is based on the distorted logic of the divine

Biblical decree that races should be socially and politically separated. It is also based on the myth of God's "chosen race" that
Whites should have a guardianship relationship over Blacks. A
number of laws, numbering over 300 pieces based on race, are
passed. Three of the key pieces were the Population Registration Act, the Native Laws Amendment Act, and the Bantu Education Act.

1950   Population Registration Act. Assigned an identity number to
            each person, classifying him/her into one of four racial groups;
            White, Asian, Colored, and Black. The latter two were further
            classified into subgroups or ethnic groups within their race
            classification based on appearance, social acceptance and des-
            cent.

1952   The Native Laws Amendment Act is passed. It mandates Afri-
            cans to carry reference books, which consolidated fingerprints,
            information about the bearer's residency rights in urban areas,
            tribal affiliation, employment history, tax payments, and any
            infractions of urban labor control laws and regulations. In
            1956, the reference book was extended to women but met re-
            sistance "You've struck a woman, you've struck a rock." These
            'passes' had to be shown when requested by authorities and
            failure to do so or refusal to carry a pass book meant impri-
            sonment, fine, or both. non-Africans were not subjected to this
            form of tracking. The ANC and its biggest ally, the South African
            Indian Council (SAIC) decide to engage in mass action, boy-
            cotts, strikes, and civil disobedience. The Defiance Campaign
            was the largest of such mass actions to be seen in South Africa
            and the first pursued jointly by all race groups.

1953   Bantu Education Act is passed declaring that education for
            Blacks and Whites should be different. For Whites the empha-
            sis was to be on mathematics and science; and for Blacks it was
            to be on languages such as Afrikaans (not English) and 'tribal'
            dialects. Education would be free and mandatory for White
            children, but neither free nor mandatory for Black children.

1954   U.S. Supreme Court rules in Brown vs. Board of Education that
            separate education was *not* equal.

1955   ANC adopts the Freedom Charter during the Annual National
            Congress in Kliptown signaling a shift in the ANC from being an
            African-only organization to one that embraces a growing uni-

ty amongst all South Africans. It declared, among other things, that South Africa belongs to all who live in it. However this multi-racial ideology did lead to a split within the ANC by those members like Robert Mangaliso Sobukwe who espoused the Pan-Africanist view of "Africa for Africans."

1959   The Pan Africanist Congress (PAC) is founded after a number of members, led by Sobukwe, broke away from the African National Congress (ANC) because of various ideological and theoretical differences. The biggest of these was preference for the Pan-Africanist view of "Africa for Africans" versus the multiracial ideology recently adopted by the ANC at the Kliptown Conference.

1960   Sharpeville & Langa protests are organized, in which large groups of Blacks hold demonstration marches against the pass books. The government responds with violent crackdowns and the declaration of a state of emergency which lasted five months. Over sixty people are killed and many more wounded. The killings produce international outrage. African States call for sanctions. The Anti-Apartheid Movement is formed in London. The American Committee on Africa initiates sanctions campaigns in the U.S.

1961   South Africa declares itself a sovereign nation and withdraws from the Commonwealth in the face of the anti-apartheid pressure. It drops the British sterling system and institutes a new financial system based on the rand. Chief Albert Luthuli, President of the African National Congress (ANC) receives the Nobel Peace Prize. Umkhonto Wesizwe, the military wing of the ANC, is formed, signaling a change in strategy from the non-violent approach favored by Luthuli, which had been the ANC policy to that point.

1962   The United Nations General Assembly passes Resolution 1761, a non-binding resolution establishing the United Nations Special Committee against Apartheid. It calls for an imposition of economic, military and other sanctions on South Africa. Nelson Mandela is arrested and later charged with treason and sabotage, and sentenced to life imprisonment.

1970s   Some MNC's did provide training and financial support for the non-White population of SA. Examples, Unilever and the African, Indian, and Colored (ACI) Program, which helped selected non-Whites prepare for management positions and more responsibility in the workplace. Mobil Oil Company instituted a program to improve the quality of teaching in Black schools. Gillette set up a Legal Aid Clinic. Kellogg adopted local schools.

1971   In response to the pressure from the Polaroid Revolutionary Workers' Movement (PRWM) to pull out of South Africa, Polaroid decides to conduct an experiment later to be dubbed the "Polaroid Experiment." The company confirms its commitment to continue to sell its film to a distributor in South Africa, but would not allow the distributor to sell to the government. The program initially showed success as some of its goals, e.g., the wages and status of Black workers did go up.

1976   Soweto students riot against the requirement to be taught in Afrikaans as a medium of instructions on a 50:50 basis with English. The government tries to stem the protests with force. Over 600 students are killed in Soweto and Langa near Cape Town. MNCs begin to be in spotlight. The 'homeland' of Transkei, led by leader Chief Kaizer Matanzima, declares independence from South Africa. It receives no international recognition. Israel signs agreement to increase scientific cooperation with South Africa.

1977   Polaroid terminates its relationships in South Africa after it is disclosed that Frank & Hirsch, the South African Polaroid distributor, was making the film available to the South African government for use in the "passbook" in violation of Polaroid's policy. Rev. Leon Sullivan, Black Baptist minister and member of GM's Board, develops a code of conduct which becomes a guide for corporations operating in South Africa. Performances of Bertha Egos' musical *Ipi Tombi* are boycotted. UN Security Council adopts mandatory arms embargo against South Africa.

1978   Number of Sullivan U.S. signatory corporations increases dramatically from the original 12. European and Canadian codes of corporate conduct also established.

1979   U.N. General Assembly calls on Security Council to consider measures to prevent South Africa from developing nuclear weapons. Iran halts its oil exports to South Africa. U.S. satellite detects a flash of what was thought to be a small nuclear explosion in the South Atlantic. South Africa denies conducting nuclear tests.

1980   The National Key Points Act is passed into law. It provides the
            state with direct access and control over private security, em-
            powering the Minister of Defense to declare any area or place
            to be of strategic importance to state sovereignty and therefore
            in need of safeguarding measures, allowing it to be taken over
            by the government if needed to defend the state.

1982   Dutch Reformed Church of Africa (DRC) or Nederduitsch Her-
            vormde Kerk van Afrika is excluded and suspended from
            World Alliance of Reformed Churches because of the theologi-
            cal and biblical backing it gives to the system of White domina-
            tion under which South Africa was governed.

1984   A new South African constitution establishes a tricameral par-
            liament with separate chambers for 'Coloreds' and Asians, but
            excludes all Africans. Violence erupts in the townships. Long
            time anti-apartheid campaigner, Bishop Desmond Tutu, rece-
            ives the Nobel Peace Prize. The Sullivan Code is strengthened
            and calls for signatory companies to practice civil corporate
            disobedience against all apartheid laws. It also calls for compa-
            nies to use resources, both financial and legal to assist Blacks
            in attaining equal rights.

1985   President P. W. Botha delivers his infamous "Rubicon" speech,
            which amounts to an announcement that there would be no
            major reforms in the country's apartheid system and that the
            government would not give in to hostile pressure from abroad.
            In his words, "South Africa had crossed the Rubicon of political
            reform." The value of the Rand begins to plummet. Sullivan is-
            sues an ultimatum to government to dismantle apartheid with-
            in two years or else face threat of MNC withdrawal from SA.
            The U.N. Security Council adds computers to its embargo,
            which prohibits sales of computer equipment to the South
            African police or military. The South African government dec-
            lares a state of emergency and institutes a news blackout. U.S.
            Banks, led by Chase Manhattan, refuse to roll over their shot-
            term loans to South Africa. South Africa declares a moratorium
            on the repayment of some of its commercial debt.

1986   Comprehensive Anti Apartheid Act (CAAA), sponsored by U.S.
            Congressman Ron Dellums, is passed by the U.S. Congress over
            President Reagan's veto, and imposes sanctions against South
            Africa, stating five preconditions for the lifting of the sanctions

including establishing a timetable for the elimination of apartheid laws and the release of political prisoner Nelson Mandela. A flood of announcements by U.S. companies of their intentions to withdraw from South Africa ensues.

1987   Believing that even though progress has been made core issues of apartheid remain, Sullivan calls for withdrawal of signatory companies from SA and the initiation of sanctions against South Africa. The code is renamed the "Statement of Principles" and continues to be used as a guideline. Sullivan's actions spur resolutions by company shareholders, universities and municipal councils for the withdrawal of their funds from U.S. companies with South African ties.

1988   Sanctions affect SA economy leading to double-digit inflation, decline in price of gold, and devaluation of currency. First time the White South African population is so affected. Still disparities in education and public health services exist.

1989   Mobil and Goodyear, the largest remaining U.S. companies, withdraw from South Africa. De Klerk succeeds Botha as President of South Africa. Realizing that apartheid cannot be sustained, he announces his intentions to repeal several apartheid laws, to release some political prisoners, and to unban some political organizations.

1990   Nelson Mandela and other political prisoners are released from prison, opposition political movements—including the ANC and PAC and others—are unbanned, the process of return from exile begins.

1991   International Olympic Committee recognizes the non-racial National Olympic Committee of South Africa. The Group Areas Act and the Population Registration Act are removed from statutes.

1992   Whites-only referendum validates De Klerk's reforms. South Africa is selected to host the 1995 Rugby World Cup.

1994   The first democratic elections are held. Nelson Mandela is elected as the first President of a free and democratic election in South Africa's history. The ANC forms a Government of National Unity (GNU) that includes representatives from other parties. The Reconstruction and Development Program (RDP) document is published, pledging to meet the country's basic needs in a people-driven manner with an emphasis on redistribution and economic growth. MNCs such as IBM begin to return to SA.

1998   In a joint statement, South African Deputy President Thabo Mbeki and US Vice President Al Gore announce the lifting of the US Arms embargo against South Africa.

1999   Rev. Leon Sullivan and United Nations Secretary General Kofi Annan together unveil the new "Global Sullivan Principles," that expanded the corporate code of conduct requiring the adopting MNCs to be full participants in the advancement of human rights and social justice internationally. Mandela steps down from the presidency and is succeeded by Thabo Mbeki ANC, who wins the election by a two-thirds majority. Mbeki becomes the second president of the new South Africa. The Public Finance Management Act (PFMA) was passed to give voice to the constitutional imperatives of budgetary efficiency and fiscal transparency.

2004   The ANC wins third democratic elections, again by close to a two-thirds majority. Thabo Mbeki begins his second term as President of South Africa.

2008   Thabo Mbeki loses ANC party leadership to Jacob Zuma in a hotly contested party election process in Polokwane, Lebowa Province. He is later forced to step down as the SA President. Kgalema Mothlantle is appointed Interim President.

2009   The ANC wins the fourth national election by close to a two-thirds majority. Jacob Zuma becomes the fourth President of post-apartheid South Africa.

APPENDICES

APPENDIX A: STRATEGY- ENVIRONMENT-PERFORMANCE QUESTIONNAIRE

Answering the questions

1. This questionnaire is concerned with IMPRESSIONS and PERCEPTIONS that you, as a senior corporate executive, might have of business operations in South Africa.
2. Most questions can be answered by circling one of the answers. If you do not find the exact answer that fits your case, circle the one that comes closest to it. For a few questions blank spaces have been left. In those few cases, you are asked to write in the answers.
3. Please try to answer all questions.
4. Feel free to write in the margins and on the back of the questionnaire any explanations or comments you may have. Such comments will be helpful in the analysis.
5. The questionnaire has four sections as follow:

    Section I: questions concerning you impressions of the environment;
    Section II: questions concerning your company's performance;
    Section III: questions concerning strategic choices and preferences;
    Section IV: questions which solicit some general information about you and your organization for classification purposes.

We thank you, once again, for your cooperation and time.

SECTION I: PERCEPTION OF ENVIRONMENT

The following statements are designed to characterize the changes in the environment of your operations in South Africa over the last 5 years. Please circle the rating/level that is closest to your feelings about the matter.

1. Changes in fiscal policy	have become restrictive	1 2 3 4 5	Have become favorable
2. Inflation rate	Has increased dramatically	1 2 3 4 5	Has fallen dramatically
3. Trade barriers	Have become restrictive	1 2 3 4 5	Have been reduced
4. Fluctuations in the prime rate	Have dramatically increased	1 2 3 4 5	Have dramatically decreased
5. Price controls	Have become stringent	1 2 3 4 5	Have become relaxed
6. Market activities of your key competitors	Have become less predictable	1 2 3 4 5	Have become more predictable
7. Market activities of your key competitors	Have become far more hostile	1 2 3 4 5	Have become far less hostile
8. Your principal industry's upswings and downswings	Have become far less predictable	1 2 3 4 5	Have become far more predictable
9. Labor disruptions	Have become extremely unpredictable	1 2 3 4 5	Have become easier to predict
10. Attitude of public toward your industry or product	Has become more hostile	1 2 3 4 5	Has become less hostile
11. Political stability	Government has become less in control	1 2 3 4 5	Government has increased its control
12. Threats your firm's survival	Threats have increased a lot	1 2 3 4 5	Threats have been reduced a lot

13. Legal and politi- cal constraints (e.g., Government regulations)	Have increased in number	1 2 3 4 5	Have been reduced greatly in number

Please rate the following resources for your operations in S.A.:

14. Skilled labor/ supervisors	Have be- come very scarce	1 2 3 4 5	Have become plen- tiful
15. Capital	Has be- come very scare	1 2 3 4 5	Has become plenti- ful
16. Top and middle level managerial talent	Has be- come very scare	1 2 3 4 5	Has become plenti- ful
17. Material sup- plies	Have be- come very scarce	1 2 3 4 5	Have become quite plentiful

In general, what would you say about the environment of your organization in South Africa?

18. The conditions facing your firm have be- come	Highly certain, stable, predictable	1 2 3 4 5	Highly uncer- tain, unstable, unpredictable
19. Number of compo- nents in the environ- ment which are im- portant for decision- making	Has become smaller and components are similar	1 2 3 4 5	Has become larger and com- ponents have become more diverse
20. Needed diversity in your production me- thods and marketing tactics to cater to your customers	Diver- sity has dramati- cally increased	1 2 3 4 5	Diversity has dramatically decreased
21. The "hassle factor" (A measure of aggrava- tion incurred in pro- curing profits in S.A.)	Has in- creased dramat- ically	1 2 3 4 5	Has decreased substantially

Section II: Perception of Current Performance

The purpose of this section of the questionnaire is to compare your firm with firms of similar sales volume in your industry in South Africa. Listed below are items which have been considered important measures of the firm's economic performance.

To the best of your knowledge, please circle the number which you feel best estimates how YOUR FIRM compares to similar firms in your industry, in South Africa on each item.

	Top 20%	Next 20%	Middle 20%	Lower 20%	Lowest 20%
22. After-tax return on total assets	1	2	3	4	5
23. After-tax return on sales	1	2	3	4	5
24. Firm's total sales growth over past 5 years	1	2	3	4	5
25. Public image and goodwill	1	2	3	4	5
26. Overall firm performance/success	1	2	3	4	5

SECTION III: STRATEGY PREFERENCES

Please evaluate the following statements by circling the number which closely represents your preference. If the strategy seems to agree with your position, circle a 1 and if you disagree with that strategy, then circle a 5. If you are indifferent to the strategy then 3 would be the best choice.

	I agree		indifferent		I disagree
27. The presence of overseas companies in S.A. can make a greater contribution to social reform than would be possible if they left	1	2	3	4	5
28. By promoting economic growth and following some codes of conduct, companies can bring about change in S.A.	1	2	3	4	5
29. Companies can improve their profitability by increasing capital expenditure thereby reducing production costs	1	2	3	4	5
30. Organizations should wait whilst monitoring the situation and only act when there is no change evident.	1	2	3	4	5
31. To reduce the financial difficulties, a company should develop an aggressive marketing strategy.	1	2	3	4	5
32. Companies should stay and invest in the improvement of the Quality of Life of Blacks both inside and outside of the work place.	1	2	3	4	5
33. Companies should maintain their holdings but should neither increase their investments nor withdraw from S.A.	1	2	3	4	5
34. Companies should selectively slow down re-investment in S.A.	1	2	3	4	5
35. Companies should selectively sell those holding which are marginally profitable or not profitable at all	1	2	3	4	5
36. Companies should sell their holdings in SA	1	2	3	4	5

37. Companies should beef up those areas where profitability is good whilst shrinking investment in less attractive areas.	1	2	3	4	5
38. Companies should stay in S.A. and use their leverage to bring about reform.	1	2	3	4	5
39. Any new investments should be frozen but companies should give the government a chance to implement its social reforms and only withdraw if the government effort fails.	1	2	3	4	5

40   Which ONE of the following statements would come closest to your position regarding your company's doing business in South Africa?
Please circle one:

1.   The most suitable strategy is to *sell off* or *liquidate* our subsidiary in South Africa in other words we should pull out completely.

2.   My organization should attempt to reverse any trend of poor performance by embarking on a *retrenchment* strategy.

3.   A *stability or hold* strategy is the most appropriate, in other words, we should neither expand operations nor pull out.

4.   *Selective growth* and *shrinkage* is the best strategy for our business in South Africa.

5.   The *growth* (or opportunistic) strategy is one that makes the most sense for my business in South Africa.

SECTION IV: DEMOGRAPHIC INFORMATION

In this section, a few questions are asked about you and your organization. Please answer them as precisely as you can. Answers to these questions will enable to group your organization with similar organizations.

41. Size of operations in South Africa:
    (a) Approximate Asset Value: $ _____
    (b) Approximate number of employees: .   _____

42. What is your principal business in South Africa?
     (a) retailing   (b) manufacturing   (c) agriculture   (d) mining
     (e) transportation (f) banking   (g) other _____
                                                           please specify

43. What type of business do you have in South Africa? Please circle one:
     (a) subsidiary investment   (b) joint venturing   (c) licensing
     (d) technical contracting   (e) marketing outlet   (f) other _____
                                                            please specify

44. How long has your company had operations/business in S.A.?   ____ yrs

45. What percentage of your total sales come from S.A.? ____ %
46. What is your current job title? .... _____
47. What is your highest level of formal education? _____
48. What is your area of education? .... _____
49. How long have you worked for this company?   ____ yrs
50. What is your present age?   ____ yrs

THANK YOU!

Please return the questionnaire in the enclosed pre-addressed envelope to:
    Institute for North American Trade and Economics
    School of Management
    University of Massachusetts
    121 Presidents Drive
    Amherst, MA, 01003, U.S.A.

APPENDIX B: ACRONYMS USED IN THE QUESTIONNAIRE

QUESTION	ACRONYM	DESCRIPTION
1	FISCHA	Changes in Fiscal Policy
2	INFLAT	Inflation Rate
3	TRBAR	Trade Barriers
4	PRIMRA	Fluctuation in the Prime Rate
5	PRICO	Price Controls
6	MKTPRED	Predictability of Competitor Activities
7	MKTHOST	Hostility of Competitor Activities
8	INDFLCT	Industry Fluctuations
9	LABDIS	Predictability of Labor Disruptions
10	PUBATT	Public Attitude to Product/Industry
11	POLSTAB	Political Stability
12	THRTSUV	Threats to Survival of a Firm
13	GOVCONT	Legal and Political Constraints
14	SKILDLA	Availability of Skilled Labor
15	CAPITAL	Availability of Capital
16	TOPMMGT	Availability of Top/Middle Management
17	MATSUPL	Availability of material Supplies
18	STABENV	Predictability of Environment
19	DIVSENV	Number of Components in Environment
20	DIVMETH	Needed Diversity to Compete
21	HASFA	Existence of the "Hassle Factor"
22	ATROTA	After-Tax Return on Total Assets
23	ATROSA	After-Tax Return on Sales
24	PGROSA	Total Sales Growth
25	PUBIG	Public Image and Goodwill
26	OVERPER	Overall Performance
27	SCONTRI	Presence in S.A. Will Help Reform
28	BRCHANG	Economic Growth Will Bring Change
29	CAPEX	Increase Capital Expenditure in S.A.
30	WAIT	Wait and See before Taking Action
31	AGGRESS	Develop Aggressive Marketing Strategies
32	QOWL	Stay and Improve Quality of Work Life
33	NINWD	Neither Withdraw nor Expand Operations
34	SLODREI	Selectively Slowdown Reinvestment
35	SELESEL	Sell Marginal/Non-profitable Holdings
36	SELLAL	Sell all S.A. holdings
37	BEEFSHR	Beef up Profitable Areas, Shrink Others
38	STALEV	Stay and Use Leverage to Bring Reform
39	GOVCHAN	Pull Out Only if Government Effort Fails
40	GRDSTRA	Overall Grand Strategy
41a	ASSETVA	Size of Assets in S.A.
41b	EMPLONO	Number of Employees in S.A.
42	PRINBUS	Principal Area of Business in S.A.
43	INVESTYP	Type of Business Venture
44	YRSINSA	Years of Operation in S.A.
45	PERCENT	Percent of Company Sales from S.A.
46	JOBTTL	Current Job Title
47	LEVELED	Highest Level of Formal Education
48	MAJORED	Major Area of Education
49	SERVICE	Service with the Company
50	AGE	Age (of Respondent)

APPENDIX C: CORRELATION MATRIX OF PERCEIVED ENVIRONMENTAL TURBULENCE

VARIABLE	1	2	3	4	5	6	7	8	9	10	11	12	13	14	15	16	17	18	19	20
1 FISCHA	1.000																			
2 INFLAT	0.316	1.000																		
3 TRBAR	0.344	0.014	1.000																	
4 PRIMRA	0.220	0.271	0.294	1.000																
5 PRICO	0.385	0.168	0.087	0.085	1.000															
6 MKTPRED	0.260	0.138	0.298	0.111	0.075	1.000														
7 MKTHOST	0.097	0.036	0.172	0.183	0.010	0.586	1.000													
8 INDFLCT	0.128	0.176	0.201	0.095	0.073	0.226	0.282	1.000												
9 LABDIS	0.036	0.087	0.294	0.246	0.085	0.111	0.057	0.345	1.000											
10 PUBATT	0.141	0.021	0.034	0.061	0.085	0.168	0.061	0.047	0.105	1.000										
11 THRTSUV	0.009	0.009	0.017	0.139	0.143	0.252	0.108	0.265	0.232	0.263	1.000									
12 GOVCONT	0.433	0.344	0.373	0.257	0.190	0.109	0.012	0.225	0.134	0.047	0.017	1.000								
13 SKILDLA	0.189	0.058	0.081	0.019	0.097	0.268	0.462	0.310	0.209	0.075	0.260	0.104	1.000							
14 CAPITAL	0.297	0.242	0.193	0.001	0.296	0.216	0.139	0.326	0.416	0.087	0.150	0.278	0.229	1.000						
15 TOPMMGT	0.112	0.009	0.284	0.078	0.136	0.216	0.325	0.226	0.263	0.143	0.216	0.017	0.612	0.190	1.000					
16 MATSUPL	0.057	0.099	0.227	0.027	0.068	0.138	0.107	0.331	0.267	0.003	0.220	0.007	0.203	0.156	0.250	1.000				
17 STABENV	0.120	0.127	0.019	0.044	0.001	0.143	0.171	0.256	0.171	0.092	0.239	0.019	0.468	0.120	0.136	0.199	1.000			
18 DIVSEN	0.148	0.036	0.196	0.069	0.199	0.161	0.194	0.260	0.194	0.270	0.201	0.111	0.298	0.139	0.232	0.292	0.399	1.000		
19 DIVMETH	0.033	0.096	0.362	0.172	0.109	0.290	0.363	0.275	0.363	0.089	0.101	0.011	0.196	0.109	0.401	0.301	0.062	0.339	1.000	
20 HASFA	0.298	0.250	0.347	0.030	0.209	0.112	0.092	0.179	0.342	0.036	0.104	0.383	0.319	0.223	0.326	0.146	0.247	0.470	0.233	1.000

APPENDIX D: CORRELATIONS FOR PERFORMANCE SCALE

	VARIABLE	1	2	3	4	5
1	ATROTA	1.000				
2	ATROSA	0.830	1.000			
3	PGROSA	0.479	0.525	1.000		
4	PUBIG	0.281	0.308	0.475	1.000	
5	OVERPER	0.581	0.674	0.512	0.554	1.000

APPENDIX E: RESULTS OF REGRESSION ANALYSES

Variables:	PET	=	Perceived Environmental Turbulence
	GRDSTRAT	=	Preferred Strategy
	AVPER	=	Perceived Performance
	GRP	=	Country Group
	ASSETVA	=	Value of Assets
	EMPLONO	=	Number of Employees

Equation 1: Dependent Variable – PET

INDEPENDENT VARIABLE	BETA	STANDARD ERROR	T	PROBABILITY
AVPER	-0.167	0.325	-1.030	0.310
GRP	-0.072	2.477	-0.445	0.659

Multiple R = 0.19; R^2 = 0.04; F = 0.67; p = 0.51

Equation 2: Dependent Variable – GRDSTRA

INDEPENDENT VARIABLE	BETA	STANDARD ERROR	T	PROBABILITY
PET	-0.067	0.027	-0.419	0.678
ASSETVA	-0.078	0.001	-0.345	0.732
AVPER	-0.119	0.056	-0.709	0.483
EMPLONO	0.381	8224	1.751	0.089

Multiple R = 0.37; R^2 = 0.13; F = 1.34; p = 0.27

APPENDIX F: NORTH AMERICAN RESPONDENTS' COMMENTS

REF #   COMMENT

R2   South Africa is changing rapidly and as a result of pressure. If you leave, the pressure ends.

R7   We have no intention to have an operation in South Africa and never had one. We have investments in Sub-Sahara Africa and plan to increase our investment in Sub-Sahara Africa.

R11   South Africa is rapidly changing and as a result of pressure. If you leave, the pressure ends.

R12   The ability to grow and make a profit determine whether businesses stay or withdraw. .... Business wages help fund reform.... Business has a long-term responsibility to its faithful employees.

R13   Unfortunately the questionnaire overly simplifies "impressions" involving marketing strategies in a complex international environment, or whether a company can influence the South African situation, much less pull out.

R16   1. Note: We divested our interests in S.A. (to our majority S.A. partner) in September 1986. Our reply to this questionnaire is based on our experience prior to that time and knowledge of what has happened since! (We manufactured both in South America and Zimbabwe).

        2. Political Stability (Q.11). Sanctions and resulting activities within South Africa have resulted in a more stubborn, more radical control exerted by the government. It is clear they have the strength and resolve to maintain control. They have become more repressive and have cancelled or curtailed progressive moves initiated before the sanctions. We perceive that sanctions have been counterproductive.

        3. Performance (Section 2): (the company was) by far the market leader – with 90% of market share with some products. Other factors show the advantage to our company.

        4. Strategy: Obviously, we divested because the "hassle factor" was taking too much management effort. We were profitable, but in a 45.5 Billion company we need to exert our energy where a greater percentage of profits can be produced. We were morally indignant that we were pushed into the divestment decision. Previously as a corporate officer – I had direct access to all top executives in the South African government (including Mr. Botha) and had a high degree of influence to bring about change. We foreclosed any capability to influence change when we divested. We had to face a tough ethical problem: was it more ethical to divest and abandon our ability to bring about change – or was it more ethical to consider the interests of our stakeholders? We firmly believe that institutional investors and governmental agencies who have forced the imposition of sanctions are condemning the people of S.A. to bloody revolution, when change could be accomplished in a different manner. Also we assert that to destroy the

South African Government – even though it is far from ideal – and to replace it with the ANC is a tragic error!!

5. General Comment: We consider *apartheid* to be evil. We have worked diligently to bring about its demise. Our facilities were totally integrated and over 15% of our managers were black. Out life saving, health care products served all people of all races – more than 75% used for the care and treatment of Blacks.

R20   We sold our operations in June 1987.

R23   We only provide sales and services.

R24   Your questions ask about the environment in South Africa. The problem is the environment in the United States.

R27   (Capital) . . . rather scarce due to U.S. government control. (Government Legal Political Constraints) have become more relaxed. Passbook elimination – a great step. (Wait) . . . Disagree completely: Organizations should be active in the Black communities. (General Comment) . . . Encourage active involvement by company employees and provide funds for creating improvement in black townships.

R28   Our Company ceased operations in South Africa about one and a half years ago.

R30   We no longer manufacture in South Africa. The strategy of withdrawal is a stupid farce by a group of political opportunists that have used well meaning humanist and immature students to further their interests. Our business in South Africa was bought by local management at a bargain price, and is doing fine. ...but we no longer influence the policy. When we owned (the company) there was 50% black employment. Now only one [Black employee] remains. I am sure that our withdrawal served no useful purpose.

Why did we withdraw? It was too small for us to put up with the harassment from every Stafford shirt politician running on a state pension fund or every academic who succumbed to the mindless chanting of their students. Once again, people get what they deserve.

R31   Change must come in South Africa since suppression of the non-White majority cannot continue indefinitely. In the meantime the economy expands slowly and the tension in the society impacts on all aspects of life. Thus the environment is pretty stable but underlying condition is a destabilizing influence.

(Slow Down Reinvestments) . . . The flight against apartheid is in South Africa and only by being there can companies be a force for peaceful change and reform. U.S. companies have invested more than $200 million in social and economic programs to help the non-Whites. These have increased economic opportunity and education for Blacks. Withdrawal would abandon the people we are trying to help and would reduce pressure on the government for reform.

R35   Selectively Sell: This is a normal part of adapting and changing to stay via-
        ble. (Beef-Shrink) . . . is simply a good business strategy. (Give the Govern-
        ment a Chance) . . . Companies need to keep the pressure on the govern-
        ment for reform. If they retrench, their voice will be ignored. (Grand Strat-
        egy) . . . Continue social and economic programs to help the Blacks. This is
        also a sensible stance since that is the largest market in South Africa.

R37   In my opinion, a strong economy in South Africa is a requisite to social and
        political reform without extreme violence. The government will not yield
        to pressure. Sanctions, etc., strengthen the right wing and harm conserva-
        tive Blacks.

R38   Answers refer to pre-withdrawal period.

R39   Answers refer to pre-withdrawal. Withdrew from South Africa in February
        1987.

R43   Company sold its two affiliates in South Africa in December 1986.

R48   South African business was sold in 1986.

R49   The primary "hassle factor" is not from the conditions in the R.S.A. It's the
        environment in the U.S.A.

R50   Withdrawal from South Africa will increase violence and hardship while at
        the same time weakening external (government and business) influences
        or pressure against apartheid.

R52   (Grand Strategy) . . . Sell off or liquidate until the South African government
        can get its act together. Up to now, business has not been able to influence
        political issues in South Africa. On the contrary, the firm's position in mar-
        kets outside of South Africa which are more relevant may be hurt by con-
        tinued operation in South Africa.

NOTES

1. Literally translated from Afrikaans, *apartheid* means separateness. It is a government system based on race "separateness". However, the implications of this system are more far reaching. The core characteristics of apartheid are described by Lipton (1985, p. 14) as (a) the hierarchical ordering of socioeconomic and political structures on the basis of race; (b) discrimination against blacks on such basic rights as freedom of movement, the vote, ownership of property in much of the country; (c) segregation of races in many spheres of life, e.g., residential areas, schooling, etc.; and (d) the legislation and institutionalization of this system, which is enshrined by law and enforced by the government.

2. For a detailed account of the principles, the reader can refer to any of the *Reports on the Sullivan Companies*, published by Arthur D. Little, Inc., Cambridge, Massachusetts (for example, the *Eighth Report* 1984).

3. It has been reported, for example, that under the Export and Import Permits Act, the Canadian Government laid charges against Space Research Corporation in connection with the shipment of arms to South Africa and the falsification of documents to obtain export permits (United Nations 1986, p. 14).

4. Versions of this chapter were presented at the 2008 Annual Conference of the Eastern Academy of Management in New Brunswick, NJ, and at the International Academy of Business and Public Administration Disciplines (IABPAD) Annual Conference in Orlando, FL.

5. A version of this chapter was presented at the 41st Conference of the Eastern Academy of Management, Providence, Rhode Island, May 2004.

6. A version of this chapter was presented at the School of Business Leadership, University of South Africa and later published in the *Southern African Business Review*. 2(2): 25-37.

7. Such strategies, when misused, may lead to the release of substandard, or even dangerous products to Third-World countries. This has been observed in the pharmaceutical industry, with the marketing of drugs

banned by the World Health Organization. Such strategies may backfire on their perpetrators as the global marketplace leads to globalized information exchange and its image consequences.

8. Soweto is a sprawling agglomeration of townships southwest of Johannesburg (roots: *South Western Townships*). Most of the 1.2 million blacks live in overcrowded homes. In 1976, African students in the townships of Soweto initiated a school boycott in protest against a new government law requiring that schools teach all subjects offered on the basis of 50 percent in English, and 50 percent in Afrikaans. Some sources assert that the students' frustration ran deeper than just that engendered by this new law (for example, see De St. Jorre 1977; Woods 1986). The government responded by using force to get the students back to classes. The aftermath of these riots left more than 600 students dead and many more injured from gun shots from the police (De St. Jorre 1977; Lindsay Smith 1979; Thomas 1981). This event rekindled the debate about whether the presence of multinational corporations helps or exacerbates the sociopolitical situation in South Africa.

9. A 1986 listing of companies with business operations in South Africa was used to identify respondents. Due to the heightened exodus rate of U.S./Canadian corporations from South Africa over the period 1985— 1987, many lists were inaccurate. Thus, it was difficult to tell, a priori, which companies had pulled out. Many of those that responded negatively to the first request stated that they had pulled out of S.A. A note in the second cover letter requesting them to participate even though they had exited the market increased the response rate by 6 additional percentage points.

10. The S.A. figures were reported in the local currency, the rand. The exchange rate of the rand fluctuated greatly over the ten years 1979— 1985, from a high of $1.42 to a low of $0.35 (*Standard Bank Review*, September 1985). In June 1988, the commercial rand conversion rate was about US$0.45 to the rand (Last, Weekly Mail, June 1988). For parsimony at the time of completing the write-up for this research in the late 1980s and early 1990s, a factor of $0.50 was applied to bring the S.A. rand figures in line with U.S. dollar figures. Since that time the rand has slipped considerably, trading for as low as $0.10 to the rand.

11. This distribution of start-ups corroborates the reported statistics on the growth of the South African secondary sector and the upsurge of American investments during that period in South Africa. It is well known that in the 1960s, companies enjoyed a high return on their S.A. investments. Specifically, in 1967 American companies earned 19.2 percent average return from their S.A. subsidiaries, compared with 10 percent from all other foreign investments (Koenderman 1982; also Schmidt 1983).

12. Some statisticians have argued that the chi-square statistic becomes less reliable when the expected frequencies are small (Cochran 1954; Everitt 1977). To minimize the problem of small cell sizes, from this point on we decided to use 2x2 chi-square tables for the purposes of cross-tabulation. When applicable, Yates's (1934) corrected chi-square was used.

13. Ten years of experience with the Sullivan Principles had proved that apartheid could coexist with all six of them. At the time of writing, it was too soon to tell if the newly added seventh principle intended to encourage corporate civil disobedience would make any significant impact on the gross socioeconomic inequities that had been created by apartheid in South Africa. It was a telling reality, however, when even Rev. Leon Sullivan, after whom the Sullivan Principles were named, decried the principles as providing little more than a license for MNCs to continue to operate in South Africa—an indication of how ineffective this approach was to the total elimination of apartheid.

14. Starting from the Industrial Conciliating Act of 1923, the right of African workers to bargain collectively was gradually scaled down until it was rendered technically nonexistent with the introduction of the Bantu Labor (Settlement of Disputes) Act of 1953, which redefined the term "employee" to exclude all Africans (Davis 1978).

15. Respondents from these two companies sent informative pamphlets on their position regarding their withdrawal strategies. One of them stated that the uniqueness of their approach precluded their participation in the questionnaire.

16. For a detailed account of the Coca-Cola withdrawal strategy, see Voorhes (1986) and Rouse (1986). With respect to African involvement in the Coca-Cola withdrawal, see *Race Relations Survey 1986* (1987, part 1); and Raspberry (1986).

17. For example, in a press release dated December 30, 1986, and made available to the researcher, Exxon cited the deteriorating economic and business climate in South Africa as the reason for its decision to sell its operation there. To avoid abandoning its employees, Exxon also established a trust. See "Exxon Announces Sale of South African Interests," *Press Release*, December 30, 1986.

BIBLIOGRAPHY

Abell, D.F. and Hammond, J.S. 1979. *Strategic Marketing Planning Problems and Analytical Approaches.* Englewood Cliffs, NJ: Prentice Hall.

Abels, E. 2002. Environmental Scanning. *Bulletin of the American Society for Information Science & Technology,* 28(3): 16-18.

Appel, M. 2008. Poverty in South Africa 'Is Declining.' http://www. Southafrica.info/about/social/poverty-021008.htm. Accessed on October 24, 2009.

Ackoff, R. 1981. On the Use of Models in Corporate Planning. *Strategic Management Journal,* 2: 353-359.

Adler, N.J. 1983. Cross-Cultural Management Research: The Ostrich and the Trend. *Academy of Management Review,* 8(2): 226-232.

Adler, N.J. 1986. *International Dimensions of Organizational Behavior.* Boston, MA: Kent Publishing Company.

Agger, B, 1991. Critical Theory, Poststructuralism, Postmodernism: Their Sociological Relevance. *Annual Review of Sociology,* 17: 105-131.

Aguilar, F. 1967. *Scanning the Business Environment.* New York: MacMillan.

Ajam, T. and Aron, J. 2007. Fiscal Renaissance in a Democratic South Africa. *Journal of African Economies,* 16(5): 745-781.

Ajiferuke, M. and Boddewyn, J. 1970. 'Culture' and Other Explanatory Variables in Comparative Management Studies. *Academy of Management Journal,* 13(2): 153-164.

Aldrich, H. 1979. *Organizations and Environments.* Englewood Cliffs, NJ: Prentice Hall.

Aldrich, H. E. and Pfeffer, J. 1976. Environments of organizations. *Annual Review of Sociology.* 2. Palo Alto, CA: Annual Review.

Aldrich, H. E. and Sasaki, T. 1995. R&D Consortia in the United States and Japan. *Research Policy,* 24(2): 301-316.

Aldrich, H.E., McKelvey, M. and Ulrich, D. 1984. Design Strategy from the Populations Perspective. *Journal of Management,* 10(1): 67-86

Anderson, C. R. and Zeithaml, C. P. 1984. Stage of the Product Life Cycle, Business Strategy, and Business Performance. *Academy of Management Journal.* 27(1): 5-24.

Anderson, C.R. and Paine, F.T. 1975. Managerial Perceptions and Strategic Behavior. *Academy of Management Journal*, 18(4): 811-823.

Anderson, C.R., and Zeithaml, C.P. 1981. Stage of Product Life Cycle as a Determinant of Business Strategy: An Empirical Test Using PIMS Data. Paper Presented at the Academy of Management Meeting. San Diego, CA.

Anderson, T.J. 2000. Real Options Analysis in Strategic Decision Making: an Applied Approach in a Dual Options Framework. *Journal of Applied Management Studies*, 9(2): 235-255.

Andreason, A.R. 1970. Personalizing Mail Questionnaire Correspondence. *Public Opinion Quarterly*, 34: 273-274.

Andrews, K. R. 1971. *The Concept of Corporate Strategy*. Homewood, IL: Irwin.

Ansoff, H.I. 1965. *Corporate Strategy: An Analytical Approach to Business Policy for Growth and Expansion*, New York: McGraw-Hill.

Ansoff, H.I. 1969. *Business Strategy*. Harmondsworth, Middlesex: Penguin Books.

Ansoff, H.I. 1984. *Implanting Strategic Management*. Englewood Cliffs, NJ: Prentice Hall

Ansoff, H.I. 1991. Critique of Henry Mintzberg's "The Design School: Reconsidering the Basic Premises of Strategic Management." *Strategic Management Journal*, 12: 449-461.

Ansoff, H.I. and Sullivan, P.A. 1993. Optimizing Profitability in Turbulent Environments: A Formula for Strategic Success. *Long Range Planning*, 26(5): 11-24.

Ansoff, H.I., Avner, J., Brandenburg, R.G., Portner, F.E., and Radosevich, R. 1970. Does Planning Pay? The Effect of Planning on Success of Acquisitions in American Firms. *Long Range Planning*, 3: 1-7.

Ashby, W. R. 1956. *An introduction to Cybernetics*. New York: Wiley.

Atherton, A. 2003. The Uncertainty of Knowing: An Analysis of the Nature of Knowledge in a Small Business Context. *Human Relations*, 56(11): 1379-1398.

Austin, J., and Ickis, J. 1986. Managing After the Revolutionaries Have Won. *Harvard Business Review*, (May-June): 103-109.

Avirgan, T. 2006. South Africa's economic gap grows wider while Brazil's narrows slightly. EPA Snapshot. April 19. Accessed On July 2, 2009 from www.epi.org/economic_snapshots/entry/webfeatures_snapshots_200 60419/.

Bain, J. S. 1956. *Barriers to New Competition: Their Character and Consequences in Manufacturing Industries*. Cambridge, MA: Harvard University Press.

Barnet, R. and Muller, R. 1974. *Global Reach: The Power of Multinational Corporations.* New York: Simon & Schuster.

Barney, J. 1991. Firm Resources and Sustained Competitive Advantage. *Journal of Management.* 17: 99-120.

Barney, J. 1991. Firm Resources and Sustained Competitive Advantage. *Journal of Marketing,* 17: 99-120.

Barney, J. B. 1986a. Strategic Factor Markets, Expectations, Luck, and Business Strategy. *Management Science.* 42:1231-1241.

Barney, J.B. 1986b. Types of Competition and the Theory of Strategy: Toward an Integrative Framework. *Academy of Management Review,* 11(4): 791-800.

Barr, P.S. 1998. Adapting to Unfamiliar Environmental Events: A Look at the Evolution of Interpretation and its Role in Strategic Change. *Organization Science,* 9(6): 644-670.

Battersby, J.D. 1987. U.S. Goods in South Africa: Little Impact of Divestiture. *New York Times,* July 27: D1, D5.

Baudrillard, J. 1986. Forgetting Baudrillard. *Social Text.* 15 (Fall): 140-144.

Baumol, W. and Benhabib, J. 1989. Chaos, significance, mechanism, and economic applications. *Journal of Economic Perspectives,* 3: 77-105.

Beaty, D. T. & Harari, O. 1978. South Africa: White Managers, Black Voices. *Harvard Business Review,* 4 (July-August): 98-105.

Beckert, J. 1996. What is Sociological about Economic Sociology? Uncertainty and the Embeddedness of Economic Action. *Theory and Society,* 25(6): 803-40.

Bergen, M., Dutta, S., & Walker, O.C. (1992). Agency Relationships in Marketing: A Review of the Implications of Agency and Related Theories. *Journal of Marketing,* 3(July): 1-24.

Bernard, Frank J. 2003. Calculating for Uncertainty. *Intelligent Enterprise,* August 10: 30-33.

Bernasek, A., Shiller, R., Zook, C., Varian, H., and Porter, M. 2001. Okay. Now What? *Fortune,* 143(12 - July 11): 98-104.

Bernstein, L. 1974. *Financial Statement Analysis.* Homewood, IL: Irwin. pp. 466-509.

Bettman, J.R. and Weitz, B.A. 1983. Attribution in the Board Room: Causal Reasoning in Corporate Reports. *Administrative Science Quarterly,* 28(3): 165-183.

Bierman, H., (Jr.), and Smidt, S. 1980. *The Capital Budgeting Decision.* New York: MacMillan.

Biggadike, E.R. 1981. The Contributions of Marketing to Strategic Management. *Academy of Management Review,* 6: 621-632.

Bigler, R. 1982. Environment, Strategy and Performance: An Empirical Analysis in Two Service Industries. *Unpublished Ph.D. Dissertation.* Baton Rouge, LA: Louisiana State University.

Bloom, A.H. 1987. Managing against Apartheid: An Interview by B. Avashi, *Harvard Business Review*, 6: 49-56.

Blunt, P. 1973. Cultural and Situational Determinants of Job Satisfaction Amongst Management in South Africa: A Research Note. *The Journal of Management Studies*, 10: 133-140.

Blunt, P. 1986. Techno- and Ethnocentrism in Organizational Studies: Comment and Speculation Prompted by Ronen and Shenkar. *Academy of Management Review*, 11: 857-859.

Bomona, T.V. and Johnston, W.J. 1979. Decision Making under Uncertainty: A Direct Measurement Approach. *Journal of Consumer Studies*, 6(2): 177-191.

Bordley, R. F. 1998. Quantum Mechanical and Human Violations of Compound Probability Principles: Toward a Generalized Heisenberg Uncertainty Principle. *Operations Research*, 46(6): 923-926.

Bouchard, T.J. (Jr.). 1976. Unobtrusive Measures: An Inventory of Uses. *Sociological Methods and Research*, 4: 267-300.

Bourgeois, L. J. (III), McAllister, D. W., and Mitchell, T. R. 1978. The effects of different organizational environments upon decisions about organizational structure. *Academy of Management Journal*. 21: 508-514.

Bourgeois, L.J. (III). 1978. Strategy Making, Environment, and Economic Performance: A Conceptual and Empirical Exploration. *Unpublished Ph.D. Dissertation*. University of Washington.

Bourgeois, L.J. (III). 1980. Strategy and Environment: A Conceptual Integration. *Academy of Management Review*, 5(1): 25-39.

Bourgeois, L.J. (III). 1985. Strategic Goals, Perceived Uncertainty, and Economic Performance in Volatile Environments. *Academy of Management Journal*, 28(3): 548-573.

Bowman E. and Hurry, D. 1993. Strategy through the option lens: integrated view of resource investments and the incremental choice process. *Academy of Management Review*. 18 (4): 760-782.

Bracken, S. (ed.). 1987. *Canadian Almanac and Directory*. Toronto: Copp Clark Pitman, 6/80-6/88.

Bracker, J. 1980. The Historical Development of the Strategic Management Concept. *Academy of Management Review*, 5(2): 219-224.

Brown, L.O., and Beik, L.L. 1969. *Marketing Research and Analysis*. New York: The Ronald Press Co.

Bukszar Jr., E. 1999. Strategic Bias: The Impact of Cognitive Biases on Strategy. *Canadian Journal of Administrative Sciences*, 16(2): 105-118.

Burgelman, R.A. 1983. A Model of the Interaction of Strategic Behavior, Corporate Context, and the Concept of Strategy. *Strategic Management Review*, 18(1): 61-70.

Burns, J.F. 1988. South Africa's Economy Faces an Unsteady Future. *New York Times*, March 13, p. F10.

Burns, T. and Stalker, G.M. 1961. *Management of Innovation*. London: Tavistock.

Burrell, G. and Morgan, G. 1979. *Sociological Paradigms and Organizational Analysis*. London: Heinemann.

Business Week. 1980. Wanted: A Manager to Fit Each Strategy. February: 173-199.

Buzzell, R.B., Gale, B., and Sultan, R. 1975. Market Share – a Key to Profitability. *Harvard Business Review*, 53 (January-February): 97-106.

Byrne, J. 1996. Strategic Planning: It's Back. *BusinessWeek*. August 26. Accessed on September 4 from http://www.businessweek.com/1996/35/960826.htm.

Camerer, C. and Weber, M. 1992. Recent Developments in Modeling Preferences: Uncertainty and Ambiguity. *Journal of Risk and Uncertainty*, 5(4): 325-370.

Cameron, K. S., Sutton, R. I. and Whetten, D. A. 1988. Issues in Organizational Decline. In K. S. Cameron, R. I. Sutton and D. A, Whetten (eds.), *Readings in Organizational Decline: Framework, Research, and Prescriptions*: 3-19. Boston, MA: Ballinger Publishing Company.

Cameron, K.S., Kim, M.U. and Whetten, D.A. 1987. Organizational Effects of Decline and Turbulence. *Administrative Science Quarterly*, 32 (June): 222-240.

Camillus, J. C. and Datta, D. K. 1991. Managing Strategic Issues in a Turbulent Environment. *Long Range Planning*. 24 (2): 67-74.

Capon, N., Christodoulou, C., Farley, J., and Hulbert, J. A. 1987. Comparative Analysis of the Strategy and Structure of United States and Australian Corporations. *Journal of International Business*, 18(1): 51-74.

Carpenter, M.A. and Fredrickson, J.W. 2001. Top Management Teams, Global Strategic Posture, and the Moderating Role of Uncertainty. *Academy of Management Journal*, 44(3): 533-545.

Carroll, A.B. 1991. The Pyramid of Corporate Social Responsibility: Toward the Moral Management of Organizational Stakeholders. *Business Horizons*. 34(4): 39-48.

Carter, K.D. 1987. The Uses of Formal and Informal Plans in Top Executive Decision Making: A Comparison between U.S. and Canadian Executives. *Unpublished Doctoral Dissertation*, University of Massachusetts, Amherst, MA

CDE - Center for Development and Enterprise. 2008. Youth Unemployment Interventions Neither Attacking Root Causes Nor Going to Scale. http://www.cde.org.za/article.php?a_id=325. Accessed on October 21, 2009.

Chaffee, E.E. 1985. Three Models of Strategy. *Academy of Management Review*, 10(1): 89-98.

Chandler, A.D. 1982. *Strategy and Structure: Chapters in the History of the American Industrial Enterprise*. Cambridge, MA: M.I.T. Press.

Channon, D. 1973. *The Strategy and Structure of British Enterprise.* Cambridge, MA: Harvard University.

Cheng, T.C.E. 1987. A Simulation of MRP Capacity Planning with Uncertain Operation Times. *International Journal of Production Research*, 25(2): 245-258.

Chenhall, R. and Morris, J. 1985. The Impact of Structure, Environment, and Interdependence on the Perceived Usefulness of Management Accounting Systems. *The Accounting Review*, January: 16-33.

Child, J. 1972. Organizational Structure, Environment, and Performance: The Role of Strategic Choice. *Sociology*, 6: 1-21.

Child, J. 1974a. Managerial and Organizational Factors Associated with Company Performance. *Journal of Management Studies*, 1(3): 175-189.

Child, J. 1974b. What Determines Organizational Performance? The Universals vs. the It-All Depends. *Organizational Dynamics*, 3(1): 2-18.

Christofides, N., Muirhead, D., Jewkes, R., Penn-Kekana, L. and Conco, N. 2006. *Including Post-Exposure Prophylaxis to Prevent HIV/AIDS into Post- Sexual Assault Health Services in South Africa: Costs and Cost Effectiveness of User Preferred Approaches to Provision.* Pretoria: Medical Research Council. Accessed on July 2, 2009 from http://www.unicef.org/southafrica/SAF_resource_violencehivaids.pdf.

Clarke, I. and Mackaness, W. 2001. Management 'Intuition': An Interpretative Account of Structure and Content Of Decision Schemas Using Cognitive Maps. *Journal of Management Studies*, 38(2): 147-173.

Coase, R. 1937. The Nature of the Firm. *Econometrica.* 4: 386-405.

Cochran, W.G. 1954. Some Methods for Strengthening the Common Chi-Squared Tests. *Biometrics*, 10: 417-451.

Cohen, J., and Cohen, P. 1983. *Applied Multiple Regression/Correlation Analysis for the Behavioral Sciences.* Hillsdale, NJ: Lawrence Erlbaum.

Cohen, J.F. 2001. Environmental Uncertainty and Managerial Attitude: Effects on Strategic Planning, Non-Strategic Decision-Making and Organisational Performance. *South African Journal of Business Management*, 32(3): 17-32.

Conrad, T. 1982. Computers programmed for racism. *Business and Society Review*, 42(Summer): 61-64.

Cool, K., and Schendel, D. 1987. Strategic Group Formation and Performance: The Case of the U.S. Pharmaceutical Industry. *Management Science*, 33(9): 1963-1982.

Courtney, H., 2003, Decision-Driven Scenarios for Assessing Four Level of Uncertainty, *Strategy & Leadership.* 31(1): 14-22.

Courtney, H., Kirkland, J. and Viguerie, P. 1999. *Harvard Business Review on Managing Uncertainty.* Boston, MA: Harvard Business School Press.

Crapanzano, V. 1987. White Industry in South Africa. *Social Science*, 72(1): 69-73.

Crawford, N. and Klotz, A. (Eds.). 1997. *How Sanctions Work: Lessons from South Africa.* London, UK: Macmillan.

Crichton, K. 1986. A Conversation with the Rev. Sullivan: Going All-out against Apartheid. *The New York Times,* May 27: F1, F27.

Currim, I.S. and Sarin, R.K. 1983. A Procedure for Measuring and Estimating Consumer Preferences under Uncertainty. *Journal of Marketing Research,* 20 (Aug.): 249-256.

Currim, I.S. and Sarin, R.K. 1984. A Comparative Evaluation of Multiattribute Consumer Preference Models. *Management Science,* 30 (May): 543-561.

Cyert, R., and March, J.G. 1963. *A Behavioral Theory of the Firm.* Englewood Cliffs, NJ: Prentice Hall.

Daft, R.L. and Lengel, R.H. 1986. Organizational, Information Requirements, Media Richness and Structural Design. *Management Science,* 32(5): 554-571.

Daft, R.L. and Macintosh, N.B. 1981. A Tentative Exploration into the Amount and Equivocality of Information Processing in Organizational Work Units. *Administrative Science Quarterly,* 26: 207-224.

Das, T.K.1986. *The Subjective Side of Strategy-making.* New York: Praeger.

D'Aveni, R. A. 1989. The Aftermath of Organizational Decline: A Longitudinal Study of the Strategic and Managerial Characteristics of Declining Firms. *Academy of Management Journal.* 32 (3): 577-605.

D'Aveni, R. A. 1994. *Hypercompetition: Managing the Dynamics of Strategic Maneuvering.* New York: Free Press.

David, P. 1993. South Africa: The Final Lap. *Economist,* March 20: 60-61.

Davis, D. 1978. African Workers and Apartheid. *Fact Paper on Southern Africa.* London: International Defense and Aid Fund.

Davis, K. 1973. The Case For and Against Business Assumption of Social Responsibilities. *Academy of Management Journal,* 16: 312-322.

Davis, K. and Blomstrom, R.L. 1975. *Business and Society: Environment and Responsibility.* New York: McGraw-Hill.

DeLong, J.B. 1997. Slouching Towards Utopia? The Economic History of the Twentieth Century. Working Paper. University of California, Berkeley. Accessed on September 4, 2009 from http://home.cvc.org/bryant/de long chapter 2 wealth.pdf.

De Meyer, A., Loch, C. H. and Pich, M. T. 2002. Uncertainty in Project Management: From Uncertainty to Chaos. *MIT Sloan Management Review.* Winter: 60-67.

De St. Jorre, J. 1977. *A Nation Divided: South Africa's Uncertain Future.* New York: Carnegie Endowment for International Peace.

De St. Jorre, J. 1987. South Africa Embattled. *Foreign Affairs,* 65(3): 538-563.

Dequech, D. 2003. Uncertainty and Economic Sociology: A Preliminary Discussion. *The American Journal of Economics and Sociology,* 62(3): 509 – 533.

Dess, G.G., and Beard, D.W. 1984. Dimensions of Organizational Task Environments. *Administrative Science Quarterly*, 29: 52-73.

Dess, G.G., and Robinson, R.B. 1984. Measuring Organizational Performance in the Absence of Objective Measures: The Case of the Privately-held Firm and Conglomerate Business. *Strategic Management Journal*, 5(3): 265-273.

Dicken, P. 1998. *Global Shift: Transforming the World Economy*. London: Paul Chapman.

Dill, W. 1958: Environment as an Influence on Managerial Autonomy. *Administrative Science Quarterly*, 2(2): 409-443.

Dillman, D.A. 1978. *Mail and Telephone Surveys: The Total Design Method*. New York: Wiley Interscience.

Dillman, D.A. 1983. Mail and Other Self Administered Questionnaires. In Rossi, P.H., Wright, J.B. and Anderson, A.B. (eds.), *Handbook of Survey Research*. Orlando, FL: Academic Press, pp. 359-377.

Dillon, W.R., and Goldstein, M. 1984. *Multivariate Analysis*. New York: John Wiley & Sons.

Dissel, M.C. 2003, Uncertainty and Managerial Decisions for New Technology-Based Ventures. *Unpublished Ph.D. Dissertation*. Universität Bw München, Germany.

Dixit, A.K. and Pindyck, R. S. 1994. *Investment under Uncertainty*. Princeton, NJ: Princeton University Press.

DOJ&CD (Department of Justice & Constitutional Development) c.1997: African Charter on Human and Peoples' Rights. Accessed on May 31, 2009. From http://www.doj.gov.za/policy/african%20charter/african charter.htm#pre.

Donaldson, T. 1989. *The Ethics of International Business*. New York: Oxford University Press.

Dosi, G. and Egidi, M. 1991. Substantive and Procedural Uncertainty: An Exploration of Economic Behavior in Changing Environments. *Journal of Evolutionary Economics*, 1(2): 145-68.

Downey, H.K., and Slocum, J.W., Jr. 1975. Uncertainty: Measures, Research, and Sources of Variation. *Academy of Management Journal*, 18(3): 562-577.

Downey, H.K., Hellriegel, D. and Slocum, Jr., J.W. 1975. Environmental Uncertainty: The Construct and Its Application. *Administrative Science Quarterly*, 20 (4): 613-29.

Doz, Y. and Prahalad, C. K. 1991. Managing DMNCs: A search for a new paradigm. *Strategic Management Journal*. 12(Summer): 145-164.

Drucker, P.F. 1969. *The Age of Discontinuity*. New York: Harper and Row.

Drucker, P.F. 1974. *Management: Tasks, Responsibilities, Practices*. New York: Harper and Row.

Drucker, P.F. 1980. *Managing in Turbulent Times*. New York: Harper and Row.

Drucker, P.F. 1985. *Frontiers of Management*. New York: Harper and Row.

Drucker, P.F. 1986. The Changed World Economy. *Foreign Affairs*, Spring: 768-791.

Du Toit, A. 1983. No Chosen People: The Myth of the Origins of Afrikaner Nationalism and Racial Ideology. *American Historical Review*, 88(4): 920-952.

Duhaime, I.M., and Schwenk, C.R. 1985. Conjectures on Cognitive Simplification in Acquisition and Divestment Decision Making, *Academy of Management Review*, 10(2): 287-295.

Dun and Bradstreet. 1986. *Principal International Businesses*. Parsippany, NJ: Dun and Bradstreet International.

Duncan, R. B. 1972. Characteristics of Organizational environments and Perceived Environmental Uncertainty. *Administrative Science Quarterly*. 17: 313-327.

Duncan, R.B. 1972. Characteristics of Organizational Environments and Perceived Environmental Uncertainty. *Administrative Science Quarterly*, 17(2): 313-327.

Duncan, R.B., 1972. Characteristics of Organizational Environments and Perceived Environmental Uncertainty, *Administrative Science Quarterly*, 17: 313-327.

Dutton, J.E. and Jackson S.E. 1987. Categorizing Strategic Issues: Links to Organizational Action. *Academy of Management Review*, 121: 76-90.

Dutton, J.E., Walton, E. J. and Abrahamson, E. 1989. Important Dimensions of Strategic Issues: Separating the Wheat From The Chaff. *Journal of Management Studies*, 264: 379-396.

Dyackman, T. R. and Thomas, L.J. 1977. *Fundamental Statistics for Business and Economics*. Englewood Cliffs, NJ: Prentice Hall.

Eberstadt, N. 1988. Poverty in South Africa. *Optima*, 36(1): 20-33.

Edmondson, L. 1988. From trans-Atlantic slavery to global apartheid: The challenges of Black liberation. Paper presented at the International Conference to Commemorate the 150th Anniversary of Emancipation from Slavery in Guyana, University of Guyana, Georgetown, Guyana, South America. July.

Eisenhardt, K.M. 1989. Making Fast Decisions in High Velocity Environments. *Academy of Management Journal*, 32: 543-576.

Ellis, J. 1975. *The Social History of the Machine Gun*. Baltimore, MD: Johns Hopkins University Press.

Ellis, R. J. 1982. Improving Management Response in Turbulent Times. *Sloan Management Review*. 23 (2): 3-12.

Emery, F.E., and Trist, E.L. 1965. Causal Texture of Organizational Environment. *Human Relations*, 18: 21-32.

Encarnation, D.J. and Vachani, S. 1985. Foreign Ownership: When the Hosts Change the Rules. *Harvard Business Review*, September-October: 7-10.

Everend, R. 1983. So What Is Strategy. *Long Range Planning*, 16(3): 57-72.

Everitt, D.S., 1977. *The Analysis of Contingency Tables*. London: Chapman and Hall.

Exxon. 1986. Exxon Announces Sale of South Africa Interests. *Press Release*, December 30.

Fahey, L. and Christensen, H.K. 1986. Evaluating the Research of Strategy Content. *Journal of Management*, 12: 167-183.

Fahey, L., and King, W.R. 1977. Environmental Scanning for Corporate Planning", *Business Horizons*, 61-71.

Faur, T. 1993. Foreign Capital in Hungary's Privatization. In *Privatization in the Transition to a Market Economy*. New York: St. Martin's Press, pp. 203-214.

Fayerweather, J. 1959. *The Executive Overseas*. Syracuse, NY: Syracuse University Press.

Fayol, H. 1949. *General and Industrial Management*. Pitman, London: C. Storrs, (Trans.)

Feather, N.T. 1971. Attribution of Responsibility and Valence of Success and Failure in Relation to Initial Confidence and Rash Performance. *Journal of Personality and Social Psychology*, 18: 173-188.

Feder, B. 1987. Sullivan asks end of business links with South Africa. *The New York Times*, June 4: A1, D6.

Fishbein, M. and Ajzen, I. 1957. *Beliefs, Attitude, Intention and Behavior – An Introduction to Theory and Research*. Reading, MA: Addison-Wesley.

Fisher, F. and McGowan, J. 1983. On the Misuse of Accounting Rates of Return to Inter Monopoly Profits. *American Economic Review*, 82-97.

Fisher, R.A. 1950. *Statistical Methods for Research Workers*. Edinburgh: Oliver and Boydm.

Fiske, S.T. and Shelley E.T. 1991. *Social Cognition*. New York: McGraw-Hill.

Forbes, D.P. 2005. Managerial Determinants of Decision Speed in New Ventures. *Strategic Management Journal*, **26**: 355–366.

Fortune. 1987. The Fortune Directory of the 500 largest U.S. Industrial Corporation. April 27.

Foster, R. 2001. The Welch Legacy: Creative Destruction. *Wall Street Journal*. September 10

Fouraker, L.E., and Stopford, J.M. 1968. Organizational Structure and Multinational Strategy", *Administrative Science Quarterly*, 13(1): 47-64.

Frederickson, J.W. and Mitchell, T.R. 1984. Strategic Decision Processes: Comprehensiveness and Performance in an Industry with an Unstable Environment. *Academy of Management Journal*, 27(2): 399-423.

Freeman, R.E. 1984. *Strategic Management: A Stakeholder Approach*. Boston, MA: Pitman.

Friedman, M. 1962. *Capitalism and Freedom*. Chicago, IL: University of Chicago Press.

Friedman, M. 1970. The Social Responsibility of Business Is to Increase Profits. *New York Times Magazine*. (September 13): 32-33, 122, 126.

Fry, J.N. and Killing, J.P. 1986. *Strategic Analysis and Action.* Englewood Cliffs, NJ: Prentice Hall.

Gadeake, R.M., and Tootelian, D.H. 1976. The Fortune 500 list – And Endangered Species for Academic Research. *Journal of Business Research,* 4: 283-288.

Galbraith, J.R. 1973. *Designing Complex Organizations.* Reading, MA: Addison-Wesley.

Galbraith, J.R. and Nathanson, D.A. 1978. *Strategy Implementation: The Role of Structure and Process.* St. Paul, MN: West.

Galtung, J. 1969. *Theory and Methods of Social Research.* New York: Columbia University Press.

General Motors Public Relations Staff. 1986. General Motors in South Africa. *Public Affairs News Letter.* 16(6).

Gersick, C. J. G. 1991. Revolutionary Change Theories: A Multilevel Exploration of the Punctuated Equilibrium Paradigm. *Academy of Management Review.* 16 (1): 10-36.

Gibson, J.L. Ivancevich, J.M. and Donnelly, J.H. 1979. *Organizations: Behavior, Structure, Process.* Dallas, TX: Business Publications.

Gifford, W.E., Slocum, J.W. (Jr.) and Bobbitt, H.R. 1979. Message Characteristics and Perception of Uncertainty by Organizational Decision Makers. *Academy of Management Journal,* 22 (3): 458-481.

Gladwin, T.N. and Walter, I. 1980. *Multinationals under Fire.* New York: Wiley.

Glennville-Grey, W. 1985. The Rockefeller Report: Important Insights, Critical Omissions. *Africa Today.* 4: 17-26.

Glover, J. 1966. The Changing Environment. *Teaching Note* (8-367-019). Boston, MA: Graduate School of Business, Harvard University.

Glueck, W.F. 1976. *Business Policy: Strategy Formulation and Management Action.* New York: McGraw-Hill.

Glueck, W.F. 1980. *Strategic Management and Business Policy.* New York: McGraw-Hill.

Glueck, W.F., and Jaunch, L.R. 1984. *Strategic Management and Business Policy.* New York: McGraw-Hill.

Godiwalla, Y.M. Meinhart, A. and Warde, C. 1981. How CEOs form Corporate Strategy. *Management World,* 10.

Goodpaster, K.E. 1991. Business Ethics and Stake Holder Analysis. *Business Ethics Quarterly,* 1(1): 53-73.

Goodsell, C. 1985. *The Case for Bureaucracy: A Public Polemic.* Chatham, NJ: Chatham House.

Goodstein, J. and Boeker, W. 1991. Turbulence at the Top: A New Perspective on Governance Structure Changes and Strategic Change. *Academy of Management Journal.* 34(2): 306-330.

Grant, J.H. and King W.R. 1982. *The Logic of Strategic Planning.* Boston, MA: Little, Brown and Co.

Grant, J.H. and Mason, P.A. 1984. Upper Echelons: The Organization is a Reflection of its Top Managers. *Academy of Management Review*, 9: 193-206.

Graves, S.B. & Waddock, S.A. 1999. A Look at the Financial Social Performance Nexus when Quality of Management is Held Constant. *International Journal of Value Based Management*, 12: 87-99.

Gray, E.R. and Smeltzer, L.R. 1987. Planning a Face-Lift: Implementing a Corporate Image Program. *Journal of Business Strategy*, 8 (1): 4 - 10

Greenhalgh, L., Lawrence, A. T. and Sutton, R. I. 1988. Determinants of Work Force Reduction Strategies in Declining Organizations. *Academy of Management Review*. 13 (2): 241-254.

Greenwood, R. and Hinings, C.R. 1988. Organizational Design Types, Tracks, and the Dynamics of Strategic Change. *Organization Studies*, 8: 293-316.

Greidner, W. 1997. *One World, Ready or Not: The Manic Logic of Global Capitalism*. New York: Simon & Schuster.

Greve, H.R. 2002. Sticky Aspirations: Organizational Time Perspective and Competitiveness. *Organization Science*, 13(1): 1-18.

Grinyer, P.H., and Noburn, D. 1975. Planning for Existing Markets: Perceptions of Chief Executives and Financial Performance. *Journal of the Royal Statistical Society, Series A*, 138(1): 70-97.

Grinyer, P.H., Yasai-Ardekani, M., and Al-Bazzaz, S. 1980. Strategy, Structure, Environment, and Firm Performance in 48 United Kingdom Companies, *Academy of Management Journal*, 13: 193-220.

Gulati, R. 1995. Does familiarity breed trust? The Implication of Repeat Ties for Contractual Choice in Alliances. *Academy of Management Journal*, 38 (1): 85-112.

Hale, F. 1985. South Africa: Defending the Laager. *Current History*, 84(501, April): 155-158, 184-186.

Haleblian, J. and Finkelstein, S. 1993. Top Management Team Size, CEO Dominance, and Firm Performance: The Moderating Roles of Environmental Turbulence and Discretion. *Academy of Management Journal*, 36 (4): 844-863.

Hall, R.H. 1972. *Organizations: Structure and Process*. Englewood Cliffs, NJ: Prentice-Hall.

Hall, W.K. 1980. Survival Strategies in a Hostile Environment. *Harvard Business Review*, September-October, 75-85.

Hambrick, D.C. 1982. Environmental Scanning and Organizational Strategy. *Strategic Management Journal*, 3: 159-174

Hambrick, D.C. and Mason, P.A. 1984. Upper Echelons: The Organization as a Reflection of Its Top Managers. *Academy of Management Review*, 9(2): 193-206.

Hambrick, D.C. and Snow, C.C. 1977. A Contextual Model of Decision Making in Organizations. *Academy of Management Proceedings*, Orlando, FL., 109-112.

Hammer, M. and Champy, J. 1993. *Reengineering the Corporation: A Manifesto for Business Revolution*. New York: Harper Business.

Hansell, S. 2000. Banking's Big Deal: The Tradition, Storied Bank Failed to Move with Times. *New York Times*, September 13.

Hansen, G. S. and Wernerfelt, B. 1989. Determinants of Firm Performance: The Relative Importance of Economic and Organizational Factors. *Strategic Management Journal*. 10: 399-411.

Harland, R. 1987. *Super Structuralism: The Philosophy of Structuralism and Post Structuralism*. London: Meltheun.

Harrigan, K.R. 1985a. Coalition Strategies: A Framework for Joint Ventures. *Academy of Management Proceedings*, San Diego, CA.

Harrigan, K.R., 1985b. *Strategic Flexibility: A Management Guide for Changing Times*. Lexington, MA: D.C. Heath.

Hart, B.H. 1967. *Strategy*. New York: Praeger.

Hart, G. 2002. *Disabling Globalization: Places of Power in Post-Apartheid South Africa*. Berkeley, CA: University of California Press.

Hatziantoniou, P. 1986. The Relationship of Environmental Turbulence Corporate Strategic Profile and Company Performance. *Unpublished D.B.A. Dissertation*, United States International University.

Hayes, R.H., and Abernathy, W.J. 1980. Managing Our Way to Economic Decline. *Harvard Business Review*, 4: 67-77.

Heenan, D. A. and Perlmutter, H. V. 1979. *Multinational Development: A Social Architecture Perspective*. Reading MA: Addison-Wesley.

Heisenberg, W. 1958. Physics *and Philosophy: The Revolution in Modern Science*. New York: Harper and Row.

Helmer, H.W. 2003. A Lecture on Integrating the Treatment of Uncertainty in Strategy. *Journal of Strategic Management Education*. 1(1): 1-24.

Hempel, C.G. and Oppenheim, P. 1948. Studies in the Logic of Explanation. *Philosophy of Science,* 15(2): 135-175.

Herold, D.M. 1972. Long-range Planning and Organizational Performance: A Cross-evaluation Study. *Academy of Management Journal*, 15: 91-102.

Hill, C. W. L. 1988. Differentiation versus Low-Cost or Differentiation and Low-Cost: A Contingency Framework. *Academy of Management Review.* **13** (2): 159-178.

Hill, C. W. L., Hitt, M. A. and Hoskisson, R. E. 1992. Cooperative versus Competitive Studies in Related and Unrelated Diversified Firms. *Organization Science*. 3 (4): 501-521.

Hofer, C. and Schendel, D. 1978. *Strategy Formulation: Analytical Concepts*. St. Paul, MN: West Publishing Co.

Hoffman, P. 1960. The Paramorphic Representation of Clinical Judgment. *Psychological Bulletin*, 47: 116-131.

Hofstede, G. 1980. *Culture's Consequences*. Beverly Hills, CA: Sage Publications.

Holt, D. 1987. *Management: Principles and Practices.* Englewood Cliffs, NJ: Prentice-Hall.

Hopkins, R. 1978. Global Networks: The Internationalization of Domestic Bureaucracies. *International Social Science Journal*, 30(1): 31-46.

Horgan, J. 1992. Quantum Philosophy. *Scientific American.* 267(1): 94-104.

Houston, M.J. and Jefferson, R.W. 1975. The Negative Effects of Personalization on Response Patterns in Mail Surveys. *Journal of Market Research*, 12(1): 114-117.

Houston, M.J. and Jefferson, R.W. 1976. On the Personalization-Anonymity Relationship in Mail Surveys-Reply. Journal of Marketing Research, 2(1): 112-113.

Hrebiniak, L .G. and Joyce, W. F. 1985. Organizational adaptation: Strategic choice and environmental determinism. *Administrative Science Quarterly.* 30: 336-349.

Huber, G. 1984. The nature and design of post-industrial environments. *Management Science.* 30: 928-951.

Huber, G. P., Miller, C. C. and Glick, W. H. 1990. Developing more encompassing theories about organizations: The centralization-effectiveness relationship as an example. *Organization Science.* 1: 11-40.

Huber, G.P. and Power, D.J. 1985. Retrospective Reports of Strategic-Level Managers: Guidelines for Increasing their Accuracy. *Strategic Management Journal*, 6(2): 171-180.

Huff, A.S. and Reger, R.K. 1987. A Review of Strategic Process Research. *Journal of Management*, 13(2): 211-236.

Hull, R. W. 1990. *American Enterprise in South Africa.* New York: New York University Press.

Human Sciences Research Council 2004. Poverty in South Africa. Fact Sheet No. 1. July 26. Accessed on September 4, 2009 from http://www.sarpn. org.za/documents/d0000990/P1096-Fact_Sheet_No_1_Poverty.pdf

Hunt, S.D., Sparkman, R.D. (Jr.), and Wilcox, J.B. 1982: The Pretest in Survey Research: Issues and Preliminary Findings. *Journal of Marketing Research*, 19(2): 269-273.

Hurlbut, C.S. 1976. *The Planet We Live On.* New York: Harry Abrahams.

Hurry, D., Miller, A. J. and Bowman, E. H. 1992. Calls on high-technology: Japanese exploration of venture capital investments in the United States. *Strategic Management Journal.* 13 (2): 85-101.

Hurst, D.K. 1986. Why Strategic Management is Bankrupt. *Organizational Dynamics*, 4-27.

IMC - International Marketing of South Africa. 2009.)

Ireland, R.D., Hitt, M., Bettis, R., and De Porras, D.A. 1987. Strategy Formulation Process: Weaknesses Indicators and Environmental Uncertainty by Managerial Level. Strategic Management Journal, 8(5): 469-485.

Jabnoun, N., Khalifah, A. and Yusuf, A. 2003. Environmental Uncertainty, Strategic Orientation, and Quality Management: A Contingency Model. *The Quality Management Journal*, 10(4): 17-31.

Jacobs, G. 1986. *South Africa-The Road Ahead*. Johannesburg, South Africa: Jonathan Ball.

Jacobson, C. 2009. In South Africa, rape is linked to manhood. *Mail & Guardian*, July 9. Accessed on July 15, 2009 from http://www.mg.co.za/article/2009-07-09-in-south-africa-rape-is-linked-to-manhood.

Jain, P.C. 1985. The Effect of Voluntary Sell-Off Announcements on Shareholder Wealth. *Journal Finance*. 40(1): 209-224.

Jauch, L. R. and Kraft, K.L. 1986. Strategic Management of Uncertainty. *Academy of Management Review*, 11(4): 777-790.

Jauch, L.R., and Glueck, W.F. 1984. *Strategic Management and Business Policy*. New York: McGraw-Hill.

Jauch, L.R., Osborn, R.L. and Glueck, W.F. 1980. Short Term Success in Large Business Organizations: The Environment-Strategy Connection. *Strategic Management Journal*, 1(1): 49-63.

Javidan, M. What Does Top Management Expect From Its Corporate Planning Department? A *Paper* presented at the Administrative Science Academy of Canada Conference, University of Ottawa, Canada.

Jelinek, M., Litterer, J.A., and Miles, R. 1982. *Organizations by Design: Theory and Practice*. Plano, TX: Business Publications.

Jemison, D.B. 1981a. Organizational versus Environmental Sources of Influence in Strategic Decision Making. *Strategic Management Journal*, 2(1): 77-90.

Jemison, D.B. 1981b. The Contributions of Administrative Behavior to Strategic Management. *Academy of Management Review*, 6: 633-642.

Jensen, M, & Meckling, P. (1976). Theory of the Firm: Managerial Behavior, Agency Costs, and Ownership Structure. *Journal of Financial Economics*. 3: 305-360.

Johnson, S. and Loveman, G. 1995. Starting Over: Poland After Communism. *Harvard Business Review*. March-April: 41-58.

Johnston, S. 1995. Managerial Dominance of Japan's Major Corporations. *Journal of Management*. 22 (2): 191-204.

Jones, G.R. and Butler, J. E. 1988. Costs, Revenue, and Business-Level Strategy. *Academy of Management Review*. 13(2): 202:213.

Jones, G.R. and Hill, C.W.L. (1988). Transaction Cost Analysis of Strategy-Structure Choice. *Strategic Management Journal*, 9:159-172.

Kahneman, D. and Tversky, A. 1979. Prospect Theory: An Analysis of Decision under Risk. *Econometrica*, 47(2): 263-291.

Kahneman, D. and Tversky, A. 1996. On the Reality of Cognitive Illusions. *Psychological Review*, 103(3): 582-592.

Kanuk, L. and Berenson, C. 1975. Mail Surveys Response Rates: A Literature Review. *Journal of Marketing Research* 12: 440-453.

Kanungo, R.N., and Wright, R.W. 1983. A Cross-Cultural Comparative Study of Managerial Job Attitudes. *Journal of International Business Studies*, 14(2): 115-130.

Kast, F.E. and Rosenzwieg, J.E. 1973. *Contingency Views of Organization and Management*. Chicago: IL: Science Research Association.

Katz, D. and Kahn, R.L. 1966. The *Social Psychology of Organizing*. New York: Wiley.

Keats, B. and Hitt, M. 1988. A causal model of linkages among environmental dimensions, macro-organizational characteristics and performance. *Academy of Management Journal*. 31: 570-598.

Kelley, H.H. 1967. Attribution Theory in Social Psychology. in Levine, D. (Ed.), *Nebraska Symposium on Motivation*. Lincoln, NE: University of Nebraska, 15.

Kerin, R.A., and Harvey, M.G. 1976. Methodological Considerations in Corporate Mail Surveys: A Research Note. *Journal of Business Research*, 4(3): 276-281.

Kerlinger, F.N. 1973. *Foundations of Behavioral Research*. New York: Holt, Rinehart and Winston.

Keynes, J.M. 1965. *The General Theory of Employment, Interest and Money*. New York: Harcourt, Brace & World.

Khandwalla, P. N. 1978. Crisis response of competing versus noncompeting organizations. In Smart, C. F. and Stanbury, W. T. (eds.): 158-178. *Studies on Crisis Management*. Toronto: Butterworth.

Khandwalla, P.N. 1972. Environment and its Impact on the Organization. *International Studies of Management and Organization*, 2: 297-313.

Khandwalla, P.N. 1976. The Techno-Economic Ecology of Corporate Strategy. *Journal of Management Studies*, 13: 62-75.

Khandwalla, P.N. 1985. Pioneering Innovative Management: An Indian Excellence. Organizational Studies, 6(2): 161-183

Kiesler, S. and Sproul, L. 1982. Managerial Response to Changing Environments: Perspectives and Problem Sensing from Social Cognition. *Administrative Science Quarterly*, 37: 548-570.

Klimoski, R. 1994. A "Total Quality" Special Issue. *Academy of Management Review*. 19 (3): 390-392.

Kneale, D. 1987. Xerox Finally Succumbing to Pressure. *Wall Street Journal*, 42.

Knight, F. 1921. *Risk, Uncertainty and Profit*. Boston, MA: Houghton Mifflin.

Koberg, C.S., and Ungson, G.R. 1987. The Effect of Environmental Uncertainty and Dependence on Organizational Structure and Performance: A Comparative Study. *Journal of Management*, 13(4): 725-737.

Kobrin, S.J. 1982. *Managing Political Risk: Strategic Response to Environmental Change*. Berkeley, CA: University of California Press.

Kobrin, S.J. 1988. Expatriate Reduction and Strategic Control in American Multinational Corporations. *Human Resource Management,* 27: (1): 63-75.

Koenderman, T. 1982. *Sanctions: The Threat to South Africa.* Johnannesburg: Jonathan Ball Publishers.

Kotter, J.P. 1982. What Effective General Managers Really Do. *Harvard Business Review,* 6: 156-167.

Kreinovich, V. 2000. Interval Methods in Knowledge Representation. *International Journal of Uncertainty, Fuzziness & Knowledge-Based Systems*; 8(5): 619-621.

Lado, A. A. and Wilson, M. C. 1994. Human Resource Systems and Sustained Competitive Advantage: A Competency-Based Perspective. *Academy of Management Review.* 19 (4): 699-727.

Lado, A.A., Boyd, N.G. and Hanlon, SC. 1997. Competition, Cooperation, and the Search for Economic Rents: A Syncretic Model. *Academy of Management Review.* 22(1): 110-141.

Lambley, P. 1980. *The Psychology of Apartheid,* Secker and Warburg, 105-106.

Langley, A. 1995. Between "Paralysis by Analysis" and "Extinction by Instinct." *Sloan Management Review.* 36(3 Spring): 63-76.

Lant, T. K. and Mezias, S. J. 1995. Managing Continuous Change: A Simulation Study of Organizational Learning and Entrepreneurship. *Strategic Management Journal.* 11 (Special Issue): 147-179.

Last, K. 1988. Economy. *Weekly Mail,* Witwatersrand, South Africa, 18.

Lawrence, P.R. and Lorsch, J.W. 1967. *Organization and Environment.* Boston, MA: Graduate School of Business Administration, Harvard University.

Leach, G. 1986. *South Africa: No Easy Path to Peace.* London: Routledge and Kegan Paul.

Leape, J., Baskin, B., & Underhill, S. 1985. *Business in the Shadow of Apartheid.* Lexington, MA: D.C. Heath.

Lenz, R.T. 1981. Determinants of Organizational Performance: An Interdisciplinary Review. *Strategic Management Journal,* 2(2): 131-154.

Lenz, R.T., and Engledow, J.L. 1986. Environmental Analysis: The Applicability of Current Theory. *Strategic Management Journal,* 7(4): 329-346.

Leonard, R. 1986. The Crisis in South Africa: Rising Pressures on Multinationals. *Multinational Business* Quarterly, 3: 17-29.

Leontiades, M. 1982. Choosing the Right Manager to Fit the Strategy, *Journal of Business Strategy,* 3(2): 58-69.

Leontiades, M., and Tezel, A. 1980. Planning Perceptions and Planning Perceptions and Planning Results. *Strategic Management Journal,* 1: 65-76.

Levy, D. 1994. Chaos Theory and Strategy: Theory, Application, and Managerial Implications. *Strategic Management Journal.* 15 (Summer): 167-178.

Lewis, G. J. 2004. Uncertainty and Equivocality in the Commercial and Natural Environments: The Implications for Organizational Design. *Corporate Social Responsibility and Environmental Management*, 11(3): 167-177.

Lewis, G.J. and Harvey, B. 2001. Perceived Environmental Uncertainty: The Extension of Miller's Scale to the Natural Environment. *Journal of Management Studies*, 382): 201-235.

Likert, R. 1967. *The Human Organization: Its Management and Value*. New York: McGraw-Hill.

Lilienthal, D.E. 1960. The Multinational Corporation. In Anshen, M. and Bach, E.L (eds.), *Management and Corporations*. New York: McGraw-Hill.

Lindsay Smith, H. 1979. *Anatomy of Apartheid*. Germiston, South Africa: Khanya Publishers.

Lindsay, W.M., and Rue, L.W. 1978. Impact of business Environment on the long Range Planning Process: A Contingency View. *Academy of Management Proceedings*, 116-120.

Linsky, A. 1975. Stimulating Response to Mail Questionnaires: A Review. *Public Opinion Quarterly*, 39: 82-101

Lipset, S.M. 1985. Canada and the U.S.: The Cultural Dimension. in Doran, C.F. and Sigler, J.H., *Canada and the U.S.: Enduring Friendships and Persistent Stress*. Englewood Cliffs, NJ: Prentice-Hall.

Lipton, M. 1985. *Capitalism and Apartheid*, Rowman and Allanheld, Totowa, NJ.

Little, A.D. 1978-1985. Reports *on the Sullivan Signatory Companies*. Cambridge, MA: Arthur D. Little, Inc.

Litvak, L., DeGrasse, R., & McTigue, K. 1978. *South Africa: Foreign investment and Apartheid*. Washington, DC: Institute of Policy Studies.

Lodge, G. 1975. *The New American Ideology*. New York: Alfred Knopf.

Lorange, P., and Vancil R.F. 1977. *Strategic Planning Systems*. Englewood Cliffs, NJ. Prentice-Hall.

Loubser, J.J. 1968. Calvinism, Equality, and Inclusion: The Case of Afrikaner Calvinism. In Eisenstadt, S.N., (ed.). *The Protestant Ethic and Modernization: A Comparative View*. New York: Basic Books.

LRP. 2002. Individual Planning Topics--Strategic Planning. *Long Range Planning*, 25(5): 124-128.

Mack, R. P. 1971. Planning for Uncertainty: Decision Making in Business and Government. New York: Wiley.

MacMillan, W. M. 1963. *Bantu, Boer and Briton: The Making of the South African Native Problem*. London: Oxford University Press.

Madhok, A. 2002. Reassessing the Fundamentals and Beyond: Ronald Coase, the Transactional Cost and Resource-Based Theories of the Firm and the Institutional Structure of Production. *Strategic Management Journal*, 23: 535-550.

Mahoney, J.T. and Pandian, J.R. 1992. The Resource-Based View within the Conversation of Strategic Management. *Strategic Management Journal*, 13(5): 363-380.

Majd, S. and Pindyck, R. S. 1987. Time to build, option value and investment decisions. *Journal of Financial Economics*. 18: 7-27.

Malcolm, A.H. 1985. *The Canadians*. Toronto, ON: Bantam Books.

Malik, Z.A., and Karger, D.W. 1975. Does Long Range Planning Improve Company Performance? *Management Review*, 64: 26-31.

Malknight, T. W. 1995. Globalization of an ethnocentric firm: An evolutionary perspective. *Strategic Management Journal*. 16 (2): 119-142.

Malone, D., and Goodin S. 1997. An Analysis of U.S. Disinvestment from South Africa: Unity, Rights, and Justice. *Journal of Business Ethics*, 16(16): 1687-703.

Mangaliso, M. P. 1992. The Corporate Social Challenge for the Multinational Corporation. *Journal of Business Ethics*, 11(7): 491-500.

Mangaliso, M. P. and Lane, P. J. 1992. The Role of Turbulence in the Strategic Management Literature. *Proceedings of the Eastern Academy of Management Meetings*. Baltimore, MD.

Mangaliso, M.P. 1995. The Strategic Usefulness of Information As Perceived by Middle Managers. *Journal of Management*, 25(2): 231-250.

Mangaliso, M.P. 1999. Disinvestment by Multinational Corporations. In Crawford, N. & Klotz, A. (eds.), *How Sanctions Work: Lessons from South Africa*, pp. 145-158. London: MacMillan.

Mangaliso, M.P., Mir, R.A. and Knipes, B.J. 1998. Towards a Framework of Firm Responsiveness to Turbulent Environments. *Southern African Business Review*, 2(2): 25-37.

March, J.G., and Simon, M.A. 1958. *Organizations*. New York: Wiley.

Mascarenhas, B. 1985. Flexibility: Its Relationship to Environmental Dynamism and Complexity. *International Studies of Management and Organization*, 14(4): 107-124.

Matlosa, K. 2001. Essay Review of *Democracy and Governance Review: Mandela's Legacy, 1994-1999*. Muthien, Y., Khosa, M., and Magubane, B. (eds.) (2000). Pretoria: Human Sciences Research Council. *African Journal of Political Science*, 6(2):109-114.

Mayer P., and Mayer, I. 1971. *Townsmen and Tribesmen*. Cape Town: Oxford University Press.

Maylam, P. 1986. *A History of African People In South Africa*. New York: St. Marfia Press.

McCann, J. E. and Selsky, J. 1984. Hyperturbulence and the Emergence of Type 5 Environments. *Academy of Management Review*, 9(3): 460-470

McFarlin, D.M., Coster, E.A. and Mogale-Pretorius, C. (1999). South African Management Development in the Twenty-First Century: Moving toward an Africanized model. *Journal of Management Development*. 18 (1): 63-78.

McGee, J.E. and Sawyer, O.O. 2003. Uncertainty and Information Search Activities: A Study of Owner–Managers of Small High-Technology Manufacturing Firms. *Journal of Small Business Management*, 41(4): 385-402.

McGrath, R. G., Ferrier, W. J., and Mendelow, A. L. 2004. Real options as engines of choice and heterogeneity. *Academy of Management Review*, 20(1): 86-101.

McKerrow, K.K. and McKerrow, J.E. 1991. Naturalistic Misunderstanding of the Heisenberg Uncertainty Principle. *Educational Researcher*, 20(1): 17-20.

McWilliams, A., Siegel, D. and Teoh, S.H. 1999. Issues in the Use of the Event Study Methodology: A Critical Analysis of Corporate Social Responsibility Studies. *Organizational Research Methods*, 2 (4): 340-365.

Mercer, D. 2001. Fear of the Future: A New Management Approach. *Management Decision*, 39(8): 654-659

Metcalfe, J.L. 1974. Systems Models, Economic Models and the Causal Texture of Organizational Environments: An Approach to Macro-Organization Theory. *Human Relations*, 639-663.

Metcalfe, J.L. and McQuillan, W. 1977. Managing Turbulence. In Nystrom, P. and Starbuck, W. (eds.), *Prescriptive Models of Organizations*, North-Holland, Amsterdam, 7-23.

Meyer, A.D., Brooks, G.R. and Goes, J.B. 1990. Environmental Jolts and Industry Revolutions: Organizational Responses to Discontinuous Change. *Strategic Management Journal*, 11: 93-110.

Meyer, A.D., Goes, J.B. and Brooks, G.R. 1994. Organizations reacting to hyperturbulence. In G.P. Huber and W. H. Glick (eds.). *Organizational Change and Redesign: Ideas and Insights for Improving Performance*, 66-111. New York: Oxford University Press.

Meyers, G. C. and Holusha, J. 1986. *When It Hits the Fan: Managing the Nine Crises for Business*. Boston: Houghton Mifflin.

Meznar, M.B., Nigh, D. and Kwok, C.C. 1994. Effect of Announcements of Withdrawal from South Africa on Stockholder Wealth. *Academy of Management Journal*. 37(6): 1633-1648.

Miles, R. E. and Snow, C. C. 1978. *Organizational Strategy, Structure, and Process*. New York: MacGraw Hill.

Miles, R. E. and Snow, C. C. 1994. *Fit, Failure, and the Hall of Fame*. New York: The Free Press.

Miles, R.E. and Snow, C.S., and Pfeffer, J. 1974. Organization-Environment: Concepts and Issues. *Industrial Relations*, 13: 244-264.

Miller, C. C. and Cardinal, L. B. 1994. Strategic Planning and Firm Performance: A Synthesis of More Than Two Decades of Research. *Academy of Management Journal*. 37 (6): 1649-1665.

Miller, D. 1983. The Correlates of Entrepreneurship in three Types of Firms. *Management Science*, 29(7): 770-791.

Miller, D. 1987. The Structural and Environmental Correlates of Business Strategy. *Strategic Management Journal*, 8(1): 55-76.

Miller, D. 1992. Environmental fit versus internal fit. *Organization Science*. 3 (2): 159-178.

Miller, D. and Friesen, P. 1980. Archetypes of Organizational Transition. *Administrative Science Quarterly*, Vol. 25.

Miller, D., and Friesen, P. 1983. Strategy-Making and Environment: The Third Link. *Strategic Management Journal*, 4: 221-235.

Milliken, F.J. 1987. Three Types of Perceived Uncertainty about the Environment: State, Effect, and Response Uncertainty. *Academy of Management Review*, 2: 133-143.

Milman, A. 1986. Perceptual Differences Between Canadian and U.S. CEOs As to Their Role Responsibilities: The Canadian Perspective. *Unpublished Ph.D. Dissertation*, University of Massachusetts, Amherst, MA.

Minter, W. 1986. "South Africa: Straight Talk on Sanctions. *Foreign Policy*, 65: 43-63.

Mintzberg, H. 1973. Strategy Making in Three Modes. *California Management Review*, 16(2): 44-53.

Mintzberg, H. 1979. *The Structuring of Organizations*. Englewood Cliffs, NJ: Prentice-Hall.

Mintzberg, H. 1984. Who Should Control the Corporation? *California Management Review*, 27(1): 90-114.

Mintzberg, H. 1990. The Design School: Reconsidering the Basic Premises of Strategic Management. *Strategic Management Journal*, 11: 171-195.

Mintzberg, H. 1991a. Crafting Strategy. In H. Mintzberg and J. B. Quinn (Ed.), *The Strategy Concept*. 105-114. Englewood Cliffs, NJ: Prentice-Hall Inc.

Mintzberg, H. 1991b. Learning 1, Planning 0: Reply to Igor Ansoff. *Strategic Management Journal*. 12 (6): 463-466.

Mintzberg, H. 1994a. That's Not 'Turbulence,' Chicken Little, It's Really Opportunity. *Planning Review*, 22(6): 7-10.

Mintzberg, H. 1994b. Rethinking Strategic Planning Part I: Pitfalls and Fallacies. *Long Range Planning*, 27(3): 12.

Mintzberg, H. 1994c. *The Rise and Fall of Strategic Planning: Reconceiving roles for Planning, Plans, Planners*. New York: The Free Press.

Mintzberg, H. 1994d. Rethinking Strategic Planning Part II: New Roles for Planners. *Long Range Planning*, 27(3): 22.

Mintzberg, H. and McHugh, A. 1985. Strategy formation in an adhocracy. *Administrative Science Quarterly*: 160-197.

Mintzberg, H., and Waters, J. 1985. Of Strategies, Deliberate and Emergent. *Strategic Management Journal*, 6(3): 257-272.

Mitroff, I. I. and Kilmann, R. H. 1984. *Corporate Tragedies: Product Tampering, Sabotage, and other Catastrophes*. New York: Praeger.

Mitroff, I. I. and Pauchant, T. 1990. *We Are So Big And Powerful Nothing Can Happen To Us*. New York: Caroll Publishing.

Mogotlane, R.A. 2009. The HIV/AIDS Malady in Southern Africa: Observations from the Epicentre. Keynote Address at the *13th International Conference on Managing in a Global Economy*. Held Rio de Janeiro. June 24.

Moller, V. 1999. South African Quality of Life Trends in the Late 1990s: Major Divides in Perceptions. *Society in Transition*, 30 (2): 93-105.

Montanari, J.R. 1979. Strategic Choice: A Theoretical Analysis. *Journal of Management Studies*, 16(2): 202-221.

Montgomery, C. 1979. Diversification, Market Strategy and Firm Performance: An Extension of Rumelt's Model. *Unpublished Ph.D. Dissertation*, Purdue University.

Moodie, D.T. 1975. *The Rise of Afrikanerdom Power, Apartheid and the Afrikaner Civil Religion*. Berkeley, CA: University of California Press.

Moor, J. F. 1993. Predators and prey: A new ecology of competition. *Harvard Business Review*. May-June: 75.

Morgan, G., and Smircich, L. 1980. The Case for Qualitative Research. *Academy of Management Review*, 5(4): 491-500.

Mthombeni, M.S. 2006. The Role of Multinational Corporations in South Africa: A Political Perspective. *Unpublished Masters' Thesis*. Bloemfontein: University of Free State. Accessed on September 9, 2009 from: http://etd.uovs.ac.za/ETD-db/theses/available/etd-02192007-132437/unrestricted/MthombeniMS.pdf

Myers, S. C. 1984. Finance Theory and Financial Strategy. *Interfaces*. 14 (1): 126-137.

Nasser, M.E. (Chair). 1986. *Economic Participation in South Africa*. Pretoria, South Africa: School of Business Leadership, UNISA.

Nayyar, P. 1993. On the measurement of competitive strategy: Evidence from a large, multi-product, U.S. firm. *Academy of Management Journal*. 36 (6): 1652-1669.

Neghandi, A.R. 1975. Comparative Management and Organization Theory: A Marriage Needed. *Academy of Management Journal*, 18(2): 334-344.

Neghandi, A.R. 1983. Cross-Cultural Management Research: Trend and Future Directions, *Journal of International Business*, 14: 17-28.

Neghandi, A.R. and Prasad, B. 1971. *Comparative Management*, Appleton, New York.

Nelson, R.R. and Winter, S. 1982. *An Evolutionary Theory of Economic Change*. Cambridge, MA: Harvard University Press.

Newman, A., and Bowers, C. 1984. *Foreign Investment in South Africa and Namibia*. Washington, D.C.: Investor Responsibility Research Center.

Newsweek 2009. Accessed on April 21, 2009 from http://www.newsweek.com/id/163194?tid=relatedcl.

Ngassam, C. 1992. *An Examination of Stock Market Reactions to U.S. Corporate Divestitures in South Africa*. Montclair State University, NJ: Center for Economic Research on Africa, Accessed on July 9, 2009 from: ftp://ftp.cba.uri.edu/classes/dash/fin625/StkRetDivestSA.pdf.

Nie, N.H., Hull, C.H., Jenkins, J.G. Steinbrenner, K., and Bent, D.H. 1975. *SPSS: Statistical Package for the Social Sciences.* New York: McGraw Hill.

Nisbett, R. and Ross, L. 1980. Human Interference: *Strategies and Shortcomings of Social Judgment.* Englewood Cliffs, NJ: Prentice-Hall.

Norburn, D. 1987. Corporate Leaders in Britain and America: A Cross-national Analysis. *Journal of International Business Studies*, 18(3): 15-32.

Norvall, M. 1985. The strategic role of South Africa. *Conservative Digest*, 11(4): 18.

Nunnally, J. 1967. *Psychometric Theory.* New York: McGraw-Hill.

Oler, D.K., Harrison, J. S. and Allen, M. R. 2008. The Danger of Misinterpreting Short-Window Event Study Findings in Strategic Management Research: An Empirical Illustration Using Horizontal Acquisitions. *Strategic Organization*, 6(2): 151 - 184.

Omond, R. 1986. *The Apartheid Handbook.* New York: Penguin Books.

Organ, D.W. and Hamner, W.C. 1982. *Organizational Behavior.* Plano, TX: Business Publications.

Orkin, M. 1986. *The Struggle and the Future: What Black South Africans Really Think.* Johannesburg: Ravan Press.

Orpen, C. 1979. The Effects of Job Enrichment to Employee Satisfaction, Motivation, Involvement, and Performance: A Field Experiment. *Human Relations*, 32: 189-217.

Orpen, C. 1987. The Attitudes of United States and South African Managers to Corporate Social Responsibility, *Journal of Business Ethics*, 6: 89-96.

Parkhe, A. 1993. Strategic alliance structuring: A game theoretic and transaction cost examination of inter-firm cooperation. *Academy of Management Journal.* 36 (4): 749-829.

Parnell, J.A., Lester, D.L, and Menefee, M.L. 2000. Strategy as a Response to Organizational Uncertainty: An Alternative Perspective on the Strategy-Performance Relationship. *Management Decision*, 38(8): 520-530.

Parnell, J.A., Lester, D.L. and Menefee, M.L. 2000. Strategy as a Response to Organizational Uncertainty: An Alternative Perspective on the Strategy-Performance Relationship. *Management Decision*, 38(8): 520-531.

Pascoe, E. 1987. *South Africa: Trouble Land.* New York: Franklin Watts.

Pasquero, J. 1988. Bilateral Protectionism: Lessons from Cause Celebre. *California Management Review*, 30(2): 107-123.

Paton, A. 1948. *Cry, the Beloved Country.* New York: Scribner's Sons.

Patterson, M. 2002. Learning In Manufacturing Organizations: What Factors Predict Effectiveness? *Human Resource Development International*, 5(1): 55-73.

Paul, K. 1987. U.S. companies in South Africa. In S. P. Sethi (Ed.), *The South African Quagmire*, 395-407. Englewood Cliffs, NJ: Prentice Hall.

Payne, J.L. 1974. Fishing Expedition Probability: The Statistics of Post-Hoc Hypothesizing. *Polity*, 7(1): 130-138.

Pearce, J.A. (II) and Robinson. 1985. *Strategic Management: Strategy Formulation and Implementation*. Homewood, IL: Irwin.

Pearce, J.A. (II), Robbins, D.K. and Robinson, R.B. (Jr.). 1987. The Impact of Grand Strategy and Planning Formality on Performance. *Strategic Management Journal*, 8: 125-134.

Pearce, J.A. (II). 1982. Executive Level Perspective on the Strategic Management Process. *California Management Review*, 24(1): 39-48.

Pearce, J.A. (II). 1982. Selecting Among Alternative Grand Strategies. *California Management Review*, 24(3): 23-31.

Penrose, E.T. 1959. *The Theory of the Growth of the Firm*. Oxford, England: Oxford University Press.

Perrow, C. 1967. A Framework for Comparative Organizational Analysis. *American Sociological Review*, 32: 194-208.

Perrow, C. 1970. *Organizational Analysis: A Sociological View*. Monterey, CA: Brooks/Cote.

Perrow, C. 1972. *Complex Organizations*. Glenview, IL: Scott, Foresman and Co.

Perrow, C. 1974. Is Business Really Changing? *Organizational Dynamics*, 3(1): 30-45.

Perrow, C. 1977. The Bureaucratic Paradox: The Efficient Organization Centralizes in Order to Decentralize. *Organizational Dynamics*, 5 (4): 3-15.

Perrow, C. 1984. *Normal Accidents*. New York: Basic Books.

Perrow, C. 1985. Comment on Langton's 'Ecological Theory of Bureaucracy.' *Administrative Science Quarterly*, 30 (2): 278-289.

Peters, T.J. 1984. Strategy Follows Structure: Developing Distinctive Skills. *California Management Review*, 26(3): 111-125.

Peters, T.J. and Waterman, R.H. 1982. *In Search of Excellence: Lessons from America's Best Run Companies*. New York: Harper & Row.

Pfeffer, J. and Salancik, G.R. 1978. *The External Control of Organizations: A Resource Dependency Perspective*. New York: Harper and Row.

Phelan, S. E. 1995. From Chaos to Complexity in Strategic Planning. Paper presented at the *55th Annual Meeting of the Academy of Management*. Vancouver, BC, Canada. August 8.

Phillips, L.W. 1981. Assessing Measurement Error in Key Informant Reports: A Methodological Note on Organizational Analysis in Marketing. *Journal of Marketing*, 5: 395-414.

Pitelis, C.N. and Pseiridis, A.N. 1999. Transaction Costs versus Resource Value? *Journal of Economic Studies*. 26 (3): 221- 240.

Polonsky, M.J. and Grau, S.L. 2008. Evaluating the Social Value of Charitable Organizations: A Conceptual Foundation. *Journal of Macromarketing*, 28(2): 130-140.

Porter, M.E. 1980. *Competitive Strategy: Techniques for Analyzing Industries and Competitors*. New York: The Free Press.

Porter, M.E. 1981. The Contributions of Industrial Organization to Strategic Management. *Academy of Management Review,* 6: 609-620.

Porter, M.E. 1985. *Competitive Advantage: Creating and Sustaining Superior Performance.* New York: The Free Press.

Posnikoff, J.F. 1997. Disinvestment from South Africa: They Did Well by Doing Good. *Contemporary Economic Policy.* 15(1): 76-86.

Prahalad, C. K. and Bettis, R. A. 1986. The Dominant Logic: The New Linkage Between Diversity and Performance. *Strategic Management Journal.* 7: 485-501.

Prahalad, C. K. and Hamel, G. 1990. The Core Competence of the Corporation. *Harvard Business Review.* 3: 79-91.

Pugh, D.S. Hickson, D.J., Hinnings, C.R., and Turner, C. 1969. Context of Organization Structures. *Administrative Science Quarterly,* 14(1): 91-114.

Quinn, J. B. 1991. Strategic Change: "Logical Incrementalism". In H. Mintzberg and J. B. Quinn (Ed.), *The Strategy Concept.* 96-104. Englewood Cliffs, NJ: Prentice-Hall Inc.

Quinn, J.B. 1980. *Strategies for Change: Logical Incrementalism,* Irwin, Homewood, IL.

Race Relations Survey 1986, Part 1. South African Institute of Race Relations, (Cooper, C., and Staff), Johannesburg South Africa.

Ramanujam, V. and Venkatraman, N. 1984. An Inventory and Critique of Strategy Research Using the PIMS Data Base. *Academy of Management Review,* 9(1): 138-151.

Randall, D.J. 1996. Prospects for the Development of a Black Business Class in South Africa. *Journal of Modern African Studies,* 34(4): 661-686.

Rashid, S. 1987. Political Economy as Moral Philosophy: Dugal Stewart of Edinburgh. *Australian Economic Papers,* 26(48): 145-156.

Raspberry, W. 1986. No Way to Disinvest. *The Washington Post.* November 14

Raymond, L., Julien, P.A. and Ramangalaby, C. 2001. Technological Scanning by Small Canadian Manufacturers. *Journal of Small Business Management,* 39(2): 123-139.

Rhyne, L.C. 1986. The Relationship of Strategic Planning to Financial Performance. *Strategic Management Journal,* 7(5): 423-436.

Richman, L. S. 1995. The Economy: Managing through a downturn. *Fortune.* August 7: 59-64.

Robins, J.A. 1987. Organizational Economics: Notes on the Use of Transaction-Cost Theory in the Study of Organizations. *Administrative Science Quarterly,* 32(1): 68-86.

Robins-Mowry, D. 1988. *Canada-U.S. Relations: Perceptions and Misperceptions.* Lanham, MD: Aspen Institute for Humanistic Studies, University Press.

Roeber, R.J.C. 1973. *The Organization in a Changing Environment.* Reading, MA: Addison-Wesley.

Rosenau, P. M. 1992. *Postmodernism and the Social Sciences.* Princeton, NJ: Princeton Univeristy Press.

Ross, M. and Sicoly, F. 1979. Egocentric Biases in Availability and Attribution. *Journal of Personality and Social Psychology.* 37: 322-336.

Ross, M. and Sicoly, F. 1982. Egocentric Biases in Availability and Attribution. In D. Kahneman, P. Slovic and A. Tversky (Eds.), *Judgment under Uncertainty: Heuristics and Biases* (pp. 179-189). Cambridge, UK: Cambridge University Press.

Rossi, P.H. Wright, J.D. and Anderson, A.B. 1983. *Handbook of Survey Research.* Orlando, FL: Academic Press.

Rossiter, C. 1985. *Bureaucratic Struggle for Control of U.S. Foreign Aid.* Boulder, CO: Westview Press.

Rothschild, W.E. 1979. *Strategic Alternatives.* New York: Amacom.

Rouse, L. 1987. Dealers and Staff Go for ABI's Share Offer. *Business Day.*

Rowe, G. and Wright, G. 1999. The Delphi Technique as a Forecasting Tool: Issues and Analysis. *International Journal of Forecasting,* 15: 353 -375.

Rubin, I. S. 1979. Retrenchment, Loose Structure, and Adaptability in Universities," *Sociology of Education.* 52: 211-222.

Rumelt, R.P. 1974. *Strategy, Structure, and Economic Performance in Large Industrial Corporations.* Boston, MA: Harvard University Press.

Rumelt, R.P. 1984. Towards a Strategic Theory of the Firm. In Lamb, R.B. (Ed.). *Competitive Strategic Management.* Englewood Cliffs, NJ: Prentice-Hall.

Rumelt, R.P. 1987. Theory, Strategy, and Change. In D.J. Teece (Ed.), *The Competitive Challenge:* 137-158. Cambridge, MA: Ballinger.

Salomon, G. 1985. Accounting Rates of Return. *American Economic Review,* 495-504.

Savage, L. 1954. *The Foundations of Statistics.* New York: Wiley.

Scheibe, K.E. 1970. *Beliefs and Values.* New York: Holt, Rinehart & Winston.

Schendel, D. and Patton, G.R. 1976. A Simultaneous Equation Model of Corporate Strategy. *Paper No. 582,* Institute for Research in Behavioral, Economic, and Management Sciences, Krannert Graduate School of Management.

Schermerhorn, J.R. (Jr.). 1986. *Management for Productivity.* New York: Wiley.

Schmidt, E. 1985. *Decoding the Corporate Camouflage.* Washington, DC: Institute of Policy Studies.

Schoefler, S. 1977. Cross-sectional Study of Strategy, Structure, and Performance: Aspects of the PIMS Program in H. Thorelli (Ed.), *Strategy + Structure = Performance,* Indiana University Press, Bloomington, Ind. 108-121.

Schoefler, S. Buzzell, R. and Heany, D. 1974. Profit Impact on Marketing Strategies, *Harvard Business Review,* (52): 137-149.

Schumpeter, J. 1950. *Capitalism, Socialism and Democracy.* New York: Harper and Row.

Schumpeter. J. A. 1934. *The Theory of Economic Development.* Cambridge, MA. Harvard University Press.

Schwenk, C. 1984. Cognitive Simplification Processes in Strategic Decision-making. *Strategic Management Journal,* 5(2): 111-128.

Seaton, K.B. 2002. Strategic Environmental Assessment: Effective Planning Instrument or Lost Concept? *Planning Practice & Research,* 17(1): 31-45.

Seedat, A. 1987. Health in apartheid South Africa. In D. Mermelstein (Ed.), *The Anti-Apartheid Reader,* New York: Grove Press, 169-176.

Segal, G. 1990. China after Tiananmen. *Asian Journal,* 21(2): 144-154.

Seidman, A. and Seidman, N. 1978. *South Africa and U.S. Multinational Corporations.* Westport, CT: Lawrence Hill and Company.

Shetty, Y.K. 1979. A New Look at Corporate Goals. *California Management Review,* 22: 71-79.

Shrader, C.B. Taylor, L. and Dalton, D.R. 1984. Strategic Planning and Organizational Performance: A Critical Essay. *Journal of Management,* 10(2): 149-171.

Shrivastava, P. 1987. *Bhopal: Anatomy of Crisis.* Cambridge, MA: Ballinger Publishing.

Shrivastava, P. 1994. Castrated environment: greening organizational studies. *Organization studies.* 15 (5): 705-721.

Shrivastava, P. and Mitroff, I. I. 1987. Strategic management of corporate crises. *Columbia Journal of World Business.* 22 (1): 5-11.

Simon, H.A. 1982. *Models of Bounded Rationality.* Cambridge, Mass. MIT Press.

Simon, H.A. 1959. Theories of Decision Making in Economics. *American Economics Review,* 59: 253-283.

Sincere, R.L. (Jr.). 1986. *The Politics of Sentiment.* Washington, DC: Ethics and Public Policy Center.

Singh, J.V. 1986. Performance, Slack and Risk-Taking in Organizational Decision Making. *Academy of Management Journal,* (29)3: 562-585.

Slovic, P. 1969. Analyzing the Expert Judge: A Descriptive Study of Stockbrokers' Decision Processes. *Journal of Applied Psychology,* 53: 255-263.

Smart, C. and Vertinsky, I. 1977. Designs for Crisis Decision Units. *Administrative Science Quarterly,* 29: 640-657.

Smart, C. and Vertinsky, I. 1984. Strategy and the Environment: A Study of Corporate Responses to Crises. *Strategic Management Journal,* 5(3): 199-213.

Smircich, L. and Stubbart, C. 1985. Strategic Management in an Enacted World. *Academy of Management Review.* 10: 724-736.

Smith, R. 1986. Why G.M. Decided to Quit South Africa. *New York Times,* October 30: 27.

Smock, D. 1983. *Black Education in South Africa: The Current Situation.* New York: Institute of International Education.

SNL. 1936. "Uncertainty Principle" Extended to Include Biology. *Science News-Letter*, 29(777 February 29): 133.

Snow, C.S. and Hambrick, D.C. 1980. Measuring Organizational Structures: Some Theoretical and Methodological Problems. *Academy of Management Review*, 5(4): 527-538.

Snyder, N. H. 1987. Validating measures of environmental change. *Journal of Business Research.* 15 (1): 31-43.

Snyder, N. H. and Glueck, W. F. 1982. Can Environmental Volatility be Measured Objectively? *Academy of Management Journal.* 25: 185-192.

Snyder, N.H. 1979. An Analysis of the Impact of Environmental Volatility on the Effectiveness of Strategic Planning for U.S. Firms in Selected Industries between 1972 and 1977. *Unpublished Ph. D. Dissertation*, University of Georgia.

Söderblom, J.D. 2005. Gini Coefficients: Their Role and Operation. *World International Community Experts.* Accessed on September 15, 2009 from http://world-ice.com/Articles/Gini Coefficients.pdf.

Southall, R. 2004. The ANC & Black Capitalism in South Africa. *Review of African Political Economy*, 31(100): 313-328.

Sparks, A. 1990. *The Mind of South Africa.* New York: Ballentine Books.

Spencer, W. J. and Grindley, P. 1993. SEMATECH after Five Years: High-technology consortia and U.S. competitiveness. *California Management Review.* 35 (4): 9-32.

Spender, J-C. 1996. Making Knowledge the Basis of a Dynamic Theory of the Firm. *Strategic Management Journal*, 17 (Special Special Issue): 27-43.

Spivey, J.K. (2008). Coke vs. Pepsi: The Cola Wars in South Africa during the Anti-Apartheid Era. *Unpublished Master's Thesis.* Atlanta, GA: Georgia State University.

Stacey, R. D. 1991. *The Chaos Frontier.* Oxford: Butterworth-Heinemann.

Standard & Poor's Index 1957-1998. Accessed on April 2004 from http://www.standardandpoors.com

Standard Bank Review. 1985. Economics and Planning Division, Standard Bank Investment Corporation Limited, South Africa, 1-2.

Starbuck, W. G., and Hedberg, B. L. T. 1977. Saving an organization from stagnating environments. In Thorelli, H. (ed.): 249-258. *Strategy + Structure = Performance.* Bloomington, IN: Indiana University Press.

Starbuck, W. G., Greve, A., and Hedberg, B. L. T. 1978. Responding to Crisis. *Journal of Business Administration.* 9: 111-137.

Starbuck, W.R. 1976. Organization and their Environments. in Dunnette, M. (ed.), *Handbook of Industrial and Organizational Psychology.* Chicago, IL: Rand McNally.

Stata, R. 1989. Organizational learning--the key to management innovation. *Sloan Management Review*, pp. 63-74.

Staw, B.M. 1981. The Escalation of Commitment to a Course of Action *Academy of Management Review*, 6(4): 577-587.

Staw, B.M. and Swajkowski, E. 1975. The Scarcity-Munifecence Component of Organizational Environments and the Commission of Illegal Acts. *Administrative Science Quarterly*, 20: 62-81.

Staw, B.M., Sandelas, L.E. and Dutton, J.E. 1981. Threat-Rigidity Effects in Organizational Behavior: A Multilevel Analysis. *Administrative Science Quarterly*, 26: 501-524.

Steiner, G.A. 1979. Strategic Planning: *What Every Manager Must Know*. New York: The Free Press.

Stogdill, R. 1965. *Handbook of Leadership: A Survey of Theory and Research*. New York: The Free Press.

Stokes, R.G. 1975. Afrikaner Colonialism and Economic Action: The Weberian Thesis in South Africa, *American Journal of Sociology*, 81: 62-81.

Stopford, J.M. and Wells, L.T. 1965. *Managing the Multinational Enterprise*. New York: Basic Books.

Stubbart, C.I. 1985. Why We Need a Revolution in Strategic Planning. *Long Range Planning*, 18(6): 68-76.

Sudman, S. 1976. *Applied Sampling*. New York: Academic Press.

Suh, W. S., Key, S. K. and Munchus, G. 2004. Scanning Behavior and Strategic Uncertainty: Proposing a New Relationship by Adopting New Measurement Constructs. *Management Decision*, Vol. 42(8): 1001-1016

Swamidas, P.M. and Newell, W.T. 1987. Manufacturing Strategy, Environmental Uncertainty and Performance: A Path Analytical Model. *Management Science* 33(4): 509-524.

Taylor, F.W. 1911. *The Principles of Scientific Management*. New York: Harper and Row.

Terryberry, S. 1968. The Evolution of Organizational Environments. *Administrative Science Quarterly*, 12: 337-396.

Thatcher, G. 1980. South Africa: How vital to the West? *Christian Science Monitor*, December 16:12-13.

Theobald, R. 1994. New Success Criteria for a Turbulent World. *Planning Review*. 22 (6): 10-13.

Thomas, F.A. (chair) 1981. *South Africa: Time Running Out: Study Commission on U.S. Policy towards South Africa*. Berkeley, CA: University of California Press.

Thompson, A.A. and Strickland, A.J. 1984. *Strategic Management Concepts and Cases*. Plano, TX: Business Publications.

Thompson, J.D. 1967. *Organizations in Action*. New York: McGraw Hill.

Thune, S.S. and House, R.J. 1970. Where Long-range Planning Pays Off. *Business Horizons*, 13(4): 81-87.

Thurow, R. 1987. What is Swaziland? Well, for One Thing It Isn't Switzerland. *Wall Street Journal*, October 1: 1.

Tichy, Noel. 1983. Essentials of Strategic Change Management. *Journal of Business Strategy*, 3(4): 55.

Toffler, A. 1970. *Future Shock.* New York: Bantam Book/Random House, Inc.

Tosi, H. Aldag, R. and Storey, R. 1973. On the Measurement of Environment: An Assessment of the Lawrence and Lorsch Environmental Uncertainty Scale. *Administrative Science Quarterly*, 18: 27-36.

Tull, D.S. and Hawkins, D.I. 1976. Marketing *Research Meaning, Measurement and Method.* New York: MacMillan.

Tung, R.L. 1987. Expatriate Assignments: Enhancing Success and Minimizing Failure. *Academy of Management Executive*, 1(2): 117-125.

Tuominen, M., Rajala, A., Möller, K. and Anttila, M. 2003. Assessing Innovativeness through Organisational Adaptability: A Contigency Approach. *International Journal of Technology Management*, 25(6/7): 643-659.

Tushman, M.L. and Anderson, P. Technological Discontinuities and Organizational Environments, *Administrative Science Quarterly*, 31: 439-465.

Tushman, M.L. and Romanelli E. 1985. Organizational Evolution: A Metamorphosis Model of Convergence and Reorientation. In L. L. Cummings and B. M. Staw (eds.), *Research in Organizational Behavior*, 7: 171-222. Greenwich, CT: JAI Press.

Tversky, A. and Kahneman, D. 1974. Judgment under Uncertainty: Heuristics and Biases. *Science*, 185: 1124-1131.

Tversky, A. and Kahneman, D. 1980. Causal Schemas in Judgments under Uncertainty. In M. Fishbein (Ed.). *Progress in Social Psychology*, 84-98. Hillsdale, NJ: Erlbaum.

Tversky, A. and Kahneman, D. 1982a. Availability: A heuristic for Judging Frequency and Probability. In D. Kahneman, P. Slovic, and A. Tversky (Eds.), *Judgment under Uncertainty: Heuristics and Biases*, 163-178. Cambridge, UK: Cambridge University Press.

Tversky, A. and Kahneman, D. 1982b. Judgments of and by Representativeness.In D. Kahneman, P. Slovic and A. Tversky (Eds.), *Judgment under Uncertainty: Heuristics and Biases*, 84-98. Cambridge, England: Cambridge University Press.

Tversky, A. and Kahneman, D. 1983. Extensional versus Intuitive Reasoning: The Conjunction Fallacy in Probability Judgment. *Psychological Review*, 91, 293-315.

Tversky, A. and Kahnemann, D. 1974. Judgment under Uncertainty: Heuristics and Biases. *Science*, 185: 1124-1131.

UNAID (2006). Overview of the Global Aids Epidemic. *2006 Report on the Global AIDS Epidemic.* Accessed on September 1, 2009 from http://data. unaids.org/pub/GlobalReport/2006/2006_GR_CH02_en.pdf

Ungson, G.R. 1978. The Relationship between Task Environmental Contingency, Structure, Organizational Role and Performance: An Empirical and Contextual Analysis. *Unpublished Ph.D. Dissertations*, Pennsylvania State University.

United Nations Center on Transnational Corporations. 1986. *Activities of Transnational Corporations in South Africa and Namibia.* New York: United Nations.

Urwick, L.F. 1960. The Problem of Management Semantics. *California Management Review*, 2(3): 77-83.

Van den Bergh, P. 1973. Social Science in Africa. Epistemological Problems. in Barr, W.M. Spam, D.H. and Tessler, M.A. *Survey Research in Africa*, 25-35. Evanston, IL: North Western University Press.

Van Gils, M.R. 1984. Interorganizational Relations and Networks. in Drenth, P.D.J., Thierry, H., Willems, P.J., and de Wolff, C.J., (eds.), 2: 1073-1100. *Handbook of Work and Organizational Psychology*, Wiley New York.

Van Vuuren, D.J. Wiehahn, N.E. Lombard, J.A. and Rhoodie, N.J. (eds.) 1983. *Change in South Africa.* Durban, South Africa: Butterworth.

Van Zwieten, J. 1999. How Not to Waste Your Investment in Strategy. *Training & Development*, 53(6): 48-54.

Vancil, R.F. and Lorange, P. 1975. Strategic Planning in Diversified Companies. *Harvard Business Review*, 53(1): 81-90.

Venkatraman, N. and Ramanujam, V. 1985. On the Correspondence between 'Primary' and 'Secondary' Measures of Business Economic Performance: An Attempt at Methodological Triangulation. *Faculty Working Paper*, Bureau of Economic and Business Research, University of Illinois, Urbana-Champaign, 1127.

Venkatraman, N. and Ramanujam, V. 1987. Measurement of Business Economic Performance: An Examination of Method Convergence. *Journal of Management*, 13(1): 109-122.

Von Neumann, J. and Morgenstern, O. 1947. *Theory of Games and Economic Behavior.* Princeton, NJ: Princeton University Press.

Voorhes, M. (ed.) 1986. *Directory Update*, South Africa Review Service, Investor Responsibility Research Center, Washington, D.C.

Vroom, V.H. 1966. Organizational Choice: A Study of Pre- and Post- Decision Processes. *Organizational Behavior and Human Performance*, 1: 212-225.

Wadhwa, V. 2009. Why Be an Ethical Company? They're Stronger and Last Longer. *BusinessWeek.* August 17. Accessed on September 4, 2009 from: http://www.businessweek.com/technology/content/aug2009/tc20090816_435499.htm

Waldman, D.A., Ramirez, G.G., House, R.J. and Puranam, P. 2001. Does Leadership Matter? CEO Leadership Attributes and Profitability under Conditions of Perceived Environmental Uncertainty. *Academy of Management Journal*, 44(1): 134-143.

Wartick, S.L. and Cochran, P.L. 1985. The Evolution of the Corporate Social Performance Model. *Academy of Management Review*, 10(4): 758-769.

Weber, M. 1947. *Theory of Social and Economic Organization*, (Translated by Henderson, A.M., and Parsons, T.) New York: The Free Press.

Weber, M. 1958. *The Protestant Ethic and the Spirit of Capitalism*. New York: Charles Scribner's and Sons.

Webster's New Collegiate Dictionary. 1977. Springfield, MA: G. & C. Merriam Company.

Weick, K. 1977. Organization Design: Organizations as Self Designing Systems. *Organizational Dynamics*. Springfield, MA: G. & C. Merriam Company, 31-46.

Weick, K. E. 1979. *The Social Psychology of Organizing*. Reading, MA: Addison-Wesley.

Wernerfelt, B. 1984. A Resource-Based View of the Firm. *Strategic Management Journal*, 5: 171-180.

Wernerfelt, B. 1995. The Resource-Based View of the Firm: Ten Years After. *Strategic Management Journal*. 16(3): 171-174.

Whitehill, A.M. (Jr.) 1964. Cultural Values and Employee Attitudes: United States and Japan. *Journal of Applied Psychology*, 48(1):

Whiteside, A. and Sunter, C. 2000. *AIDS: The Challenge for South Africa*. Tafelberg: Human and Rousseau.

Whitmore, W.J. 1976. Mail Survey Premiums and Response Bias. *Journal of Marketing Research*, 8: 46-50.

Whittaker, J.B. 1978. *Strategic Planning in a Rapidly Changing Environment*. Lexington, MA: D.C. Heath.

Williamson, O.E. 1985. *Economic Institutions of Capitalism*. New York: The Free Press.

Wills, L.A. and Beasly, J.E. 1982. The Use of Strategic Planning Techniques in the United Kingdom. *Omega*, 10: 433-440.

Winch, R. and Campbell, D.T. 1969. Proof? No. Evidence? Yes. The Significance of Tests of Significance. *American Sociologist*, 4: 14-143

Wiseman, F.A. 1976. Reassessment of the Effects of Personalization on Response Patterns in Mail Surveys. *Journal of Marketing Research*, 13(1): 110-111.

Woiceshyn, J. 2000. Technology Adoption: Organizational Learning in Oil Firms. *Organization Studies*, 21(6): 1095-1113.

Wood, D.J. 1991.Social Performance Revisited. *Academy of Management Review*, 16(4): 691-718.

Wood, D.R. and LaForge. 1979. The Impact of Comprehensive Planning on Financial Performance. *Academy of Management Journal*, 22: 516-526.

Woods, D. 1986. *South African Dispatches: Letters to My Countrymen*. New York: Holt.

Woodward, J. 1965. *Industrial Organizations: Theory and Practice*. London: Oxford University Press.

Woodward, S.N. 1982. The Myth of Turbulence. *Futures*, August: 266-279.

Woolard, I. 2002. An Overview of Poverty and Inequality in South Africa. *Working Paper*. Prepared for DFID (SA): July.

Wooldridge, B., Schid, T. and Floyd, S.W. 2008. The Middle Management Perspective on Strategy Process: Contributions, Synthesis, and Future Research *Journal of Management*, 34(6): 1190-1221.

World Bank 2002. Accessed on August 31 2009 from: www.worldbank.org/

Wright, P. and Ferris, S.P. 1997. Agency Conflict and Corporate Strategy: The Effect of Divestment on Corporate Value. *Strategic Management Journal.* 18: 77-83.

Yankelovich, D. 1982. *New Rules.* New York: Bantam Books.

Yates, F. 1934. Contingency Tables Involving Small Numbers and the Chi-Square Test. *Journal of Royal Statistical Society Supplement*, 1: 217-235.

Yaukey, D. 1985. *Demography: The Study of Human Population.* New York: St. Martin's Press.

Young, S. and Litterer, J.A. 1991. Organizational Development Diagnostic Categories: A Clinical Approach. *Journal of Organizational Change Management*, 4(4): 58-72.

Yuchtman, E., and Seashore, S.E. 1967. A System Resource Approach to Organizational Effectiveness. *American Sociological Review*, 30(6): 67-85.

Zaltman, G. and Burger, P.C. 1975. *Marketing Research: Fundamentals and Dynamics.* Hinsdale, IL: The Dryden Press.

Zammuto, R. F. and Cameron, K. S. 1985. Environmental decline and organizational response. In Cummings, L. L. and Staw, B. M. (eds.). 7:223-262. *Research in Organizational Behavior.* Greenwich, CT: JAI Press.

Zedeck, S. 1971. Problems with the Use of 'Moderator Variables.' *Psychological Bulletin*, 76: 295-310.

INDEX

BIOGRAPHICAL NOTE

The author has been teaching at the Isenberg School of Management, University of Massachusetts-Amherst since 1984, where he has also served as director of MBA Programs, coordinator of the Ph.D. Program in Strategic Management, and Associate Director of the Massachusetts Institute for Social and Economic Research (MISER). Born in Benoni, South Africa, he had extensive experience there prior to joining the academia. He worked for the Standard Bank of South Africa in Johannesburg, and at the Uranium Plant and Metallurgical Research Laboratories of the Harmony Gold Mines in the Free State. He subsequently spent 8 years working for Unilever initially as a chemical analyst at the Lever Brothers laboratory, and later as a production manager in the company's soap manufacturing plant in Durban, South Africa. Since joining the academia he has had more than 100 publications in refereed scholarly outlets, including a co-edited book, *Prophesies and Protests: Ubuntu in Glocal Management*. He has presented his research work at different venues around the world, including Austria, Brazil, Canada, Costa Rica, the Czech Republic, France, Germany, Ireland, Japan, the Netherlands, Norway, Portugal, Singapore, South Africa, and the United States.

Professor Mangaliso has received scholarships from the Ford Foundation (1984-1988), Educational Opportunities Council—Institute of International Education (1982-1984), Barlow-Rand (1974-1975), Shell Oil Company, and the Ernest Oppenheimer Trust Fund (1970-1973). His teaching honors include being the winner of the Distinguished Teaching Award at the University of Massachusetts, Amherst. He is a Fellow and past President of the Eastern Academy of Management (US), past President and CEO of National Research Foundation of South Africa, and member of the Academy of Science of South Africa. His degrees include a B.Sc. in Chemistry and Physics from the University of Fort Hare, South Africa; an M.B.A. from Cornell University, Ithaca, NY; and a Ph.D. from the University of Massachusetts, Amherst. He presently lives in Amherst with his wife, Nomazengele Mangaliso (nee Jordan), a professor of sociology at Westfield State University. They have two grown daughters one in Atlanta, Georgia and the other in Los Angeles, California; and one grandson.

39482575R00137

Made in the USA
Middletown, DE
16 January 2017